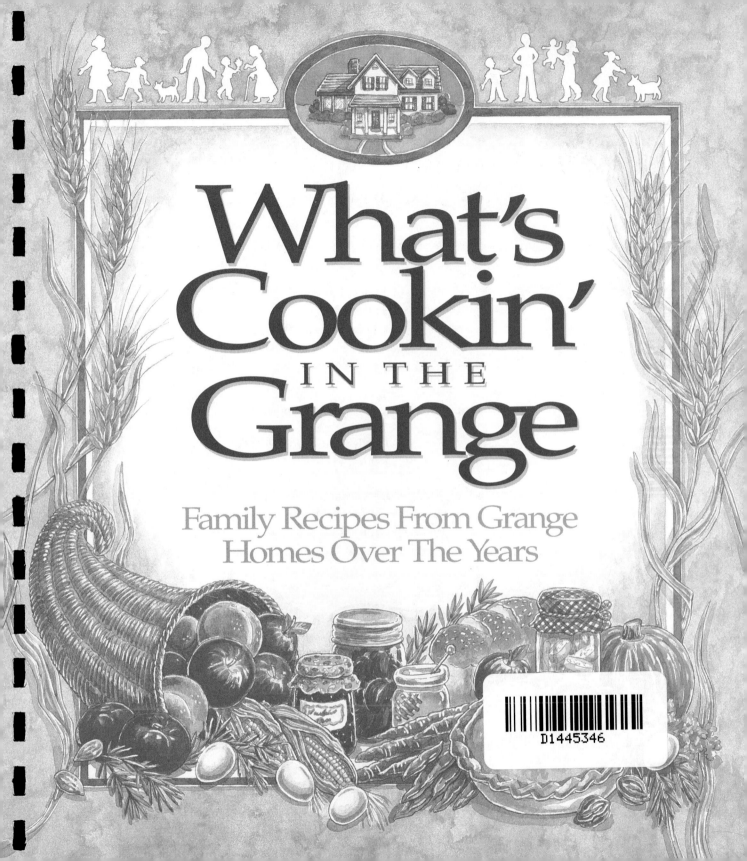

What's Cookin'
IN THE
Grange

Family Recipes From Grange
Homes Over The Years

D1445346

This cookbook is a collection of favorite recipes,
which are not necessarily original recipes.

What's Cookin' IN THE Grange

Family Recipes From Grange
Homes Over The Years

Copyright© 2000
The National Grange
1616 H Street, NW
Washington, D.C. 20006-4999

Library of Congress Catalog Number: 99-75220
ISBN: 0-9674841-0-3

Edited, Designed, and Manufactured by
Favorite Recipes® Press
an imprint of

FRP

P.O. Box 305142, Nashville, Tennessee 37230
800•358•0560

Managing Editor:	Mary Cummings
Project Manager:	Debbie Van Mol
Art Director:	Steve Newman
Cover and Book Design:	Dave Malone
Cover Art:	Susan Harrison
Project Production:	Sara Anglin

Manufactured in the United States of America
First Printing: 2000
35,000 copies

Contents

 Men's Specialties   Historical or Heritage Recipes

 Children's Recipes   Quick or Easy Recipes

National Grange
of THE ORDER of PATRONS of HUSBANDRY

1616 H Street, N.W., Washington, D.C. 20006-4999 - (202) 628-3507 - FAX: (202) 347-1091

Kermit W. Richardson, Master

Dear Friends,

As we pass from the 20th to the 21st Century, it is a highly appropriate time to present the new National Grange cookbook, *What's Cookin' in the Grange*. I would like to thank Betty-Jane Gardiner, Director of Women's Activities of the National Grange and the hundreds of Grange people all across this country who have made contributions to this beautiful cookbook. Without everyone working together, it would not have been a possibility.

Over the years Grange cooks have become legendary in their abilities and excellence in cooking. Thousands of Grange suppers are held every year where the talents of these cooks are put on display and enjoyed and admired by the public. This cookbook is a composite of their expertise.

The Grange had its beginning as a family organization, and like a family, we value sharing and caring about one another. Our commitment today to all families is steadfast, because we realize that the strength of a society is in direct relationship to the strength of its families. Mealtime is family time and what better way to honor the families of this country than with this new cookbook, as we celebrate "A New Century—A New Grange."

Sincerely,

Kermit W. Richardson, Master
National Grange of the Order of Patrons of Husbandry

National Grange

of THE ORDER of PATRONS of HUSBANDRY

1616 H Street, N.W., Washington, D.C. 20006-4999 - (202) 628-3507 - FAX: (202) 347-1091

Betty-Jane Gardiner, Director of Women's Activites
15 Meadowlark Rd., W. Simsbury, CT 06092
Tel: (860) 658-2855 (R), FAX: (860) 651-9859

Dear Friends,

Over the years the National Grange has been known for its wonderful cookbooks. We are delighted to present to you the latest of our publications, *What's Cookin' in the Grange.*

As we look to the new millennium we present recipes from our officers and members which have been used over the years in Grange homes all across the country. In addition to the "tried and true" favorites, we offer short-cut recipes for use during the busy days of the 21st century.

We sincerely thank the thousands of members who submitted recipes to be considered for printing, and only wish it had been possible to use all of them.

As you use this cookbook, please also notice that it has Grange information as well as recipes. These facts, interspersed throughout the recipe pages, were provided by the National Lecturer (Program Chairman) and the Directors of National Grange about the work done in their departments. We look forward to further accomplishments in the days ahead and will continue to make the Grange, the oldest farm fraternity in the country, a vital part of our way of life.

Our appreciation goes to the leaders in our Grange states for preparing short histories of their organizations to share with you, and for selecting a recipe emblematic of each area. We hope you will enjoy preparing many of them.

Last, but not least, we say thank you to our publisher, Favorite Recipes Press, for the help and guidance which made possible this cookbook from the National Grange. Now that you know *What's Cookin' in the Grange,* we wish for you healthy and happy eating during the new century.

Best wishes to you all,

Betty Jane Gardiner

Betty-Jane Gardiner
Director of Women's Activities
The National Grange

Board of Advisors
Cookbook Committee

Coordinator
Betty-Jane Gardiner
Director of Women's Activities

Margaret Richardson
Wife, National Master

Georgia M. Taylor
Sales Department Director

Mary Wilson
Favorite Recipes Press

Debbie Van Mol, RD
Favorite Recipes Press

Richard Wiess
Marketing

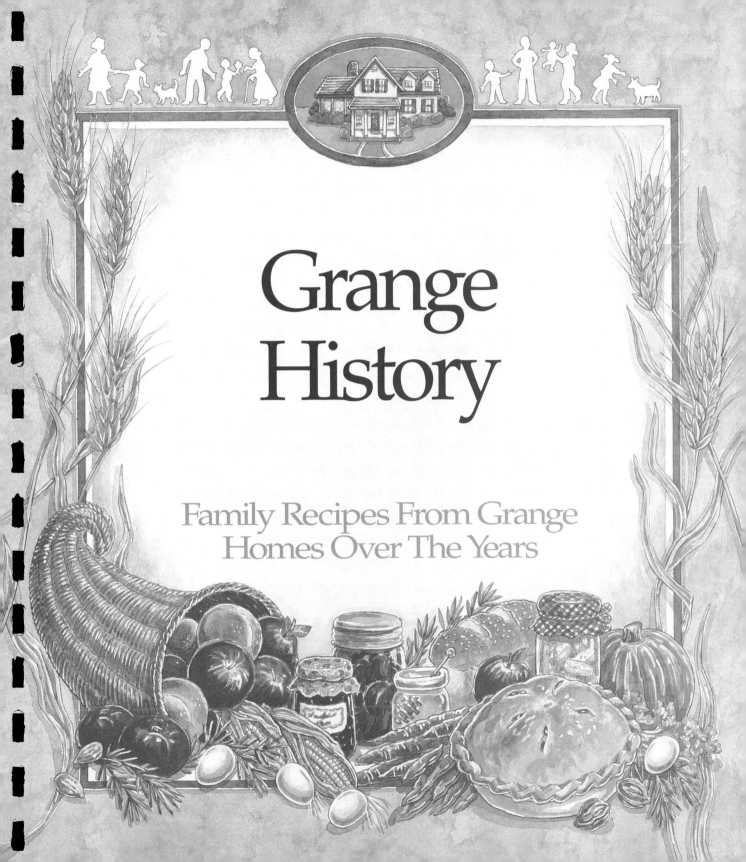

Grange History

Family Recipes From Grange Homes Over The Years

Alaska State Grange

Granges in Alaska date back to 1934 when the Northland Pioneer Grange No. 1 was organized in Palmer, Alaska, by colonists from the Midwest who had been relocated to the Matanuska Valley.

The Two Rivers Grange No. 3 was organized in 1960 in a community outside of Fairbanks by a group of people who had settled on federal homesteads just prior to 1959, the year Alaska was granted statehood.

Two more Granges were organized in 1961—the Tanana Valley Grange No. 4 near Fairbanks, and the Eielson Area Grange No. 6 in North Pole, Alaska. The area-wide Fairbanks Pomona Grange was also organized in 1961.

Grangers in Alaska recognized the importance of a statewide organization and requested permission from the National Grange to organize the Alaska State Grange Council. National Master Herschel Newsom granted permission for the Council in 1962 and the organizational meeting was held in Fairbanks in July of 1962. Bylaws for the Council were adopted in compliance with the *National Grange Digest.*

The Delta Buffalo Grange was organized in 1980 and the Salcha Grange in 1981. These two Granges never became active.

In 1981 the National Grange requested information about the Alaska Council so that other states having few Subordinate Granges could form a state Council.

Various Alaskan Grangers have attended the National Sessions on occasion. In 1987 the Alaska Council began to provide financial assistance for a delegate/delegates to attend the sessions. The delegates to the 1989 National Convention were elated when Councils were granted a vote at the next National Convention. However, before our 1990 annual state meeting, we received word that we would not be allowed that privilege. Despite that disappointment, Alaska continues to have delegates at the National Convention with the hope that one day Alaska will be granted a vote.

A new Grange was organized in Delta in 1997, bringing the number of Alaskan Subordinate Granges to five.

State Grange Councils were eliminated in 1995. A state must have six Subordinate Granges to become an official State Grange. So until Alaska reaches that magical number, we will continue to function in an unofficial capacity.

Moose Roast

1/2 to 2 cups wine or cider vinegar
1 moose, caribou or bear roast or steaks
1 or 2 envelopes onion soup mix

Pour the wine over the roast in a bowl, turning to coat. Marinate, covered, in the refrigerator for 8 to 10 hours, turning occasionally. Transfer the roast and liquid to a slow cooker. Sprinkle the soup mix over the roast. Cook on High until the roast is tender. Remove the roast to a serving platter. Slice as desired. The amount of wine or soup mix used depends on the weight of the roast. Serve leftovers on sandwiches or add to your favorite stew. **Yield:** variable.

Alice McKee

California State Grange

The first recorded communication relative to a Grange in California came from the pen of Mr. A. A. Bayley of Pilot Hill, California, to Oliver Hudson Kelley, Secretary of the National Grange. As a result of this communication, Mr. Bayley organized the Pilot Hill Grange on August 10, 1870, with twenty-nine charter members. Pilot Hill Grange No. 1 is still in existence today. In the spring of 1871, Mr. W. H. Baxter, a farmer of Napa County, made contact with Mr. Kelley with respect to the wants and needs of the farmers of California. As a result of an exchange of letters between Baxter and Kelley, Mr. Baxter was commissioned as a Deputy of the National Grange of California, and he began at once to diffuse information about the new organization and its advantages to the farmers of the state. After two years, however, he had been successful in organizing only one Grange—Napa Grange No. 2. Mr. Baxter, however, was patient and willing to persevere and watched for every opportunity to promote the Grange. Finally, on April 8, 1873, he was invited to speak on the subject at the Farmers Union Convention in San Francisco. His presentation was so persuasive that the Convention at once passed a resolution authorizing the Executive Committee to incorporate a part or whole of itself as a branch association cooperative with the Farmers Union. They proceeded to elect officers, and John Bidwell was elected President. The Convention adjourned and the Farmers Union never met again except for a final settlement of its affairs. The continuation of its work was formally turned over to the Granges, and the Farmers Union ceased to exist.

The California State Grange was organized at Napa on July 15, 1873. In the previous two years, thirty-three new Granges were organized, twenty-nine by Deputy Baxter. A total of thirty-five were eligible to sit in Convention. Of this number, twenty-nine were represented at the organization meeting. This Convention proposed legislation to reduce railroad fares, freights, and port charges, and for the development of irrigation. Other specific objectives were to establish a cooperative system of trade and to organize banks from which farmers could obtain loans at reasonable rates. The first Annual Convention of the California State Grange was held October 14, 1873, at San Jose, with 104 Granges represented.

The Grange prospered for a few years and then, in 1876, membership began to decline. By 1880 it had lost its influence and membership had dropped to fewer than three thousand. Throughout the forty years that followed, the Grange became nearly extinct as a fraternal order and quite helpless as a general farmers' organization.

A revival in Grange work began in the years shortly thereafter, when membership started to increase, only to drop to an all-time low of approximately 1,280 members in 1889. The State Master, in his report to the National Grange, said, "The California State Grange is in the morgue and ready for burial." Because of this weakened condition, Grange prestige remained at a very low ebb.

In 1908, the State Grange decided to reorganize a cooperative enterprise—fire insurance—on a fraternal/mutual basis without capital stock. It was necessary to first pass a law through the legislature permitting such companies to operate. After two unsuccessful attempts to get the law enacted, success was attained in 1913. The Grange Fraternal Fire Insurance Association was organized in 1916, with the first policy issued in May of that year. The company grew steadily from that date.

The State Convention held in Redding in 1929 made a declaration that startled California. It reaffirmed a position held on conservation in keeping with the Grange program adopted in 1873, 1874, and 1875 by urging the development of the water resources of the state with the construction of a dam at Kennet, using combined state and federal funds, to conserve water for irrigation in the

Sacramento and San Joaquin Valleys. The delegates asked that electric power and power sites be developed with the project. In adopting this policy, the California State Grange became the first statewide organization to support the construction of the dam, now known as Shasta Dam. It was no small responsibility to start legislation in motion to supply the arid sections of the valleys with water and electricity at a price farmers could afford to pay. But the delegates returned to their homes full of confidence and enthusiasm. They had elected George Sehlmeyer of Elk Grove, who was a staunch supporter of the new movement, as State Master. Upon his shoulders they placed the administrative task of carrying out the wishes of the delegates. The State Grange then consisted of eighty-two Subordinate Granges with a membership of 8,348, and ten Pomona Granges.

The Shasta Dam was built, and many other local projects have been achieved by individual Subordinate Granges or by the concerted effort of all the Granges in the State of California. Membership has been up and down the past seventy years and now stands at approximately 25,000.

As the year 2000 approaches, an indication of renewed interest in the Grange as a fraternal, family, community service organization is becoming evident. Goals are being set across the state to increase membership and to affirm the dedication of all members to the values and principles inherited from our forefathers.

Toffee

2 cups (4 sticks) butter or margarine
2 cups sugar
1 cup (heaping) sliced or chopped almonds
2 cups chocolate chips
Finely ground nuts

Beat the butter and sugar in a mixer bowl until creamy, scraping the bowl occasionally. Stir in the almonds. Spoon into a saucepan. Cook to 290 degrees on a candy thermometer, soft-crack stage, stirring constantly. Spread evenly on a buttered baking sheet or marble slab. Heat half the chocolate chips in a double boiler until melted. Spread the melted chocolate over the candy. Sprinkle with nuts. Let stand until firm. Turn the candy over. Heat the remaining chocolate chips in a double boiler until melted. Spread over the candy. Sprinkle with nuts. Let stand until firm. Break into the desired number of pieces.
Yield: 3 pounds.

Joy Beatie, *State Women's Activities Director*

Colorado State Grange

Seven years after the National Grange was founded—and two years before Colorado was admitted to the Union as a state—the Masters of thirty-three of the forty-six Subordinate Granges of the Territory of Colorado met in Denver. On January 27, 1874, they organized a State Grange of the Patrons of Husbandry for the Territory of Colorado.

The first Grange in Colorado was Ceres Grange No. 1, just west of Denver. The banner from that Grange has been restored and hangs in the State Office. Seventy-one Granges were organized before Colorado became a state and four of these are still in existence.

In 1981, Jeanne Davies became the fourteenth State Master, and the first woman to hold that office. She served for twelve years.

In the early seventies an Outstanding Granger of the Year Contest was begun that continues to honor an outstanding person or persons each year. In 1997, the CSG Emergency Relief Program was started to offer help when needed to members or non-Grangers.

Along with its emphasis on the Youth and Junior programs, Colorado Granges have been strong supporters of the Deaf Activities program. A pilot program for a Colorado Mandy Project was started in 1998, and two students were awarded financial help for purchasing hearing aids in the first six months of the program.

Throughout the past 125 years, the focus of the Grange in Colorado has been, and will continue to be, reaching out to help others.

Marge Sassman, *State Secretary*

Baked Rocky Mountain Rainbow Trout

12 slices smoked bacon
6 (1- to 1¹/2-pound) rainbow trout
1 tablespoon butter-flavor salt
6 yellow onions, cut into quarters
6 lemons, cut into wedges

Tear 6 sheets of foil large enough to enclose each fish. Place 1 slice of bacon on each sheet. Rub the cavity of each fish with some of the salt. Insert 1 onion and 1 lemon in each fish cavity. Place 1 fish on each section of foil. Top each with 1 slice of the bacon. Fold the foil to enclose. Arrange the foil packets on a baking sheet. Bake at 350 degrees for 20 to 30 minutes or until the fish flakes easily. For variety, grill over hot coals for 5 to 7 minutes per side. **Yield:** 6 servings.

Marge Sassman, *State Secretary*

13

Connecticut State Grange

The first Connecticut State Grange was organized on April 15, 1875. Due to lack of understanding, poor communication, no cooperation, and all-too-human failings, this effort lasted only about three years, and then passed into history.

The second Connecticut State Grange was organized on June 24, 1885. It started with strength and has maintained that strength through the 114 years that have passed.

As in all states where the Grange has been an active participant, a number of accomplishments are noteworthy. The Patrons Mutual Insurance Company was started as a "Grange company," and has been a strong source of assistance to the people of the state since its inception. Today it is The Patrons Group, and a strong bond is maintained between the company and the Grange.

The University of Connecticut, originally a land-grant college, and the Experimental Stations in the state were all a part of the strength of the Grange in their growth and history.

The Campaign for Better Roads was organized by the State Grange in the 1930s, and today's highways in the state are all a part of the campaign designated to "Get Connecticut Out of the Mud" by the State Grange.

Through the years, as in all organizations, there have been ups and downs, successes and failures, good years and bad, for the Grange in Connecticut. However, through the years there has been a dedication, a love, and a strength among the members that guarantees there will always be a Connecticut State Grange.

Marion W. Beecher, *State Secretary*

Crisp Apple Scallop

8 medium apples, peeled, sliced
1/2 cup water
1 teaspoon lemon juice
1/2 teaspoon cinnamon
1/4 teaspoon nutmeg
1 cup sugar
3/4 cup flour
1/2 cup (1 stick) butter, softened

Arrange the apples in a 2-quart baking dish. Drizzle with a mixture of the water, lemon juice, cinnamon and nutmeg. Combine the sugar, flour and butter in a bowl and stir until crumbly. Sprinkle over the prepared layers. Bake at 350 degrees for 30 minutes or until the apples are tender. Serve plain or topped with ice cream or whipped cream. **Yield:** 6 to 8 servings.

Jane Miller, *State Women's Activities Director*

Delaware State Grange

Farmers were struggling to recover from the Panic of 1873. Poor prices plus the tyranny of the railroads had goaded farmers into action across the nation. Delaware Granges were under the jurisdiction of the Maryland State Grange but were anxious to be independent. The Delaware State Grange was organized March 2, 1875, with seventeen Subordinate Granges.

For the past 124 years we have continued to meet and grow with the times. While many of our Granges have come and gone, we continue to have three Pomona Granges and sixteen Subordinate Granges.

Our officers and directors are dedicated members who do their best to see that the Delaware State Grange is an organization of which to be proud.

The Grange was instrumental in getting legislation passed in July 1991 to create the Farmland Preservation Act.

Our biggest activity is our food booth at the Delaware State Fair. Hundreds of Grangers put in many hours for the ten days of the fair. We feed thousands of people and are known for our "Delmarvalous Chicken Dinners."

The following is a recipe for our potato salad we serve with the dinners. Last year we peeled, diced, and cooked approximately four thousand pounds of Delaware potatoes during those ten days.

Delaware Potato Salad

150 pounds potatoes, chopped, cooked,
    drained
1 (106-ounce) can chopped celery in
    salad sauce
1 gallon sweet pickle relish
3 cups reconstituted dehydrated onions
2 gallons mayonnaise-type salad
    dressing
4 cups prepared mustard
4 cups sugar
$^1/_3$ cup (scant) salt
$1^1/_2$ teaspoons pepper

Combine the cooled potatoes, undrained celery, undrained pickle relish and onions in a large container and mix gently. Combine the salad dressing, mustard, sugar, salt and pepper in a bowl and mix well. Add to the potato mixture and stir until coated. Store, covered, in the refrigerator until serving time. **Yield:** 4 gallons.

Florida State Grange

A Florida State Grange has existed in three different periods.

The First Period, 1873–1889

The first Florida Subordinate Grange was organized by Colonel D. H. Jacques, assisted by Special Deputy Thomas A. Corruth, on August 25, 1873, at Welbourn, Swanee County. It was named Flora Grange No. 1, with William H. Wilson as Master. Organization of subordinate Granges continued, and by the fall of 1873, Florida had fourteen Granges. On November 26, 1873, nineteen delegates met in Lake City and organized the first Florida State Grange, with Benjamin F. Wardlaw of Madison as the first State Master. Wardlaw was born in South Carolina, moved to Florida as a young man, and served as a colonel in the Confederate army. From 1873 to 1889, 161 Granges were organized, primarily in the northern two-thirds of the state. In 1874 the Grange concentrated on a campaign against the theft of cattle, hogs, mules and horses, and "dark lantern" traffic, which was the stealing of seed cotton from farmers' fields and gin houses.

The Florida State Grange employed several purchasing agents to obtain goods for Grangers at a lower cost. Eventually fraudulent deals swindled the funds invested from the purchasing agents, who were also victims of the swindle. This created suspicion and loss of confidence in the purposes of our Order. There were several reasons why this first period of the Florida State Grange came to a close.

Middle Period, 1936–1955

The several attempts made to re-organize the Grange in Florida were short-lived. The following Granges were organized in this period: Sunnyfield No. 162, Fort Pierce, in 1936; Lakeland No. 163, in 1937; and Pioneer No. 164, Osceola County, in 1955. Grange Clubs were organized at St. Petersburg and St. Cloud. These were attended by winter visitors. Since they were not Chartered it is the author's opinion that they were social Granges.

The Present Period, 1959–1999

In 1960, at the 94th National Grange Convention, held in Winston-Salem, North Carolina, a resolution was introduced changing the *National Grange Digest.* This resolution opened the gate to organize Granges in Florida. National Deputy Sherman K. Ives, and his wife, Special Deputy Lida S. Ives, were sent, along with National Deputy Harold Brundage, to organize Granges. Brother Brundage's assignment was to plow, plant, cultivate, and create Granges on the west coast, while the Ives were given the same assignment for the east coast and central area of the state. Sunshine State Grange No. 165, White City, was organized October 1, 1959. Nineteen other Granges were organized in 1960 and 1961. Established northern Granges were generous in giving regalia and equipment to the new Florida Granges.

On August 30 and 31, 1961, representatives of twenty Subordinate Granges and one Pomona Grange (the only one in the state) met at Ellinor Village, Ormond Beach, to organize the second Florida State Grange. National Master Herschel Newsom presided over the meeting. This was a working delegate session with bylaws adopted, Granges reporting their activities, and resolutions referred to proper committees for appropriate action.

On August 31 the delegation met in the ballroom of the Coquina Hotel where E. Carrol Bean, High Priest of Demeter, installed Sherman K. Ives as Master of the second Florida State Grange. A class of 61 candidates received the 6th degree, with Mary Key, Master of South Carolina State Grange, serving as Degree Master.

From 1959 to the present, Granges numbering No. 165 through No. 213 have been organized, but many no longer exist. Much of this information was excerpted from "Florida State Grange, 1873–1976," by John J. Geil.

James S. Barnt, *State Historian*

Calamondin Pie

1¹/₄ cups sugar
¹/₂ cup ground calamondins
¹/₂ cup flaked coconut
¹/₂ cup water
3 tablespoons flour
2 eggs, beaten
1 unbaked (8-inch) pie shell

Combine the sugar, calamondins, coconut, water, flour and eggs in a bowl and mix well. Spoon into the pie shell. Bake at 375 degrees for 15 minutes. Reduce the oven temperature to 325 degrees. Bake for 35 minutes longer or until a knife inserted in the center comes out clean. To prepare the calamondins, cut the fruit into halves and remove the seeds. Process in a food processor until ground. **Yield:** 6 servings.

Carryl Heath, *State Master*

Idaho State Grange

The State of Idaho celebrated its ninetieth birthday at our last state session on October 28, 1998. Records in the National Grange Office show twenty-one Granges were organized in Idaho between 1874 and 1886. Our State Grange was organized October 28, 1908. Idaho has been host to the National Grange session in 1933 and 1970 in Boise.

Our State Grange building was built and dedicated in 1962 while Ermil Jerome was State Master. We have had fourteen State Masters.

Mary Johnson is currently serving her second term as State Master. She was the first lady State Master to be elected in Idaho in eighty-eight years.

Our State Grange is still very active in legislative work and in the Deaf Activities program. Many Granges are continually doing community service work in their communities.

Mary Johnson, *State Master*

Scalloped Potatoes

10 to 12 unpeeled potatoes
2 cups sour cream
1 (10-ounce) can cream of chicken soup
1 cup shredded Cheddar cheese
Minced onion to taste
Milk to taste
1 cup crushed potato chips

Combine the potatoes with enough water to cover in a saucepan. Cook until tender; drain. Peel and chop the potatoes. Transfer the potatoes to a bowl. Combine the sour cream, soup, cheese, onion and milk in a bowl and mix well. Add to the potatoes and mix gently. Spoon into a 9x13-inch baking dish. Sprinkle with the potato chips. Bake at 350 degrees for 1 hour. **Yield:** 12 to 15 servings.

Mary Johnson, *State Master*

Illinois State Grange

The official recorded date of birth of the Illinois State Grange was March 5, 1872. Alonzo Golder was elected the first Illinois State Grange Master. The 128th Annual Session was held in Rockford, Illinois, September 16–19, 1999. A. R. Henninger is the thirteenth Master of the Illinois State Grange. At the 129th National Grange Convention on November 15, 1998, he was elected to the National Grange Executive Committee.

Illinois State Grange Members have held many National Grange Officers and Directors positions.

Alonzo Golder	1873	National Grange Executive Committee
A. P. Forsyth	1877	National Chaplain
Mary J. Thompson	1889	National Pomona
Martha Wilson	1891	National Pomona
Oliver Wilson	1901	Priest Annalist
Oliver Wilson	1909	National Lecturer
Oliver Wilson	1911	National Master
Oliver Wilson	1919	Priest Archon
Dosia Eckert	1921	National Flora
Dosia Eckert	1925	National Juvenile Superintendent
Eugene A. Eckert	1922	National Grange Executive Committee
Dorsey Kirk	1951	National Overseer
Olga Niffenegger	1963	National Ceres
James Newport	1951	National Grange Youth Committee
Allen Grommet	1966	National Grange Youth Committee
Russell Stauffer	1976	National Treasurer
Russell Stauffer	1980	National Overseer
Mary Beth Heber	1981	National Junior Grange Director
Emalee Colver	1992	National Junior Grange Director
A. R. Henninger	1995	National Executive Committee

A. R. "Al" Henninger, *State Master*

Cream Puffs

1 cup water
1/2 cup (1 stick) butter or margarine
1 cup flour
4 eggs
1/8 teaspoon salt
8 ounces cream cheese, softened
3 cups milk, heated to lukewarm
1 (4-ounce) package vanilla instant
    pudding mix
16 ounces frozen whipped topping,
    thawed
Chocolate syrup

Bring the water and butter to a boil in a saucepan. Add the flour gradually, stirring constantly. Cook until the mixture forms a ball, stirring constantly. Remove from heat. Add the eggs 1 at a time, mixing well after each addition. Stir in the salt. Spread the mixture on a greased 11x17-inch baking pan. Bake at 400 degrees for 30 minutes. Let stand until cool. Place the cream cheese in a mixer bowl. Add the milk gradually, beating constantly until blended. Add the pudding mix. Beat for 2 minutes or until thickened, scraping the bowl occasionally. Spread over the baked layer. Top with the whipped topping. Drizzle with the chocolate syrup. Cut into squares. Chill, covered, until serving time. **Yield:** 36 servings.

A. R. "Al" Henninger, *State Master*

Indiana State Grange

The Indiana State Grange was organized by Oliver Hudson Kelley in Terre Haute, Indiana, Vigo County, on March 1, 1872.

There have been 2,428 Granges in Indiana. There have been twelve national officers from Indiana, including two National Masters and two High Priests of Demeter. Aaron Jones was National Master from 1897 to 1905 and Hershel Newsome from 1950 to 1968. C. Jerome Davis was High Priest of Demeter from 1969 to 1981 and John Valentine from 1995 to present.

In 1874, delegates from ninety of Indiana's ninety-two counties attended the State Session.

By 1878, there were 521 Granges with membership of 16,426. Membership probably reached the thirty thousand mark.

In 1902 all permitted degrees were put on at the Indiana State Session and we continue to do so. I am the eighteenth State Master in our 128-year history.

F. Dean Kistler, *State Master*

Easy Cabbage Roll Casserole

1 to 1¹/₂ pounds ground beef
1 onion, chopped
¹/₂ green bell pepper, chopped
2 garlic cloves, minced
1 tablespoon parsley flakes
1 teaspoon salt
1 teaspoon Italian seasoning
¹/₂ teaspoon pepper
2¹/₂ to 3 cups boiling water
¹/₄ to ¹/₂ head cabbage, chopped
1 (15-ounce) can diced tomatoes
1 (8-ounce) can tomato sauce
1 cup long grain white rice

Brown the ground beef in a skillet, stirring until crumbly; drain. Stir in the onion, green pepper, garlic, parsley flakes, salt, Italian seasoning and pepper. Add the boiling water, cabbage, undrained tomatoes, tomato sauce and rice and mix well. Bring to a boil, stirring occasionally. Spoon into a baking dish. Bake, covered, at 350 degrees for 45 to 60 minutes or until bubbly and of the desired consistency. **Yield:** 6 to 8 servings.

F. Dean Kistler, *State Master*

Iowa State Grange

On May 1, 1868, Oliver Hudson Kelley received a letter from Mr. A. Failor of Newton, Iowa, stating that he (Failor) had organized a Grange in Newton on April 17, 1868. This Grange was called Newton No. 1 and became the second working Grange in the nation.

This historic letter marked the beginning of the Order of Patrons of Husbandry in Iowa and gave birth to an organization that would help improve the social, educational, and agricultural way of life for the farmer in Iowa.

On January 12, 1871, the Iowa State Grange was organized in Des Moines with Mr. Dudley W. Adams of Waukon being elected Master, and General William Duane Wilson of Des Moines being elected Secretary. Adams went on to serve as the second Master of the National Grange.

General Wilson, editor of the state's leading farm journal, the *Iowa Homestead,* would keep readers of the paper informed as to the various activities of the Granges in the state. General Wilson had a nephew, Woodrow, who would bring further and greater fame to the name of Wilson.

Gene C. Edelen of Cedar Rapids currently serves as Master of the Iowa State Grange.

Gene C. Edelen, *State Master*

America's Cut Pork Chops and Dressing

8 (3-ounce) America's cut pork chops
1/4 cup water
2 (10-ounce) cans cream of
    mushroom soup
3 cups croutons
1 1/4 cups chopped celery
1 medium onion, finely chopped
1/4 teaspoon sage
Salt and pepper to taste

Brown the pork chops on both sides in a skillet. Transfer the pork chops with a slotted spoon to a baking pan. Add the water to the pan drippings, stirring to loosen any brown particles. Stir in the soup, croutons, celery, onion, sage, salt and pepper. Mound some of the crouton mixture on each pork chop. Bake at 350 degrees for 1 hour or until the pork chops are cooked through. **Yield:** 8 servings.

Gene C. Edelen, *State Master*

Kansas State Grange

The first Subordinate Grange in Kansas was organized in Brown County on March 28, 1872. The organization meeting was held in the "old courthouse" on the public square in Hiawatha. This courthouse was built in 1858 and was a two-story structure. There were twenty-seven men and seventeen women who became charter members.

On December 4, 1872, representatives of nine Granges met to consider formation of a state organization to promote the Grange in Kansas. The next statewide meeting was called on July 30, 1873. The Secretary reported the Kansas State Grange had a total of 409 Subordinate Granges. In 1874, the Kansas Grange reached its peak of membership. It was reported to the National Secretary, that Kansas had 1,385 Subordinate Granges with a membership of 39,840. Fredrick H. Dumbauld was the first Kansas State Grange Master, serving from December 4, 1872, to July 30, 1873.

State Grange Relief Agent, Brother W. P. Popponoe, reported at the 1875 session that the State Grange had received $12,115.38 for the relief of the victims of the grasshopper invasion of 1874. Ten states contributed cash or supplies, which were dispersed to thirty-five suffering Kansas counties.

Prairie Central in Sumner County, the first Juvenile Grange organized in Kansas, was organized in 1916 by Mrs. L. E. Thomas. By 1920, Kansas had five organized Juvenile Granges and the sixth was ready for organization. In 1967, Kansas had 106 Junior Granges and, under the direction of Patty West, held the first Kansas Junior Camp at Lone Star Lake with thirty-two campers and fourteen staff members in attendance.

In 1963, Brother Claude Brey made the Kansas State Grange an offer on an acreage of ground from his farm for the future State Grange Youth Camp. Dedication of the facility was held on May 31, 1970. National Master John W. Scott was the dedication speaker and presented a dedication plaque from the National Grange. The main building is 60x100-feet, is constructed of steel, and has brick facing. It has a large assembly room with a fireplace and an adjoining fully modern kitchen. A partial basement provides a work area for crafts, storage space, and storm shelter.

The Kansas State Grange had their Centennial celebration in 1973, in Lawrence, Kansas. The goal was: "To have the full Grange program, and all the Grange members involved in celebrating the Centennial and commemorating the work of the past one hundred years, but everyone also looking forward to build a bigger and better Kansas State Grange by using the publicity, enthusiasm, and increased activity generated by the centennial observance."

Today, Kansas has twenty-eight Granges in fifteen counties and a membership of more than nine hundred. Two Junior Granges have more than forty members.

Kevin Klenklen, *State Master*

Kansas Sunflower Seed Cookies

1 1/3 cups unbleached flour
1 teaspoon salt
1 teaspoon baking soda
1 1/4 cups packed brown sugar
1 cup (2 sticks) butter, softened
2 eggs
2 teaspoons almond extract
3 cups rolled oats
3/4 cup sunflower kernels
1/2 cup wheat germ

Sift the flour, salt and baking soda together. Beat the brown sugar and butter in a mixer bowl until creamy, scraping the bowl occasionally. Beat in the eggs and flavoring until blended. Stir in the flour mixture. Fold in the oats, sunflower kernels and wheat germ. Drop by rounded teaspoonfuls 2 inches apart onto an ungreased cookie sheet. Bake at 375 degrees for 10 to 12 minutes or until light brown. Cool on the the cookie sheet for 2 minutes. Remove to a wire rack to cool completely.
Yield: 4 dozen cookies.

Kevin Klenklen, *State Master*

Maine State Grange

Delegates from eighteen Subordinate Granges organized the Maine State Grange in Lewiston, Maine, on April 21, 1874. Nelson Ham of Lewiston was elected the first Master.

The Maine State Grange has been a supporter of education from the early years. It supports scholarships, through donations from local Granges, and gives between eight and ten thousand dollars each year to students seeking higher education.

The State Grange has supported a home at Good Will Hinckley School since 1896. After its destruction by fire on two occasions, the members rallied and raised the money necessary to rebuild. Good Will Hinckley School was begun as a school for orphaned children and continues today as a home and school for teenagers who are having difficulty coping with the world.

Deaf Activities and concerns for the hearing impaired have been a concern for many years. The State Grange was one of the supporters that succeeded in bringing the deaf community their own school, Baxter School for the Deaf, located in Portland, Maine.

Members of the Maine State Grange consistently participate in all activities and have won National Grange awards on many occasions.

Clyde Berry, *Past Master*

Melt-In-Your-Mouth Blueberry Cake

1¹/₂ cups fresh blueberries
1¹/₂ cups sifted flour
1 teaspoon baking powder
2 egg whites
¹/₄ cup sugar
¹/₂ cup shortening
1 teaspoon vanilla extract
¹/₄ teaspoon salt
³/₄ cup sugar
2 egg yolks
¹/₃ cup milk
Sugar to taste

Toss the blueberries with 2 tablespoons of the flour in a bowl. Sift the remaining flour and baking powder together. Beat the egg whites in a mixer bowl until soft peaks form. Add ¹/₄ cup sugar gradually, beating constantly until stiff peaks form. Beat the shortening in a mixer bowl until creamy. Add the vanilla and salt and mix well. Add ³/₄ cup sugar gradually, beating constantly until blended. Add the egg yolks. Beat until light and fluffy. Add the flour mixture alternately with the milk, mixing well after each addition. Fold in the egg whites. Fold in the blueberries. Spoon the batter into an 8x8-inch cake pan. Sprinkle lightly with sugar to taste. Bake at 350 degrees for 50 to 60 minutes or until the cake tests done. **Yield:** 8 servings.

Sherley D. Geyer

Maryland State Grange

On a bitter day in December 1873, Dan Watkins started out on horseback to Baltimore for a meeting to organize the Maryland State Grange. After three hours of slugging through the mud, with the mud finally as deep as the horse's belly, he turned back home and wrote to report why he had not gotten to the meeting.

The Maryland State Grange was actually organized January 7, 1874, at the Mansion House in Baltimore. National Deputy E. J. Ohr of Iowa was installed. That same day, the Fifth Degree was conferred on ten men and three women. At that time the Fifth Degree was the State Degree.

The first two annual State Grange meetings were held in Baltimore. The third meeting was held in Kemp Hall in Frederick in December 1875. Standing committees were Constitution and Bylaws, Resolutions, Grievances and Claims, Good of the Order, and Finance. Special committees were Tobacco, Stock Law, Dog Law, Articles of Incorporation, Legislation, Vagrants, Birds, and Transportation.

In 1878 there were 112 Granges that would last four years or more. This was the highest number of Granges to operate in Maryland history.

John Thompson, *State Master*

Maryland Crab Cakes

1 cup fresh white bread crumbs
1/4 cup mayonnaise
8 ounces crab meat, drained, flaked
1 egg yolk, lightly beaten
1 teaspoon Worcestershire sauce
Sprigs of parsley to taste, minced
1/8 teaspoon salt
1/8 teaspoon paprika
1 egg white, stiffly beaten
1 tablespoon (about) butter

Mix the bread crumbs and mayonnaise in a bowl. Let stand for 5 minutes. Stir in the crab meat, egg yolk, Worcestershire sauce, parsley, salt and paprika with a fork. Fold in the egg white. Heat the butter in a 10-inch skillet until melted. Drop the crab meat mixture by 1/4 cupfuls into the melted butter. Cook until brown on both sides, turning once. **Yield:** 6 crab cakes.

John Thompson, *State Master*

Massachusetts State Grange

The first Grange in Massachusetts was organized on June 17, 1873, in Greenfield, Massachusetts, and is named Guiding Star Grange No. 1. Eighteen Granges had been organized by December 4, 1873, and the Massachusetts State Grange was organized in Greenfield, Massachusetts, on this date.

The Grange is dedicated to the preservation and expansion of the American Democracy, and is interested in agriculture and the welfare of our fellow beings. To celebrate our interest in agriculture, we cooperated with the other five New England states in erecting the New England Grange Building on the grounds of the Eastern States Exposition in West Springfield, Massachusetts, in September 1938.

As agriculture became more and more self-supporting, we expanded our interests to the service of mankind as well. Over the years we have worked for the Infantile Paralysis, Arthritis, Diabetes, Spina Bifida, Cancer, and other foundations. At present we are interested in aiding the deaf and hearing impaired.

In October 1963, we acquired and dedicated the Albert J. Thomas Library/Museum in Rutland, Massachusetts, to display our historical artifacts and provide a meeting place for our many committees. Brother Thomas was State Grange Secretary for many years and started the collection of State Grange memorabilia.

We are actively supporting the New England Dairy Compact and other measures to ensure the viability of the family farm. Agriculture has become so diverse that we are now involved in many areas that did not even exist years ago, aquaculture for example.

Our support of Agriculture in the Classroom is important in helping our children realize the importance that agriculture has for all of us. As education has always been an important facet of the Order, we maintain support of this activity through our Educational Aid Program by giving scholarships and loans to our members to enable them to receive post-secondary training.

The Massachusetts State Grange is taking its place in our society to make our citizens aware of the importance of sound agricultural, civil, and societal practices through our programs and our observance of the teachings of our ritual. We are as old-fashioned as straw hats and aprons, yet as modern as the Internet and our website. Come visit us at: www.massgrange.org

Kathleen M. Peterson, *State Master*

Cranberry Nut Squares

1½ *cups flour*
1¼ *cups sugar*
1 cup (2 sticks) butter, melted
2 eggs, beaten
2 cups whole cranberries
1 cup chopped nuts

Combine the flour, sugar, butter and eggs in a bowl and mix well. Stir in the cranberries and nuts. Spoon the batter into a 9x13-inch baking pan. Bake at 325 degrees for 40 to 50 minutes or until golden brown. Cut into squares. **Yield:** 12 servings.

Frank Jefferson, *Co-Director Women's Activities Committee*

Michigan State Grange

The Michigan State Grange was organized on April 15, 1873. A meeting was held at the courthouse in the Village of Kalamazoo for this purpose. At this time there were twenty Granges in Michigan—ten were organized in 1872 and ten more in March and April 1873. The first Grange in Michigan, Burnside No. 1, was organized January 10, 1872 in Lapeer County. A Historical Marker on the courthouse lawn in Lapeer marks this historical event.

The first Annual Session of the Michigan State Grange was held at Allen's hall, corner of Water and Burdick Streets in Kalamazoo, on January 21–23, 1874. There were 334 delegates at this session. A Historical Marker will be placed at this corner in the near future in honor of our 125th Anniversary celebrated in 1998.

Throughout the history of the Michigan State Grange an office was established, usually in the Master's or Secretary's home. At the Annual Session held in Alpena in 1946 a resolution was unanimously adopted for the Executive Committee of the Michigan State Grange to establish an office in Lansing as soon as possible. In July, 1953, a headquarters building located at 314 North Walnut Street, Lansing, was purchased. In 1978 Capitol Grange No. 540 gave a piece of land located in Grange Acres, Haslett to the State Grange for the purpose of building a new headquarters. Ground was broken in 1980 and the ranch-style building was dedicated in 1981. Our present address is 1730 Chamberlain Way, Haslett.

The first three Masters of the Michigan State Grange were Stephen F. Brown, Schoolcraft; Jonathan J. Woodman, Paw Paw (also elected National Grange Master) and Cyrus G. Luce, Gilead and Lansing. He was also elected Governor of Michigan during his term as Master for the Michigan State Grange.

Mrs. Mary Bryant Mayo was an early zealous leader of the women's movement. She proposed a Children's Day and the first one was held on June 10, 1886. She also called for state funds to build dormitories at the college. She became lecturer at the college's Farmer's Institutes, and began at once to hold sessions for women. In 1889 Mary Mayo had begun Women's Work, which she continued to chair for fourteen years. From this committee developed the Home Economics and Community Service committees, one of the most important events of Grange history. Her Fresh Air Project saw more than 200 persons from the Detroit area sent to Grange farm homes for rest during the summer of 1897. She continued to serve the Grange in many areas until her death in 1903 in her 64th year. In 1931 a new dormitory for girls was presented to students of Michigan State College as the Mary Mayo Hall.

In 1885 Miss Jennie Buell came on the scene as the able assistant to J. T. Cobb in editing *The Grange Visitor,* and as superintendent of the amusement department. Thus began a Grange career that was to span some fifty years. She served as State Grange Secretary from 1890 to 1906 and again from 1914 to 1924. She was State Grange Lecturer from 1908 to 1914 and again from 1930 to 1934. In 1912 Jennie was chairman of the intensive campaign by the Grange for woman's suffrage. As a result of the Granges' work, the issue was placed on the ballot for the November election but was defeated. Jennie was the first person in Michigan to receive a Golden Sheaf Pin for 50 years of continuous membership. She died in 1935, after having served as a State Grange officer for 36 of her 51 years in the Grange. She was the author of two books: *One Woman's Work for Farm Women,* in 1908 (about Mary Mayo) and *The Grange Master and The Grange Lecturer,* in 1921.

Dora Stockman started on the Grange lecture circuit in 1908 and at the Annual State Grange Session in 1910 she gave a talk on the Farm Art Gallery. She was a surprise and a delight to all. She proved to be one of the most outstanding leaders in State Grange history. She wrote three books and was a prolific writer of songs, selling more than 50,000 copies of one song. She served on the State Board of Agriculture, on the State Fair Board and was a State Representative from 1938 to 1946, longer than any other woman has served. She is believed to have organized more Granges than any other person in the history of the State Grange. Her mighty voice for the Grange was stilled in May of 1948. She had been active in the State Grange for 40 years.

Beulah Winter

Cheery Cherry Crunch

1/2 cup (1 stick) butter or margarine
1 (2-layer) package yellow cake mix
2 (21-ounce) cans cherry pie filling
1/2 cup chopped walnuts

Cut the butter into the cake mix in a bowl until crumbly. Reserve 1 cup of the crumb mixture. Pat the remaining crumb mixture over the bottom and 1/2 inch up the sides of an ungreased 9x13-inch baking pan. Spread the pie filling over the crumb mixture to within 1/2 inch of the edges of the pan. Mix the reserved crumb mixture and walnuts in a bowl. Sprinkle over the top. Bake at 350 degrees for 45 to 50 minutes. Serve warm topped with whipped cream or ice cream. Try these combinations for variety: Devil's food cake mix and apricot pie filling; Lemon Velvet cake mix and peach pie filling; White cake mix and blueberry pie filling; Honey Spice cake mix and apple pie filling. **Yield:** 12 to 15 servings.

Robert Brown, *State Master*

Minnesota State Grange

The State Grange of Minnesota was organized on February 23, 1869, by Oliver Hudson Kelley and was the first state of the Union to organize. Oliver Hudson Kelley, foremost among the seven founders of the organization, owned and operated a farm near Elk River.

In 1961 the National Grange presented the 190 acre farm to the Minnesota Historical Society for the preservation of the birthplace of organized agriculture.

The farm is now a national historic site. It is a "living history farm" of the 1870 period open to the public with a museum and an interpretive center depicting the importance of the Grange in American life.

During those early years the influence of the Grange spread throughout the state. Then, as the newness of the organization and the co-operative movements were not as successful as expected, there was a decline followed by a revival beginning in the 1930s.

The next four to five decades were high points in Grange life as all Granges became very involved in community service and youth programs as an important part of their communities.

Richard Field, *State Master*

Cream of Wild Rice Soup

1/2 cup wild rice
1 (10-ounce) can chicken broth
1 cup water
1/4 cup chopped onion
1/4 cup shredded carrot
1 small bay leaf
1/2 teaspoon basil, crushed
1 (4-ounce) can sliced mushrooms,
    drained
1/4 cup snipped fresh parsley
2 cups light cream or milk
1 tablespoon flour

Rinse the wild rice. Combine the wild rice, broth, water, onion, carrot, bay leaf and basil in a saucepan and mix well. Bring to a boil; reduce heat. Simmer, covered, for 45 minutes, stirring occasionally. Discard the bay leaf. Stir in the mushrooms and parsley. Combine the cream and flour in a bowl, stirring until blended. Stir into the soup. Cook just until bubbly, stirring frequently. Ladle into soup bowls. **Yield:** 4 servings.

Richard Field, *State Master*

Missouri State Grange

Missouri State Grange was organized on May 20, 1873. The first Master was T. R. Allen of St. Louis. We have had seventeen different State Masters from various parts of the state.

The National Grange wanted to hold the National Session in St. Louis but couldn't unless Missouri organized as a State Grange. A Grange organizer came into Missouri and at one time there were more than two thousand Subordinate Granges in the state. Some only lasted a few months and some only a few years. There were a large number of Subordinate Granges for a long time. Several of the Granges were one hundred years old or older when they closed.

We only have six Granges in the state at this time. The increasing numbers of larger farms has been hard on Grange membership in Missouri because there simply are not as many people as there used to be. Also, the Insurance Company pulled out in the 1980s and we lost a large number of members then.

Missouri is proud to have had four Grange sisters to serve as National Ceres as well as delegates to serve as other National Officers. We have had youth from our state on the National Youth Team, as well.

Missouri State Grange has hosted International visitors. They have also worked with the U.S. Information Service.

Missouri hosted the Mid-West Leaders Conference in Hannibal in 1977.

We have enjoyed having National Grange Representatives at our State Session for many years.

Even though we are small in number, we are very active in our communities and are dedicated Grange members.

We would like to organize some granges around St. Louis and Kansas City areas.

Virginia Henderson, *State Secretary*

Barbecued Meatballs

2 pounds ground beef
1 (12-ounce) can evaporated milk
1 cup quick-cooking oats
1 cup fine cracker crumbs
1/4 cup chopped onion
2 eggs, beaten
2 teaspoons salt
2 teaspoons chili powder
1/2 teaspoon pepper
1/2 teaspoon garlic powder
2 cups catsup
1 cup packed brown sugar
1/2 teaspoon liquid smoke
1/2 teaspoon garlic powder
1/8 teaspoon minced onion

Combine the ground beef, evaporated milk, oats, cracker crumbs, 1/4 cup onion, eggs, salt, chili powder, pepper and 1/2 teaspoon garlic powder in a bowl and mix well. Shape the ground beef mixture into 1-inch balls. May freeze at this point for future use. Arrange the meatballs in a 9x13-inch baking pan. Combine the catsup, brown sugar, liquid smoke, 1/2 teaspoon garlic powder and 1/8 teaspoon onion in a saucepan and mix well. Cook until the brown sugar dissolves, stirring constantly. Pour over the meatballs. Bake at 350 degrees for 1 hour.
Yield: 8 to 10 servings.

Neoma Foreman, *First Lady*

Montana State Grange

The Montana State Grange held its first State Session in 1938. In 1942 it held its Annual Session in Whitefish, Montana. This marked the first session of the State Grange under wartime conditions. The frills of a State Session were lacking during this tough time, but to replace it were the honest, able consideration of many problems facing farmers at this time. The Grange made a difference then and continues to do so as we approach the new millennium.

The Grange in the Big Sky Country has survived the wartime and will hold its final State Session of this century along the beautiful Clarkfork River in Sanders County in the city of Plains. This will be the 61st Annual Session of Montana State Grange.

We continue to strive to serve individual communities throughout the state with fifteen Granges, located from just east of the Continental Divide to the Canadian border. We are striving to meet the challenge—A New Century—A New Grange.

Marilyn Johnson, *State Master*

Cowboy Cookies

2 cups flour
1 teaspoon baking soda
1/2 teaspoon baking powder
1 cup shortening
1 cup sugar
1 cup packed brown sugar
1 teaspoon vanilla extract
1/2 teaspoon salt
2 eggs
2 cups quick-cooking oats
2 cups chocolate chips or
   butterscotch chips

Mix the flour, baking soda and baking powder together. Beat the shortening, sugar, brown sugar, vanilla and salt in a mixer bowl until creamy, scraping the bowl occasionally. Beat in the eggs. Add the flour mixture and beat until blended. Stir in the oats and chocolate chips. Drop by spoonfuls 2 inches apart onto an oiled cookie sheet. Bake at 350 degrees for 10 to 15 minutes or until light brown. Cool on cookie sheet for 2 minutes. Remove to a wire rack to cool completely. **Yield:** 6 dozen cookies.

Marilyn Johnson, *State Master*

Nebraska State Grange

It was not until the end of the Civil War and the passage of the Homestead Laws that settlers began to come west in large numbers.

Two events occurred in 1867 which were to leave indelible imprints on the plains and also on the history of the United States of America. The first took place on March 1, 1867, when the status of statehood was granted to the Territory of Nebraska. The second happened on December 4 of that same year, when the National Grange of Patrons of Husbandry was founded.

To encourage building of railroads in these parts to connect our now vast nation, the Government granted them thousands of acres of some of the choicest farm land. The railroads in turn sold these lands to farmers with promises of generous benefits. Instead the railroad then felt they had power to repudiate any promises and dictate terms of their own.

It was at this time that the prairie farmers found themselves burdened by poverty and mortgages. The Grange stepped in, promising equality for farmers and when the new Nebraska Constitution was adopted in 1876 it provided for regulation of the railroads.

The first Subordinate Grange in Nebraska was organized in Alma City, Harlan County, on January 1, 1872. The first Nebraska State Grange was organized on August 2, 1872, at Alma, Nebraska.

The last chartered Grange of the nineteenth century on record was Prairie Center Grange No. 99. Thereafter the Grange in Nebraska was virtually nonexistent for twelve years, but time proved the Grange was not dead.

It is difficult to pinpoint a date of the demise of the early Grange in Nebraska, but credit for the revival of the Grange in Nebraska goes to James D. Ream of Broken Bow. In 1911 he became interested in the Grange because he felt that Nebraska farmers needed a local organization that still had a strong influence at both the state and national level. He also liked the stress the Grange placed on community life, educational opportunities, and their support of women's suffrage.

On February 27, 1911, J. D. Ream organized Custer Center Grange No. 103, which still remains the oldest Grange in the state of Nebraska. He organized twenty-one Granges that year, nineteen of them in Custer County.

The first State Session of the renewal was held in Broken Bow on November 1, 1911. Records show there were 204 granges chartered before 1920.

We sadly must say as of today we have only twenty Subordinate Granges and four Pomona Granges.

Nebraska is very proud of the fact that one of our own, Ed Anderson and wife, Darlene, served as National Master from 1980–1988, and Nebraska has been fortunate to have others serve as National officers.

Although the Grange membership has declined in recent years, it still remains a strong and vibrant influence in the state and the nation. Grange accomplishments since 1872 have been impressive. It is doubtful if any other single organization has done as much to contribute to the "Good Life" that we enjoy in Nebraska today. May the Grange continue to flourish for many years into the future for all generations.

Robert W. Jeary, *State Master*

Beef Stroganoff

2 eggs
1/2 teaspoon salt
1 cup (or more) flour
1 pound beef sirloin, cut into
  1/4-inch strips
1 tablespoon flour
1/2 teaspoon salt
2 tablespoons butter or margarine
1/2 cup chopped onion
2 tablespoons butter or margarine
3 tablespoons flour
1 tablespoon tomato paste
1 (10-ounce) can beef broth
1 cup sour cream

Whisk the eggs with a fork in a bowl. Stir in 1/2 teaspoon salt. Add 1 cup flour, stirring until the mixture forms a ball. Add additional flour if needed if the dough is sticky. Roll the dough on a lightly floured surface. Let dry for 1 hour. Cut the dough into long strips. Stack the strips and cut into the desired lengths. Add the noodles to boiling water or broth in a stockpot; reduce heat. Cook until tender; drain. Cover to keep warm. Coat the beef with a mixture of 1 tablespoon flour and 1/2 teaspoon salt. Heat a skillet until hot. Add 2 tablespoons butter. Add the beef strips. Cook until brown on both sides. Stir in the onion. Cook until the onion is tender, stirring frequently. Remove the beef to a platter with a slotted spoon. Add 2 tablespoons butter to the pan drippings. Stir in 3 tablespoons flour, tomato paste and broth. Cook until thickened, stirring constantly. Return the beef to the skillet. Stir in the sour cream. Cook just until heated through, stirring frequently; do not boil. Spoon over the hot noodles on a serving platter. Homemade noodles are not a requirement for this recipe. **Yield:** 4 servings.

Jeannie Jeary, *First Lady*

New Hampshire State Grange

The New Hampshire State Grange was organized on December 23, 1873, at the G.A.R. Hall in Manchester by Brother T. A. Thompson, Lecturer of the National Grange. In a response to a call to organize a State Grange, Subordinate Grange masters and their wives, who were matrons, assembled in Manchester two days before Christmas.

At that time, there were seventeen Subordinate Granges in New Hampshire, fifteen of which were represented at this meeting. The first session was devoted to formulating a constitution and bylaws, discussion of resolutions, and election of officers. Dudley T. Chase was elected the first Master for the New Hampshire State Grange.

Looking back through the years, I wonder if these early patrons realized the impact they were going to make. Many legislative laws in New Hampshire were introduced by Grangers. The Grange was the center of activity in many towns early in the history of the New Hampshire State Grange.

The New Hampshire State Grange can look with pride at the accomplishments that have been recorded throughout its 125-year history. Establishment of the RFD (Rural Free Delivery) mail system, organizing the New Hampshire State Police Force, moving of the Agricultural College from Hanover to the University of New Hampshire in Durham, support for the State Library and libraries throughout the state, enactment of motor vehicle laws, and care and services for the elderly in nursing homes are just a few of the many accomplishments of the New Hampshire State Grange.

Although agriculture remains the basic principle for which the Grange was founded, community service has become equally important. The Grange has sponsored projects and programs to benefit people of all ages. Granges in New Hampshire continue to practice the Grange Motto: "In essentials, Unity; In non-essentials, Liberty; In all things, Charity."

Although the Grange has changed in some ways since those early days, it will always be an organization for the whole family. It will continue that same dedication and commitment to the members that was begun in 1873.

Richard Patten, *State Historian*

Knobby Apple Cake

1 cup flour
1 teaspoon baking soda
1/2 teaspoon cinnamon
1/2 teaspoon nutmeg
1/2 teaspoon salt
3/4 cup sugar
2 tablespoons shortening
1 egg, beaten
3 cups chopped apples
1/4 cup chopped walnuts (optional)
1 teaspoon vanilla extract

Sift the flour, baking soda, cinnamon, nutmeg and salt into a bowl and mix well. Beat the sugar and shortening in a mixer bowl until creamy. Add the egg and mix well. Stir in the apples, walnuts and vanilla. Add the flour mixture and mix well. Spoon into a 9x13-inch cake pan. Bake at 350 degrees for 35 to 40 minutes or until the cake tests done. Serve hot or at room temperature. Serve with lemon sauce or whipped cream if desired. **Yield:** 24 servings.

Carolee Barrett, *Director of Women's Activities*

New Jersey State Grange

The New Jersey State Grange was organized on November 25 and 26, 1873 in Camden, New Jersey, and incorporated on February 27, 1874. Prior to this official organization, there were 25 Subordinate Granges in operation. In January of 1874 there were 39 Subordinate Granges. The Grange grew rapidly in New Jersey from 1873 to 1877. Then a decline set in which lasted until around 1890.

From 1870 to 1900, wholesale prices were slowly declining and it was not until around 1903 that the number of Granges in New Jersey began to increase substantially. During its early growth, the Grange displaced many local agricultural societies and farmer's clubs. By 1953, the total number of Granges in New Jersey had reached 158 which was comprised of fifteen Pomona, 120 Subordinate and 23 Junior Granges. The total membership at this point was around 21,000.

At the 1905 Annual Session, the Committee on the Good of the Order advocated Juvenile Granges, there being none in the state at that time. Nothing happened until 1922 when a resolution was adopted calling for the appointment of a committee to encourage the institution of Juvenile Granges and to supervise their actions. As a result of this action, four Juvenile Granges with a total membership of 107 were organized in 1923. By 1924, the number had increased to nine.

The New Jersey State Grange was instrumental in the creation of several businesses and agencies to meet the needs of the rural communities. Through the untiring efforts of the New Jersey State Grange, the New Jersey State Police Department came into being in 1921. Cordial relations continue to exist today between the Grange and the New Jersey State Police.

The need for insurance coverage of Grange members prompted the New Jersey State Grange to organize two different insurance companies in the late 1800s and early 1900s. The Farmer's Reliance Insurance Company was organized in December of 1879 for the purpose of providing fire insurance for Grange members' buildings and personal property. In November of 1929, the Selective Risks Insurance Company came into being through the efforts of the Grange to provide automotive insurance coverage to Grangers and the rural people.

Great relations existed over many decades between these two Insurance Companies and the Grange. But those times, unfortunately, have passed in the latter years of this century. The Farmers Reliance Company went under as a result of the business they had in the hurricane areas of Florida and the relationship between the Grange and Selective Risks has ceased due to the action of the insurance company.

The New Jersey Museum of Agriculture was established in 1984 on the campus of Cook College of Rutgers, the State University. This museum evolved through the leadership efforts of the New Jersey State Grange. Dr. Wabun C. Krueger, a member of Pioneer Grange No. 1, had amassed an extensive collection of agricultural artifacts, which is the nucleus of the Museum's collection.

The New Jersey State Grange has enjoyed a rich history of service to people and rural America over the past 125 years, and is ready to meet the needs of mankind which lie ahead.

John A. Robinson, *State Master*

Jersey Fresh Fried Tomatoes

Ripe firm tomatoes, cut into 1/2- to
    3/4-inch slices
Salt to taste
Flour to taste
Bacon drippings or vegetable oil
    for frying
Sugar to taste
Milk

Sprinkle both sides of the tomatoes with salt. Coat with flour. Fry the tomatoes in bacon drippings in a heavy skillet over medium heat until brown. Turn and sprinkle lightly with sugar. Fry until brown. Remove the skillet from the heat. Transfer the tomatoes to a baking dish with a slotted spoon, reserving the pan drippings. Cover to keep warm. Stir enough flour into the pan drippings to make a paste. Add milk gradually until the gravy is of the desired consistency, stirring constantly. Stir in 1 tablespoon sugar for each 3 cups of gravy. Cook until thickened and of the desired consistency, stirring constantly. Spoon over the tomatoes. Serve with toast points and fried potatoes. **Yield:** variable.

John A. Robinson, *State Master*

New York State Grange

The meeting to organize the New York State Grange was held on November 6, 1873, in Syracuse, New York. There were twenty-one Subordinate Granges in New York at that time. The first annual session was held in Albany in March, 1874. George D. Hinckley, a charter member of Fredonia Grange No. 1 was elected the first Master. Mrs. Hinckley was elected the first Ceres of the State Grange.

The State Grange was instrumental in forming Mutual Fire Insurance Companies, the Geneva Agriculture Experiment Station, the GLF, (a cooperative of Grange,) Dairyman's League, and Farm Bureau. The Cornell Scholarship Fund, the Revolving Scholarship Fund, The Susan Freestone Fund and the DeNise Scholarship are programs supporting education. Maple Leaf Grange in Canada was formed in 1941 and was affiliated with the New York State Grange.

The State Grange Headquarters was built in 1973 during our centennial year. The 125th anniversary of the State Grange and the 25th anniversary of the headquarters were celebrated in 1998.

We look forward to a continuing involvement in many areas of concern in New York.

Bruce Croucher, *State Master*

Sauerkraut Cakes

2¼ cups flour
1 teaspoon baking soda
1 teaspoon baking powder
1½ cups sugar
⅔ cup shortening
3 eggs
½ cup baking cocoa
1¼ teaspoons vanilla extract
¼ teaspoon salt
1 cup water
½ cup chopped, rinsed drained
   sauerkraut

Sift the flour, baking soda and baking powder together. Beat the sugar and shortening in a mixer bowl until creamy, scraping the bowl occasionally. Add the eggs and beat until blended. Beat in the baking cocoa, vanilla and salt. Add the flour mixture alternately with the water, mixing well after each addition. Stir in the sauerkraut. Spoon the batter into 2 greased and floured 8x8-inch cake pans. Bake at 325 degrees for 25 to 30 minutes or until the cakes test done. Cool in the pans on a wire rack. Spread with your favorite frosting. **Yield:** 18 servings.

Bruce Croucher, *State Master*

51

North Carolina State Grange

The first Granges were organized in North Carolina in 1873. In 1877, with nearly five hundred Granges in place, the North Carolina State Grange passed a resolution that led to the establishment of the Department of Agriculture in our state. Other important events took place because of the Grange during the next twenty years but in the early 1900s the Grange ceased to exist in our state.

In 1929, North Carolina leaders recognized the need for a national organization to speak for the rural people of our state. Dr. Clarence Poe, Jane McKimmon and others invited the Grange back into our state after studying various organizations. Dr. Poe was elected as the first Master in the new Grange in North Carolina and W. Kerr Scott was his successor. Both of these men set into place an organization that would be a significant voice for rural issues and people. Mr. Scott later became Governor and then United States Senator.

Through the years the North Carolina State Grange has produced many great leaders, including: Robert Scott who served as Deputy, then State Master before being elected Lieutenant Governor and then Governor; Jim Graham, our Commissioner of Agriculture, was the Most Representative Boy in the Grange; James B. Hunt, Jr., our present Governor, was raised in a Grange home and served as President of the Youth Grange and on the National Grange Youth team. He met his wife to be, also a Grange Youth Team member, from Iowa.

Lloyd Massey, an outstanding dairy leader from Wayne County and Jim Oliver, tobacco farmer from Robeson County both helped move the Grange into new avenues of service. Harry Caldwell served as State Master for nearly twenty years. His leadership helped bring state and national attention to the Grange and his wife, Margaret, brought her special love of children and rural people to the Grange. She served as State Master first in 1947 and again in the 1960s and 1970s.

The North Carolina State Grange today is an outgrowth of the great heritage of our past. We continue to work with other commodity and farm organizations, co-ops, agribusiness, public schools, and our governmental leaders to represent the varied interest of our members. Family conferences, youth and junior camps, and Grange trips offer opportunities to study and learn more about the needs of our people. Cooperation with 4-H, FFA, and other self-help organizations give greater strength to the Grange. Serving as a member of the Governor's Task Force for Volunteerism is a natural for the Grange, as is taking part in DARE and designing our own programs for youth and seniors.

Community service continues as a strong emphasis of the North Carolina State Grange. Building on the past successes of Schley Grange in Orange County, Arcadia in Davidson and Old Richmond in Forsyth, Edneyville Grange in Henderson County won the National Grange Community Service Award in 1996. Cove Creek Grange in Watauga County was also recognized for their work in 1997. The work of our Family Living Committee (CWA) also provides good local and state recognition for the Grange.

The North Carolina State Grange was organized to meet the needs of rural people. That is still our major emphasis. The need for a strong, consistent voice giving sound counsel is more important today than ever.

Joanne Caldwell, *Director of Women's Activities*

Sweet Potato Casserole

3 cups mashed peeled cooked
    sweet potatoes
1 cup sugar
$^1/_4$ cup ($^1/_2$ stick) margarine, melted
2 eggs, lightly beaten
1 teaspoon vanilla extract
1 cup packed brown sugar
$^1/_3$ cup flour
$^1/_3$ cup margarine
1 cup chopped pecans

Combine the sweet potatoes, sugar, $^1/_4$ cup margarine, eggs and vanilla in a bowl and mix well. Spoon into a 7x7-inch baking dish. Combine the brown sugar, flour, margarine and pecans in a bowl and stir until crumbly. Sprinkle over the prepared layer. Bake at 350 degrees for 30 minutes or until golden brown and bubbly. **Yield:** 6 servings.

Joanne Caldwell, *Director of Women's Activities*

Ohio State Grange

Oliver H. Kelley, under the direction of National Patrons of Husbandry, arrived in Ohio in March 1870 and organized Grange No. 1 in Cleveland. Shortly thereafter, he organized Grange No. 2 near Canton. The Ohio State Grange was chartered in 1873 with 517 Granges.

Through the years, Ohio State Grange has had many worthwhile accomplishments. There has always been a strong legislative tie with our lawmakers. Ohio Grangers have always been ready to aid another member in time of need. Community service is practiced by all Granges and the accomplishments are great.

Many Granges own and maintain their own hall which may serve as meeting centers for their community as well.

Ohio Grangers are proud of Friendly Hills Grange Camp and Conference Center where five Grange camps are held each year in addition to several day or weekend conferences. When not used by Grangers, the camp is rented to community groups.

The Ohio State Grange also owns their office with an apartment for the State Master. It is located in Columbus near the Capital and therefore close to the legislature.

The Ohio State Grange is inspired by accomplishments of the past and hopes for greater leadership and service in the future.

Bernard Shoemaker, *State Master*

Buckeyes

1 pound (4 sticks) margarine
1 (1-pound) jar creamy peanut butter
2 (1-pound) packages confectioners'
   sugar
2 cups semisweet chocolate chips
1/4 block paraffin

Combine the margarine and peanut butter in a saucepan. Cook until creamy, stirring frequently. Remove from heat. Stir in the confectioners' sugar. Let stand until cool. Shape the peanut butter mixture into balls the size of a buckeye. Heat the chocolate chips and paraffin in a double boiler until blended, stirring frequently. Cool slightly. Dip the balls using a wooden pick into the chocolate, leaving 1/4 of the ball uncoated to resemble a buckeye. Arrange on sheets of waxed paper. Let stand until firm. **Yield:** 100 buckeyes.

Bernard Shoemaker, *State Master*

Oklahoma State Grange

The Oklahoma State Grange was founded with the First State Session in January 1916 at Oklahoma City, Oklahoma. Oklahoma State Grange, Patrons of Husbandry was incorporated on April 5, 1917. The purpose was to secure educational, social, legislative, and co-operative benefits for its members. The place of principal business was Banner, Oklahoma, with a branch at Chelsea, Oklahoma.

Eighty-three State Sessions have been held by the Oklahoma State Grange with fourteen State Masters terms ranging from eight months to twelve years. We have had three National Grange Officers. In 1967, three National Grange Youth Officers from the Oklahoma State Grange won the National Highway Users Safety award.

We have had 352 Subordinate Granges and 22 Junior Granges. The Oklahoma State Grange has eighteen Subordinates, one Pomona, and one Junior Grange. We publish the *Sooner State Grange* newspaper quarterly. Grange Mutual Insurance Association was incorporated in 1917 to mutually protect its members from loss by fire, lightning, and tornado.

Yvonne Meritt, *State Secretary*

Oklahoma Red Earth Cake

1/4 cup baking cocoa
3 or 4 tablespoons hot strong coffee
1 1/2 teaspoons red food coloring
2 to 2 1/2 cups cake flour
1 1/2 teaspoons baking soda
1/2 teaspoon salt
1 1/2 cups sugar
1/2 cup shortening
1 egg, beaten
1 cup buttermilk
1 teaspoon vanilla extract

Combine the baking cocoa, coffee and food coloring in a bowl and mix well. Let stand until cool. Sift the cake flour, baking soda and salt together. Beat the sugar and shortening in a mixer bowl until creamy, scraping the bowl occasionally. Add the egg and beat until blended. Add the dry ingredients and buttermilk alternately, beginning and ending with the dry ingredients and mixing well after each addition. Add the baking cocoa mixture and vanilla and mix well. Spoon the batter into two greased and floured 9-inch cake pans. Bake at 350 degrees for 35 minutes. Cool in the pans on a wire rack. Spread with your favorite chocolate frosting. **Yield:** 12 servings.

Yvonne Meritt, *State Secretary*

Oregon State Grange

On Wednesday, September 24, 1873, the Masters of Subordinate Granges in Oregon and Washington Territory met in the Masonic hall at Salem for the purpose of organizing a State Grange in Oregon.

N. W. Garretson, Deputy of the National Grange, called the meeting to order and started the process of forming the State Grange.

Forty-one Grangers from Oregon and seven from the Washington Territories were seated as delegates of Subordinate Granges. Garretson then appointed committees to write bylaws, rules, deal with resolutions, and other matters.

On Thursday morning, September 25, 1873, the rules of the order were adopted and what remained of the morning was spent in instruction of the unwritten work of the order. The afternoon was taken up with accepting the bylaws of the Oregon State Grange. In the evening, the delegates passed a resolution and then requested the National Deputy to drill them on the unwritten work.

Wednesday morning, September 26, 1873, the delegates met and discussed resolutions and committee reports. After the noon break, elections were held and Daniel Clark of Marion County was elected Master.

The morning session of September 27, 1873, started with approval of the minutes and then installation of the officers of the Oregon State Grange. After the installation, Clark appointed several committees. That evening Garretson conferred the degree of Pomona upon the members, after which the Grange enjoyed social activities. Garretson was presented with an elegant gold-headed cane and a set of gold sleeve buttons. W. H. Nash of Napa Grange, California, was also presented with a beautiful set of sleeve buttons.

Nash was a farmer from California who decided that the Grange offered such promise that he left his farm in his wife's care for the summer of 1873, and traveled at his own expense with Garretson to aid in organizing Granges in Oregon.

The Oregon State Grange was created by men and women of action, who sought to make their lives and the lives of their children a little bit better. It is a sizable legacy that we have inherited.

Ed Luttrell, *State Master*

Lemon Herbed Salmon

2¹/2 cups fresh bread crumbs
¹/2 cup chopped fresh parsley
6 tablespoons grated Parmesan cheese
4 garlic cloves, minced
¹/4 cup chopped fresh thyme, or
    1 tablespoon dried thyme
2 teaspoons grated lemon zest
¹/2 teaspoon salt
¹/4 cup (¹/2 stick) butter or
    margarine, melted
1 (3- to 4-pound) salmon fillet
2 tablespoons butter or
    margarine, melted

Combine the bread crumbs, parsley, cheese, garlic, thyme, lemon zest and salt in a bowl and mix well. Add ¹/4 cup butter and toss lightly. Pat the salmon with a paper towel. Arrange skin side down in a greased baking dish. Brush with 2 tablespoons butter. Sprinkle with the crumb mixture. Bake at 350 degrees for 20 to 25 minutes or until the salmon flakes easily. **Yield:** 8 servings.

Betty Huff

Pennsylvania State Grange

Eagle Grange No. 1 was officially organized on March 4, 1871, near Williamsport, and is still active today.

The Pennsylvania State Grange was organized on September 18, 1873 in Reading by representatives of twenty-two of the twenty-five Subordinate Granges which had been organized to that point.

David B. Mauger of Berks County was elected as the first State Master.

The first annual session was convened on January 7, 1874, in Harrisburg. There were 74 Subordinate Granges in the state at that time.

Pennsylvania State Grange published its first cookbook in 1925. Some 42,000 copies were sold in the next few years. The profit of thirty cents on each book was used to cover the costs of a dormitory on the campus of Penn State University. This 1925 edition was reprinted in 1995 to help defray the cost of hosting the National Grange Convention.

Grange members are noted for being great cooks! Additional cookbooks were published in 1950, 1972, 1984, 1992, and finally, in 1997 in time for the 125th anniversary of the State Grange.

Past National Grange Master John W. Scott, and his wife, Dorothy, both Pennsylvania natives, were instrumental in the publication of a cookbook which raised the funds to retire the mortgage on the National Grange headquarters in 1977.

As early as January, 1917, the State Grange established an office in the capital city of Harrisburg to "inform the members of bills before the legislature." In 1952 a vacant home was purchased and equipped to become a State Grange headquarters. It continues to house the offices of the State Master and the legislative and public relations directors. In the 1980s it became the offices for the Pennsylvania State Grange Service Corporation and the Pennsylvania State Grange Federal Credit Union.

In 1999 there are some four hundred Subordinate Granges in the State with twenty-five thousand members, and nearly two thousand associate members enrolled in programs provided by the Service Corporation.

William Steel, *State Master*

Pennsylvania Potpie

1 gallon water
3 to 5 pounds chicken pieces
Chopped onion, celery and carrots
    (optional)
4 cups chopped potatoes
    (optional)
4 cups flour
2 teaspoons baking powder
1 teaspoon salt
1/4 cup shortening
2 eggs, beaten
Milk
1/4 cup chopped fresh parsley

Bring the water to a boil in a stockpot. Add the chicken, onion, celery and carrots. Simmer for 1 hour or until the chicken is tender, stirring occasionally. Remove from the heat. Strain, reserving the broth and chicken. Cut the chicken into bite-size pieces, discarding the skin and bones. Return the broth and chicken to the stockpot. Add the potatoes. Cook for 20 minutes, adding additional water as needed to measure 1 gallon. Combine the flour, baking powder and salt in a bowl and mix well. Cut in the shortening until crumbly. Combine the eggs with enough milk to measure 1 cup. Add to the flour mixture and mix well. Divide the dough into 2 equal portions. Roll each portion on a lightly floured surface. Cut into 1-inch diamonds. Drop the diamonds individually into the boiling stock; reduce the heat. Simmer for 20 minutes or until the noodles are tender. The noodles will settle to the bottom when tender. Stir in the parsley just before serving. May substitute 3 to 5 pounds beef short ribs, beef chuck or ham with bone for the chicken.
Yield: 12 to 15 servings.

William Steel, *State Master*

Rhode Island State Grange

Rhode Island, one of the original thirteen colonies, was established under the leadership of Roger Williams to escape religious persecution. In that same courageous and determined manner, in the late 1800s, its citizens discovered and embraced the philosophy and teachings of the Grange, Order of Patrons of Husbandry. Under the guidance and encouragement of neighboring Massachusetts, and with the reimbursement of fifty cents for postage spent by Massachusetts State Master, James Draper, for materials about the Grange, the Rhode Island State Grange was organized on November 10, 1887, with fifteen Subordinate Granges and 514 members. The geographical size of Rhode Island worked to its advantage and Granges were organized so rapidly that, at one point, twelve received their Charters in one month's time.

Early records testify to a lively interest in public affairs with the Grange debating issues and taking stands on increased funding for education, raising the standard of living, adherence to morality, and maintaining strong family values.

Grange activity, enthusiasm, and interest continued to grow, reaching the heights in the 1940s and 1950s with the New England Granges being acknowledged as "The Gibraltar of the Grange." In addition to agriculture, community service became the focus of Grange activity and the National Health Cause, Help for the Hearing Impaired, was supported nationwide.

As we approach the twenty-first century, Rhode Island Grangers look to the future with renewed enthusiasm for the Grange and its teachings. Old-fashioned values though they may be, they are the foundations on which this country was built and they will serve us well as we look to the year 2000 and beyond.

Marjorie Tucker

Rhode Island-Style Quahog Chowder

8 ounces salt pork, cut into
   $^{1}/_{4}$x$^{1}/_{4}$-inch pieces
2 large onions, thinly sliced
15 pounds quahogs
1 quart water
3 to 4 pounds potatoes, peeled,
   chopped
1 quart water (optional)
Salt and pepper to taste

Fry the salt pork in a skillet until crispy, stirring frequently. Drain, reserving the pan drippings and discarding the salt pork. Fry the onions in the reserved drippings until tender; drain. Combine the quahogs and 1 quart water in a large stockpot. Steam, covered, for 5 to 10 minutes or until the clams open; drain. Remove the clam meat from the shells, reserving the juices. Grind the meat coarsely. Combine the ground clams, reserved juices, potatoes, onions and 1 quart water in a saucepan. Bring to a boil; reduce heat. Cook until the potatoes are tender, stirring occasionally. Season with salt and pepper. Ladle into soup bowls. **Yield:** 10 to 12 servings.

John J. Cottrell III, *State Master*

South Carolina State Grange

The South Carolina State Grange was organized in 1872. The National Convention held its Eighth Annual Session in Charleston, South Carolina, in February 1875. The founders of the Grange were present for this session.

Thomas Taylor was State Master at this time and was Overseer of the National Grange. His wife was Pomona of the National Grange. D. Wyatt Aiken of South Carolina served on the Executive Committee.

The South Carolina Grange closed in 1918 because of World War I. In 1930 the Grange was reorganized with B. D. Anderson of Spartanburg as Master until 1941. William A. Hambright was the next Master.

August 1999 will be the seventieth consecutive meeting of the South Carolina State Grange.

John M. Hammett, Sr., *State Master*

Frogmore Stew

6 to 8 red potatoes, cut into quarters
6 to 8 ears of fresh corn, shucked
2 medium onions, sliced
2 pounds unpeeled large shrimp
2 pounds Polish sausage, cut into
  bite-size pieces
2 pounds oysters in shells (optional)
2 pounds clams or mussels (optional)
Salt and pepper to taste

Combine the potatoes, corn and onions with enough water to cover generously in a stockpot. Cook until the vegetables are tender-crisp. Add the shrimp, sausage, oysters and clams. Boil for 3 minutes or until the shrimp turn pink; drain. Season with salt and pepper. Increase or decrease the amounts of ingredients according to the size of your guest list. **Yield:** 4 to 6 servings.

John M. Hammett, Sr., *State Master*

Tennessee State Grange

There were Granges in Tennessee as early as 1870, although there was no official state organization until July 2, 1873 when William Maxwell from Gibson County was elected the first State Master. The first State Grange Session in Tennessee was held in Gallatin in February of 1874. There was rapid growth of the order throughout the state, and people who joined believed they would reap great financial rewards with the Granges co-operative ventures. Unfortunately, these great rewards were never realized and the Grange declined to the point that only four Granges were still active by 1907. During the ensuing years, there was no official State Grange, but the Grange did still exist and patrons continued to meet together and discuss problems.

The Tennessee State Grange was officially reorganized in 1934 and is still active today. The first Master of the period of the 1930s-1940s was John B. Brooks from Greene County. The Grange grew rapidly during these years probably due to the Depression. In 1937, Tennessee ranked among the top six states in the USA in organization of Subordinates. Two other men were State Masters during the 1930s and 1940s. They were Walter Thompson from Knox County and Paul Dykes from Greene County. During these years the Grange had a great deal of influence in state government and many of the programs they supported were passed into law.

The period from 1950 to 1966 saw only two Masters being elected in the state, M. S. Howell from Wilson County and Allan McComb from Prospect Grange in Blount County.

During the 1950s there was apparently a rift that developed between the Grange, the Farm Bureau, and State Extension Service that resulted in a loss of members in the Grange. Master McComb had as one of his major goals to re-establish good will between these organizations.

He believed that he had succeeded in this venture with the organization of Volunteer Grange in Knox County. This Grange had among its members several members of the University of Tennessee College of Agriculture which was affiliated with the State Extension Service. Another of Master McComb's accomplishments was the organization of the Grange Credit Union.

Since the term of Allan McComb, five other persons have held the position of Master of the Tennessee State Grange. Michael LaForest succeeded Master McComb. He was followed by Donald Bates, Charles Poston, and Larry King. The office of Master is currently held by Mrs. Marian Moore of Knox County.

Some of the accomplishments by Subordinate Granges in Tennessee in the past 25 years include National Community Service honors won by Volunteer Grange. Dupont and Volunteer Granges won National Awards in Lecturers and Women's Activities contests. Junior Grangers have also won several National Awards as well.

The major goals of the Tennessee State Grange in 1999 are just the same as they were in 1873, to increase membership and to involve the entire family in programs that will improve each community where a Grange exists.

Marian H. Moore, *State Master*

Fall Harvest Casserole

4 medium green tomatoes, sliced
1 large onion, thinly sliced
1 (12-ounce) can reduced-sodium Spam,
    cut into bite-size pieces
1 (10-ounce) can cream of celery soup
1 cup shredded sharp Cheddar cheese
4 red banana chiles, seeded, coarsely
    chopped
1 cup crumbled corn bread

Layer the green tomatoes, onion and Spam in a 9x13-inch baking dish sprayed with nonstick cooking spray. Spread with the soup. Sprinkle with the cheese. Top with a mixture of the chiles and corn bread. Bake, covered with foil, at 400 degrees for 30 minutes; remove foil. Bake for 10 minutes longer.
Yield: 8 servings.

Marian H. Moore, *State Master*

Texas State Grange

The Texas State Grange was organized on October 7, 1873 in Dallas. Within two years after being organized, its membership exceeded forty thousand. The records of the Fourth Annual Session held in January 1878 reflect 1,304 Granges had been organized in the state.

On March 2, 1885, the State Grange participated in the ceremonies of laying the cornerstone of the capitol building in Austin. A $7^1/_2$x6-inch leaden box engraved "Texas State Grange" was deposited in the cornerstone. The box contained several Grange articles including copies of a current manual, minutes of the 1884 convention, bylaws of the Order, *The Texas Farmer* publication as well as several varieties of crop and garden seeds.

The fast growth of the Grange in Texas during its early years was attributed to a need for farmers to secure relief from high transportation costs and low prices for their crops. The co-operative movement promoted by the Grange was very appealing to new members. It also promoted Agricultural Fairs. It was very dedicated in its efforts to insure that Texas A&M College was developed into an Agricultural and Mechanical College to benefit agriculture.

The Grange—Friend of the Farmer notes that the first Juvenile Grange movement officially recognized as such, had its beginning in Texas about 1886. The idea seemed so feasible that at the State Session in August, 1888, a Juvenile Grange ritual was adopted. At the National Grange session in November 1888, in Topeka, Kansas, the delegates instructed the Executive Committee to cooperate with the National Lecturer in a study of the Texas Juvenile Grange ritual. At the 24th Annual Session of the National Grange in Atlanta, Georgia, the draft of a revised Juvenile Grange ritual was adopted on November 17, 1890.

During the mid 1880s membership began to decline due to the lack of a sufficient number of Deputies who were informed as to the organizational operation of the Grange and mismanagement of the Grange Stores and Co-operatives. Despite the efforts of State Grange leadership, the decline could not be reversed. The last Annual Session of the original Texas State Grange was opened September 1, 1896.

In 1935 a Deputy for the National Grange was successful in re-organizing the Grange in Texas in the general area from Dallas to San Antonio. Membership in the new Granges was predominantly in rural areas and consisted mostly of young adults who were very active in conferrals of degrees.

When the United States became involved in World War II, a large number of its members went into the armed services or sought employment in defense positions. This had a far-reaching effect on many of the Granges since few of these young adults returned to their home areas, thus causing the Granges to surrender their charters.

The Texas State Grange was among the first State Granges to send a resolution to the National Grange requesting the name of the Juvenile Grange be changed to Junior Grange.

We presently have only sixteen Granges in the state.

We are proud of the fact that from 1947 to the present time, we have had four of the First Ladies of our State Grange to have the honor of serving as Pomona of the National Grange.

Archie D. Knight, *State Master*

Lemon Meringue Pie

1/2 cup sugar
7 tablespoons cornstarch
1/4 teaspoon salt
3 cups milk
3 egg yolks, lightly beaten
1 (14-ounce) can sweetened
    condensed milk
Juice and zest of 3 lemons
3 tablespoons butter
1 baked (10-inch) deep-dish pie shell
3 egg whites
1/4 teaspoon cream of tartar
1/3 cup sugar

Combine 1/2 cup sugar, cornstarch and salt in a saucepan and mix well. Add the milk gradually, stirring constantly. Cook over medium heat until thickened, stirring constantly. Stir a small amount of the hot mixture into the egg yolks. Stir the egg yolks into the hot mixture. Cook for 1 minute, stirring constantly. Add the condensed milk, lemon juice, lemon zest and butter and mix well. Spoon into the pie shell. Beat the egg whites and cream of tartar in a mixer bowl until soft peaks form. Add 1/3 cup sugar gradually, beating constantly until stiff peaks form. Spread over the filling, sealing to the edge. Bake at 350 degrees for 12 minutes or until light brown. **Yield:** 8 servings.

Archie D. Knight, *State Master*

Vermont State Grange

The first Grange in Vermont and New England was permanently organized in St. Johnsbury, Vermont, on August 12, 1871.

Jonathan Lawrence was appointed Grand Deputy of the State of Vermont by authorities of the National Grange in Washington, D.C. It was his duty to organize Subordinate Granges in this state. He met with farmers in the Old Union Schoolhouse on Summer Street in St. Johnsbury on July 4, 1871 to discuss the feasibility of forming a Society of the Order of Patrons of Husbandry.

The application for a charter was signed by fifteen people of which four were women.

There being no table in the hall, a bass drum was used in place of one for signing. The permanent organization was formed August 12, 1871 and a full list of officers was elected. The name of the first Grange in Vermont was Green Mountain Grange No. 1.

Founder and Secretary of the National Grange, O. H. Kelly, gave instructions on November 4th in degree work from the manual and initiated two new members in the first two degrees.

The first anniversary of the founding of Green Mountain Grange No. 1 was appropriately celebrated at the Town Hall in St. Johnsbury. At this time there were thirteen Granges in Vermont and the Vermont State Grange was organized with National Secretary O. H. Kelly presiding. This was a temporary organization and on December 10, 1872 the organization was made permanent with E. P. Colton elected as Master.

The Vermont State Grange was the first in New England and the seventh in the United States.

Chittenden County Pomona No. 1 barely missed establishing the first Pomona in New England. This Pomona Grange was established January 3, 1776 which was four months after Androscogan Pomona in Maine.

Information from: "The Grange in Vermont," Guy B. Horton, Henry A. Stoddard and Harold J. R. Stillwell.

Beverly Wright, *State Secretary*

Maple Oat Bread

2 cups boiling water
1 cup rolled oats
2 tablespoons shortening
1/2 cup maple syrup
2 teaspoons salt
1 envelope dry yeast
1/2 cup lukewarm water
5 to 6 cups flour

Pour the boiling water over the oats in a bowl. Stir in the shortening. Let stand until cool. Add the maple syrup and salt and mix well. Dissolve the yeast in the lukewarm water. Stir into the oats mixture. Add the flour gradually, mixing well after each addition. Knead the dough on a lightly floured surface until smooth and elastic. Place in a greased bowl, turning to coat the surface. Let rise, covered, in a warm place for 1 hour or until doubled in bulk. Divide the dough into 2 equal portions. Shape each portion into a loaf in a greased loaf pan. Let rise, covered, until doubled in bulk. Bake at 350 degrees for 50 minutes or until brown. **Yield:** 2 loaves.

Donna Bulger, *Women's Activities Director*

Virginia State Grange

When the Virginia State Grange was first organized it was struggling to become established, like many of the young Granges in rural areas following the War Between the States. The Virginia State Grange was first organized in the early 1870s. In 1874, the Grange was represented at the Seventh Annual Session held in St. Louis, Missouri, by J. W. White of Charlotte.

The attendance of the Virginia State Grange to the annual session following 1874 was inconsistent. In 1878, J. M. Blanton represented the state at the twelfth annual session held in Richmond, Virginia.

In a few years, the Virginia State Grange lost its status as a state Grange due to lack of support by the independent Virginia farmers.

On September 19, 1928, thirty some years after disbanding, the Virginia State was reorganized with twenty-two Subordinate and four Pomona Granges. It has remained an active state Grange to this day. The present Master is James Taylor of Chesterfield, Virginia.

Ham and Sweet Potato Pie

1 (8-ounce) can juice-pack fruit
    cocktail or mixed fruit
1 (1/4- to 1/2-inch-thick) slice ham
1 (18-ounce) can sweet potatoes,
    drained
2 to 3 tablespoons brown sugar
1 tablespoon cornstarch
2 tablespoons margarine

Drain the fruit cocktail, reserving the juice. Arrange the ham in a 9x13-inch baking pan. Layer with the sweet potatoes and fruit cocktail. Combine the brown sugar and cornstarch in a saucepan and mix well. Stir in the reserved juice and margarine. Bring to a boil, stirring constantly. Pour over the prepared layers. Bake at 350 degrees for 45 minutes, adding water if needed after 30 minutes. **Yield:** 4 to 6 servings.

Washington State Grange

In 1889 Washington farmers, with the help of Oregon State Grange, organized the Washington State Grange two months before Washington became a state. There were sixteen original Granges with many more to come in the next few years. With many ups and downs, 1898 saw only twenty Granges surviving.

In the next seven years the State increased the Granges to 54. In the seven following years the Grange added another 281. Washington State has had many successes in enacting legislation and establishing a name for fighting for agricultural rights.

The delegates for the 1936 Washington State convention voted that the Home Economics Department be a department of the State Grange with an elected State Director. This became the seventeenth officer of the Washington State Grange and Washington became the only state with a seventeenth officer.

Bob Joy, *State Master*

Apple Cake

4 cups chopped apples
1 1/2 cups sugar
2 cups flour
2 teaspoons baking soda
2 teaspoons cinnamon
1/2 teaspoon salt
1/2 cup vegetable oil
2 teaspoons vanilla extract
1 cup chopped walnuts

Toss the apples with the sugar in a bowl. Combine the flour, baking soda, cinnamon and salt in a bowl and mix well. Stir in the oil and vanilla. Add the walnuts and mix well. Stir in the apple mixture. Spoon the batter into a greased 9x10-inch cake pan. Bake at 350 degrees for 50 minutes or until the cake tests done. **Yield:** 15 servings.

Bob Joy, *State Master*

West Virginia State Grange

In early June 1873, E. J. Ohr, a Deputy from Iowa, was sent to West Virginia for the purpose of organizing Granges. By September of 1873, fifteen Subordinate Granges were formed. On September 30, 1873, Masters from fourteen of the Granges met at Martinsburg to organize the West Virginia State Grange. The Charter was signed on October 1, 1873 and the West Virginia State Grange has been active ever since.

Bethuel M. Kitchen (a former member of Congress) was the first Master of the West Virginia State Grange. The first secretary of the West Virginia State Grange was J. W. Curtis. The West Virginia State Grange held its first meeting in Charles Town, West Virginia, in 1874. At this time there were twenty Subordinate Granges in the state.

The first Subordinate Grange was formed at Summit Point, Jefferson County, on June 21, 1873. The first initiated member in West Virginia was Robert W. Baylor. He became the first member and Master of Summit Point. He later served as Master of the West Virginia State Grange. At the annual State Session in Parkersburg, 1876, it was reported that there were 378 active Subordinate Granges with a membership total of 10,753.

Currently, there are twelve Subordinate Granges and five Pomona Granges in the State of West Virginia. We have several excellent prospects for new Granges. Our current membership is approximately five hundred.

James Foster, *State Master*

Winter Beauty Salad

1 cup hot water
1/2 cup red hot cinnamon candies
1 (3-ounce) package lemon gelatin
1 1/2 cups sweetened applesauce
1 cup cottage cheese
1/2 cup chopped nuts
1/2 cup finely chopped celery
1/2 cup mayonnaise-type salad dressing

Combine the hot water and cinnamon candies in a bowl and stir until dissolved. Add the gelatin, stirring until dissolved. Stir in the applesauce. Pour half the applesauce mixture into an 8x8-inch dish. Chill until set. Combine the cottage cheese, nuts and celery in a bowl and mix well. Stir in the salad dressing. Spread over the chilled layer. Top with the remaining applesauce mixture. Chill until set. May add red food coloring if desired. **Yield:** 16 servings.

Earlene Foster, *First Lady*

Wisconsin State Grange

The first contact with the Grange in Wisconsin was in 1868, as Oliver Hudson Kelley made his way from Washington, D.C. back to his home in Minnesota. As he traveled westward, organizing Granges in the states, he stopped in Madison. There he met with a man who was recommended to him as, "a man of standing and connections." It turned out that the man thought highly of himself and was not interested in forming Granges or being involved in any way. Brother Kelley ended up having to borrow money from the Masons in the area to continue on his way. The experience led him to realize he needed to talk to the "dirt farmers" and not count on his city friends.

The next attempt to organize Granges in Wisconsin occurred between December 1870 and June of 1871. Again, though several Granges were organized, two attempts to organize a State Grange meeting lead to failure, mostly because of the inability of the members to agree on the direction of the new organization.

Finally a National Deputy was appointed and between June of 1872 and October 1872, twenty-six Granges were organized. A statewide meeting was held and with the election of a new State Master, the Grange began to quickly flourish. Between December 1872 and the third annual meeting in January 1875, 508 Granges had been organized and a Grange membership of around 18,650 put the Grange Order firmly in place in Wisconsin.

In 1874, the Grange's first real opportunity to become a force in the political arena presented itself in the form of the railroads discriminatory policy, which affected farmers across the nation. Wisconsin's Grange took this opportunity to elect a Grange member to the office of governor.

In an unusual election, the Grangers and other citizens, looking for railroad reform, formed the "Reform Party." The Democratic minority joined with this movement to bolster its chances of winning the governorship.

The ironic twist comes when the railroad interests, upset with the incumbent Republican Governor, sided with the Democrats. This, in essence, helped elect to the governorship the man who was out to destroy the railroad's monopoly. Governor Taylor spent his first term assisting in the enactment of the Granger laws and leading the Grange's fight for fair trade and access with the railroads.

By 1890, the first problems of uncontrolled growth were being felt in the loses of Granges and members by the score. In hindsight, the Grange leaders realized that rampant organization without adequate follow-up visits and instruction, lead to disenchantment with the organization as a whole. The fraternity never had a chance to develop and foster the belief that the organization was a national entity. Local politics and cliquishness didn't help the cause either. These reasons, along with economic hard times, left the State Grange struggling.

However, a strong resurgence through the 1890s into the early 20th century put Wisconsin back on the map in the Grange family. Increasing membership and financial security allowed Wisconsin to host the National Grange Session in 1931. The Grange was a strong and admired political influence in the state through this period and into the 1970s.

Like other Grange states, the new industrial age in America and the loss of family farms and farm jobs, did not bolster strong membership gains. The loss of rural schools to consolidated districts in the cities, the advent of television and the easy entertainment it afforded, along with the increased need to work to keep up with the Joneses, continued to adversely affect membership.

A dedicated core of members continued to believe in and adhere to the Grange philosophy. The members were active in state and national Grange programs, and kept the Grange in the political arena. A dedicated group even boosted membership through the 1980s and Wisconsin hosted the National Convention again in 1986. This was a very exciting time for Grangers in Wisconsin.

Grange membership is still a serious concern for Wisconsin, but we are hoping that a new sense of grassroots involvement and a continuing need to support the farmers of Wisconsin will help with this endeavor. Wisconsin will continue to promote the family values and provide an avenue for political activities for every member of the community. The future of the Grange is in the youth of today.

Duane Scott, *State Master*

Ham and Cheese Bread Bake

1 medium yellow onion, finely chopped
1 tablespoon unsalted butter or
    margarine
1 (10-ounce) package frozen asparagus
    tips, thawed, drained
1 pound baked or boiled ham, cut into
    1-inch cubes
4 slices whole wheat bread, cut into
    1-inch squares
1 cup coarsely shredded Monterey Jack
    or Wisconsin Cheddar cheese
2 cups milk
3 eggs
1 egg white
1 tablespoon Dijon mustard
1/2 teaspoon salt
1/2 teaspoon pepper

Sauté the onion in the butter in a 12-inch nonstick skillet over medium heat for 2 to 3 minutes or until tender-crisp. Add the asparagus. Sauté for 2 minutes. Stir in the ham and bread. Remove from the heat. Reserve 2 tablespoons of the cheese. Whisk the milk, eggs and egg white in a bowl until blended. Add the remaining cheese, Dijon mustard, salt and pepper and stir just until mixed. Stir into the ham mixture. Spoon into a 2-quart shallow baking dish. Sprinkle with the reserved cheese. Bake, covered with foil, at 350 degrees for 30 to 35 minutes or until a knife inserted in the center comes out clean. Broil 4 inches from the heat source for 2 minutes or until light golden brown. May substitute blanched fresh asparagus for the frozen asparagus. **Yield:** 4 servings.

Duane Scott, *State Master*

Wyoming State Grange

The Wyoming State Grange was re-organized and held its first Annual Session in September, 1940, at Casper, Wyoming. Walt Samuelson of Riverton was the driving force behind the re-organization and served as Master for the organizational meeting.

Maurice Doane, serving as National Deputy, organized several Granges around the state and was elected as Master in 1941. Other Masters to head the State Grange were Clarence Jones, Morris Kershner, Elden Keith, Ken Koch, Charles Buell, William Leake, Clint Loyd, Donna Obert, and Pearl Buell.

Wyoming is basically an agricultural state and the Grange has always worked to help the farmers, ranchers, and our communities.

State Grange sessions have been held around the state, alternating between the three Pomona Grange areas. Several Granges have been organized and lost over the years. We now have fifteen Subordinate and three Pomonas.

National officers from Wyoming have been Doris Kershner, Ken Koch, and Donna Obert. Cynthia Kershner, and Kristie Wilson were chosen as National Princesses.

Antelope Gap Junior Grange and Little Bear Grange have won the National Community Service Award.

We are looking forward to a prosperous Grange in the new millennium.

Pearl Buell, *State Master*

Prime Rib Roast

1 (16-pound) prime rib
1 ounce pepper
1 ounce (or more) garlic powder

Cut the ribs from the roast or ask your butcher to perform this task. Place the ribs curved side up in a baking pan. Rub the entire surface of the roast with the pepper and garlic powder. Arrange the roast over the ribs. Bake, covered with foil, for 1³/4 hours for rare to medium-rare. Serve with baked potatoes, tossed vegetable salad and rolls. **Yield:** 32 servings.

Pearl Buell, *State Master*

A New Century
A New Grange

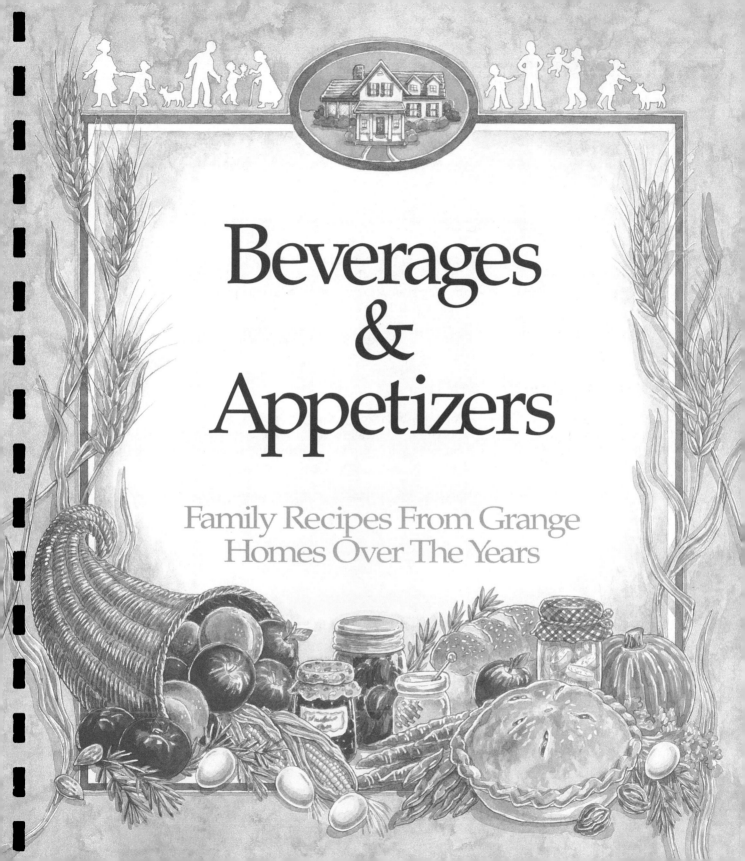

Beverages
&
Appetizers

Family Recipes From Grange
Homes Over The Years

Old Red Mill Punch

4 cups sweet apple cider, chilled
2 cups orange juice, chilled
1 cup lemon juice, chilled
1/2 cup sugar

Combine the apple cider, orange juice, lemon juice and sugar in a punch bowl and mix well. Ladle into punch cups. **Yield:** 10 servings.

Annie Kempton Rice, *Wattannick Grange, New Hampshire*

Fruit Punch

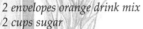

2 envelopes orange drink mix
2 cups sugar
1 (46-ounce) can orange juice
1 (46-ounce) can pineapple juice
Juice of 6 lemons
1 (2-liter) bottle ginger ale

Combine the drink mix and sugar in a large container and mix well. Stir in the orange juice, pineapple juice and lemon juice. Chill, covered, in the refrigerator. Pour into a punch bowl. Add the ginger ale and mix well. Ladle over crushed ice in punch cups. **Yield:** 25 servings.

Betty S. Tomlinson, *Colonial Grange, South Carolina*

Good and Plenty Punch

6 quarts spring water
1 (46-ounce) can pineapple juice
1 (12-ounce) can frozen orange juice
    concentrate
1 cup liquid cherry punch mix
2 envelopes strawberry drink mix
6 quarts ice cubes
2 (12-ounce) cans diet lemon-lime soda

Combine the spring water, pineapple juice, orange juice concentrate, punch mix and drink mix in a large punch bowl and mix well. Stir in the ice cubes and soda just before serving. Ladle into punch cups. **Yield:** 40 servings.

James A. Kirsch, *Banner Grange, Pennsylvania*

Guiltless Punch

2 quarts water
1 small envelope drink mix
1 small envelope sugar-free drink mix
1 (46-ounce) can unsweetened pineapple
    juice
1 (2-liter) bottle diet lemon-lime soda

Combine the water and drink mixes in a large container and mix well. Stir in the pineapple juice and soda. Chill, covered, in the refrigerator. Pour into a punch bowl. Ladle into punch cups. **Yield:** 30 servings.

Carol Warden, *Charity Grange, Oregon*

Lemon-Lime Punch

1 (6-ounce) package lime gelatin
2 cups boiling water
2 cups sugar
1 (46-ounce) can unsweetened
    pineapple juice
1 (12-ounce) can frozen orange juice
    concentrate
Juice of 1 lemon
3 quarts water
1 quart ginger ale

Dissolve the gelatin in the boiling water in a bowl and mix well. Stir in the sugar, pineapple juice, orange juice concentrate and lemon juice. Divide the gelatin mixture equally between two 1-gallon containers. Pour 1$\frac{1}{2}$ quarts of the water into each container. Add the half the ginger ale to each container just before serving and mix well. Pour into a punch bowl. Ladle into punch cups. **Yield:** 2 gallons.

Anna Davis, *Dupont Grange, Tennessee*

The Grange was founded in 1867 as a result of a perceived need to involve rural people, both farm and non-farm, in the community. Our founders saw the necessity of working with all three branches of government, the Executive Branch, the Legislative Branch, and the Judicial Branch. While the Grange is non-partisan, its purpose is to deal with community life.

Perky Party Punch

4 cups cranberry juice
4 cups pineapple juice
2 cups orange juice
1 cup frozen lemonade concentrate
1 quart ginger ale
Ice cubes

Combine the cranberry juice, pineapple juice, orange juice and lemonade concentrate in a punch bowl and mix well. Stir in the ginger ale and ice cubes just before serving. Ladle into punch cups. **Yield:** 32 servings.

Marion A. Shaw, *Beaver Falls, New York*

Bread Dip

1 cup mayonnaise
1 cup sour cream
2 tablespoons dried minced onion
2 tablespoons parsley flakes
1 tablespoon dillweed
1 teaspoon Beau Monde seasoning
1 round loaf bread

Combine the mayonnaise, sour cream, onion, parsley flakes, dillweed and Beau Monde seasoning in a bowl and mix well. Chill, covered, in the refrigerator. Cut the top from the bread loaf and remove the center carefully, leaving a shell. Cut the bread from the center into cubes. Spoon the chilled dip into the bread shell. Serve with the bread cubes. **Yield:** 16 servings.

Camilie Twiss, *Watatic Grange, New Hampshire*

Happy Horseradish and Beef Dip

8 ounces cream cheese, softened
1 cup sour cream
1/2 cup chopped green onions
1 (2-ounce) package dried beef,
    finely chopped
1 tablespoon creamy horseradish
1 teaspoon lemon juice
1/4 teaspoon garlic powder
1/4 teaspoon pepper

Combine the cream cheese, sour cream, green onions, dried beef, horseradish, lemon juice, garlic powder and pepper in a bowl and mix well. Chill, covered, for 1 to 2 hours. Serve with assorted party crackers. **Yield:** 8 to 10 servings.

Rodney Brown, *Bayard Grange, Ohio*

Hot Prairie Fire Dip

1 pound ground pork
1 small onion, chopped
1 teaspoon salt
1 pound Velveeta cheese, shredded
1 (16-ounce) can chili without beans
1 (10-ounce) can tomatoes with green
    chiles, drained

Brown the ground pork with the onion and salt in a skillet, stirring until the pork is crumbly; drain. Stir in the cheese, chili and tomatoes. Cook just until heated through, stirring frequently. Spoon into a slow cooker to keep warm. Serve with tortilla chips or corn chips. **Yield:** 20 servings.

Scott Denkman, *Bloomington Junior Grange, Iowa*

Olé Taco Salad Bean Dip

1 (16-ounce) can refried beans
1 (8-ounce) jar taco sauce
1 medium onion, chopped
2 cups sour cream
1/2 cup mayonnaise-type salad dressing
1 envelope ranch salad dressing mix
1 1/2 cups shredded Cheddar cheese
2 cups shredded lettuce
2 cups chopped drained tomatoes
1 1/2 cups shredded Cheddar cheese

Combine the beans, taco sauce and onion in a bowl and mix well. Spread over the bottom of a 9x13-inch dish. Top with a mixture of the sour cream, salad dressing and salad dressing mix. Layer with 1 1/2 cups cheese, lettuce and tomatoes in the order listed. Sprinkle with 1 1/2 cups cheese. Serve with tortilla chips. **Yield:** 12 servings.

Mrs. Scott Kemph, *Bayard Grange, Ohio*

Community Service to benefit our land includes improving rural health and education programs, both within and outside the government. Our leaders work to improve the security of the family-type farm, to strengthen cooperatives, and expand research—in short, to do everything prudent and reasonable to protect and enhance the efficiency, the productive capacity, the human dignity, and the economic freedom of those who produce food and fiber.

Potato Chip Dip

8 ounces cream cheese, softened
1/3 cup catsup
2 tablespoons Catalina salad dressing
2 tablespoons milk
Finely chopped onion to taste
Salt to taste

Beat the cream cheese, catsup, salad dressing, milk, onion and salt in a mixer bowl until smooth. Chill, covered, in the refrigerator. Serve with potato chips and/or pretzels.
Yield: 10 servings.

Wendy Chaffin, *Fairview Grange, Ohio*

Shrimp Dip

32 ounces cream cheese, softened
1/2 cup small curd cottage cheese
3 (4-ounce) cans shrimp, drained, chopped
2 (4-ounce) cans crab meat, drained, flaked
1 bunch green onions, chopped
1 teaspoon prepared horseradish
1 teaspoon salt
1/4 teaspoon red pepper
1/4 teaspoon dillweed

Combine the cream cheese and cottage cheese in a mixer bowl. Beat until blended. Stir in the shrimp, crab meat, green onions, horseradish, salt, red pepper and dillweed. Chill, covered, until serving time. Serve with chips and/or fresh vegetables.
Yield: 50 servings.

Audrey C. Wilson, *Beach Grange, Virginia*

Southwestern Salsa

1 pound ground beef
1 large onion, chopped
1 (16-ounce) jar mild or hot salsa
1 teaspoon chili powder
1 cup shredded Cheddar cheese

Brown the ground beef with the onion in a cast-iron skillet, stirring until the ground beef is crumbly; drain. Stir in the salsa and chili powder. Cook just until heated through, stirring frequently. Sprinkle with the cheese. Serve in the skillet with tortilla chips. **Yield:** 25 servings.

Roxanne Cottrell, *Richmond Grange, Rhode Island*

Veggie Dip

2 eggs
1/4 cup sugar
3 tablespoons vinegar
3 tablespoons margarine
24 ounces cream cheese, softened
1 green bell pepper, finely chopped
1 small onion, finely chopped

Whisk the eggs in a saucepan until blended. Stir in the sugar, vinegar and margarine. Cook until thickened, stirring constantly. Let stand until cool. Beat the cream cheese in a mixer bowl until creamy. Add the green pepper and onion and mix well. Stir in the egg mixture. Chill, covered, until serving time. Serve with assorted party crackers, chips and/or pretzels.
Yield: 25 servings.

Ann Distler, *Boot Jack Grange, Pennsylvania*

Cheese Ball

8 ounces cream cheese, softened
1 cup shredded Cheddar cheese
1 tablespoon Worcestershire sauce
1 tablespoon minced onion
1/2 cup finely chopped walnuts or pecans

Combine the cream cheese, Cheddar cheese, Worcestershire sauce and onion in a mixer bowl. Beat until blended, scraping the bowl occasionally. Shape the cheese mixture into a ball. Chill, covered, for 15 to 30 minutes. Coat the cheese ball with the walnuts. Serve with assorted party crackers. May be prepared in advance and stored, covered, in the refrigerator.
Yield: 15 servings.

Susan C. Culler, *Glade Valley Grange, Maryland*

Our Centennial Activities for 100 years of service to the nation took place in 1967. We found Subordinate Granges throughout the land taking pride in membership. As a lasting reminder to the nation of the first 100 years of the Grange, we reflected on the fact that William Saunders, one of the founders of our Order, designed the National Soldiers Cemetery at Gettysburg, Pennsylvania, in addition to the Grange Family Meditation Center and Chapel erected there.

Cheese Spread

1 cup half-and-half
1/2 cup vinegar
1/2 cup water
1/4 cup sugar
2 eggs, beaten
2 tablespoons flour or cornstarch
1 teaspoon salt
8 ounces Cheddar cheese, shredded

Whisk the half-and-half, vinegar, water, sugar, eggs, flour and salt in a saucepan. Bring to a boil over medium heat, stirring constantly. Remove from heat. Add the cheese and stir until smooth. Spoon mixture into a serving bowl. Serve with assorted party crackers and/or chips or use as a sandwich spread. **Yield:** 10 servings.

Mildred Meeker, *Little Bear Grange, Wyoming*

Salmon Party Ball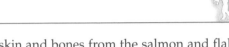

1 (16-ounce) can salmon, drained
8 ounces cream cheese, softened
1 tablespoon lemon juice
2 teaspoons grated onion
1 teaspoon grated horseradish
1/4 teaspoon salt
1/4 teaspoon liquid smoke
1/2 cup chopped pecans
3 tablespoons snipped fresh parsley

Discard the skin and bones from the salmon and flake. Combine the salmon, cream cheese, lemon juice, onion, horseradish, salt and liquid smoke in a bowl and mix well. Chill, covered, in the refrigerator. Shape the salmon mixture into a ball. Roll in a mixture of the pecans and parsley. Chill, covered, until serving time. Serve with assorted party crackers. **Yield:** 12 servings.

Patty Friede, *Stony Point Grange, Pennsylvania*

Shrimp Mousse

1 1/2 tablespoons unflavored gelatin
1/2 cup cold water
1 (10-ounce) can tomato soup
6 ounces cream cheese
8 ounces deveined peeled cooked shrimp
1 cup mayonnaise
3/4 cup finely chopped onion
3/4 cup finely chopped celery

Soften the gelatin in the cold water. Bring the soup to a boil in a saucepan. Add the cream cheese. Cook until blended, stirring constantly. Stir in the gelatin mixture. Cool in the refrigerator until slightly thickened. Reserve several of the shrimp for the garnish and finely chop remaining shrimp. Stir the chopped shrimp, mayonnaise, onion and celery into the soup mixture. Spoon into a mold or bowl. Chill, covered, until set. Invert onto a lettuce-lined serving platter. Garnish with the reserved shrimp. Serve with assorted party crackers. **Yield:** 8 to 10 servings.

Thelma Olson, *Norwich Grange, Connecticut*

Tex-Mex Cheesecake

16 ounces cream cheese, softened
2 cups shredded sharp Cheddar cheese
3 eggs
1 (4-ounce) can chopped mild green
    chiles, drained
1 envelope taco seasoning mix
1 cup sour cream
2/3 cup drained chunky salsa

Combine the cream cheese and Cheddar cheese in a mixer bowl. Beat until blended. Add the eggs, chiles and seasoning mix. Beat until mixed, scraping the bowl occasionally. Spread in a 9-inch springform pan. Bake at 350 degrees for 35 to 40 minutes or until the edge pulls from the side of the pan. Spread with a mixture of the sour cream and salsa. Bake for 10 minutes longer. Chill, covered, for 24 hours. Serve with assorted party crackers and/or tortilla chips. **Yield:** 25 servings.

Janet Price, *Director of Deaf Activities, National Grange*

Cheese Puffs

3/4 cup water
3/4 cup milk
1/2 cup (1 stick) butter
1 1/3 cups flour
1/4 teaspoon salt
1/8 teaspoon cayenne pepper
1/8 teaspoon white pepper
1/8 teaspoon nutmeg
6 eggs
1 3/4 cups shredded Swiss cheese
1 tablespoon Dijon mustard

Bring the water, milk and butter to a boil in a saucepan. Boil until the butter melts, stirring occasionally. Remove from heat. Add the flour, salt, cayenne pepper, white pepper and nutmeg, stirring until a soft ball forms. Cool for 5 minutes. Add the eggs 1 at a time, mixing well after each addition. Stir in 1 1/2 cups of the cheese and Dijon mustard. Drop by teaspoonfuls onto a parchment-lined or greased baking sheet. Sprinkle with the remaining 1/4 cup cheese. Bake at 400 degrees for 30 to 40 minutes or until brown. Serve warm or at room temperature. **Yield:** 35 cheese puffs.

Doris Simpson, *Ringoes Grange, New Jersey*

Community Service continues to grow, including activities such as working on toy projects, visiting shut-ins in their homes, working and giving to Children's hospitals, and International Friendship in the form of entertaining international guests in our Granges.

Chicken Wings

1 cup orange marmalade
1 cup soy sauce
3 garlic cloves, crushed, or garlic salt
1 teaspoon pepper
1 teaspoon ginger
40 chicken wings

Combine the marmalade, soy sauce, garlic, pepper and ginger in a bowl and mix well. Pour over the chicken wings in a shallow baking dish, turning to coat. Marinate, covered, in the refrigerator for 8 to 10 hours, turning occasionally. Bake at 300 degrees for 1¹/2 hours. May marinate the chicken wings in sealable plastic bags. **Yield:** 40 chicken wings.

Peggy Cornette, *Bounty Land Grange, South Carolina*

Holiday Buffet Eggs

12 hard-cooked eggs
¹/2 cup sweet pickle cubes
1 tablespoon pickle juice
¹/2 cup mayonnaise
2 tablespoons prepared mustard or
    Dijon mustard
Salt and coarsely ground pepper
    to taste

Slice the eggs lengthwise into halves. Remove the yolks carefully, reserving the whites. Combine the yolks, pickle cubes and pickle juice in a bowl and mix well. Stir in the mayonnaise, mustard, salt and pepper. Mound the yolk mixture by rounded spoonfuls into each egg white. Arrange on a serving platter. Garnish with sliced pimento-stuffed olives. **Yield:** 24 servings.

Grace D. Nichols, *Mountville Grange, South Carolina*

Miniature Ham Puffs

1 (2-ounce) package sliced ham
1 small onion
¹/2 cup shredded Swiss cheese
1 egg, lightly beaten
1¹/2 teaspoons Dijon mustard
¹/8 teaspoon ground pepper
1 (8-count) can crescent rolls

Chop the ham and onion finely with a food chopper. Combine the ham, onion, cheese, egg, Dijon mustard and pepper in a bowl and mix well. Unroll the roll dough. Press the dough into a large rectangle, pressing the edges and perforations to seal. Cut the rectangle into 24 equal pieces. Pat each dough piece over the bottom and up the side of a miniature muffin cup sprayed with nonstick cooking spray. Spoon some of the ham mixture into each prepared muffin cup. Bake at 350 degrees for 15 minutes or until light brown. **Yield:** 24 ham puffs.

Pat Flynn, *Moosup Valley Grange, Rhode Island*

Barbecued Hot Dogs

4 ounces bacon, chopped
1 large onion, chopped
2 to 3 pounds beef frankfurters,
    cut into 1/2-inch slices
1 (18-ounce) bottle barbecue sauce
1 (12-ounce) bottle chili sauce
1 (5-ounce) jar prepared horseradish
1/4 teaspoon crushed red pepper
1/2 teaspoon (about) liquid smoke

Layer the bacon, onion and frankfurters in the order listed in a 9x12-inch baking pan. Combine the barbecue sauce, chili sauce, horseradish, red pepper and liquid smoke in a bowl and mix well. Spoon over the frankfurters. Bake at 350 degrees for 30 to 45 minutes or until bubbly, stirring occasionally. Serve with wooden picks. **Yield:** 25 servings.

John J. Cottrell, III, *Master, Rhode Island State Grange*

Stuffed Mushrooms

12 large mushrooms
2 tablespoons margarine
1 medium onion, finely chopped
2 ounces pepperoni, chopped
1/4 cup finely chopped green bell pepper
1 small garlic clove, minced
1/2 cup finely crushed butter crackers
3 tablespoons grated Parmesan cheese
1 tablespoon chopped fresh parsley
1/2 teaspoon salt
1/4 teaspoon oregano
1/8 teaspoon pepper
1/3 cup chicken broth

Rinse the mushrooms and remove the stems. Chop the stems finely. Drain the mushroom caps on paper towels. Heat the margarine in a skillet until melted. Add the mushroom stems, onion, pepperoni, green pepper and garlic and mix well. Cook until the vegetables are tender but not brown, stirring frequently. Stir in the cracker crumbs, cheese, parsley, salt, oregano and pepper. Add the broth and mix well. Spoon the vegetable mixture into mushroom caps, rounding the tops. Arrange the caps in a single layer in a shallow baking dish. Add just enough water to the dish to measure 1/4 inch. Bake at 325 degrees for 25 minutes or until heated through. **Yield:** 12 servings.

Patty Cottrell, *First Lady, Rhode Island State Grange*

Another community service by our leaders that helped the grass roots people of the land was the state-by-state Grange fight for railroad legislation. The United States Supreme Court handed down decisions in seven Grange railroad cases in November, 1876. These decisions established the fundamental principle that the states had the right to regulate monopolies.

Salami Cornets

15 slices Genoa salami, cut into halves
8 ounces cream cheese, softened
4 ounces Boursin cheese
Sprigs of parsley
Black olive slivers (optional)

Roll the salami halves into cornets. Beat the cream cheese and Boursin cheese in a mixer bowl until smooth. Spoon the cheese mixture into a pastry bag fitted with the desired tip. Pipe the cheese mixture into the cornets. Top each with a sprig of parsley and a black olive sliver. Arrange on a serving platter. **Yield:** 30 servings.

Mrs. Christopher Glover, *Lyme Grange, Connecticut*

Spinach Bars

¼ cup (½ stick) butter or margarine
1 (10-ounce) package frozen chopped
    spinach, thawed, drained
1 cup flour
1 teaspoon salt
1 teaspoon baking powder
1 cup milk
3 eggs, lightly beaten
1 pound sharp Cheddar cheese,
    shredded
1 small onion, minced
6 medium mushrooms, chopped

Heat the butter in a 9x13-inch baking pan at 350 degrees until melted, tilting the pan to coat the bottom. Squeeze the excess moisture from the spinach. Combine the flour, salt and baking powder in a bowl and mix well. Stir in the milk and eggs. Add the spinach, cheese, onion and mushrooms and mix well. Spoon into the prepared pan. Bake at 350 degrees for 35 minutes. Cool slightly. Cut into bars. **Yield:** 48 bars.

Joy P. Murray, *Cox Chapel Grange, Virginia*

Caramel Corn

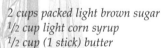

2 cups packed light brown sugar
½ cup light corn syrup
½ cup (1 stick) butter
1 teaspoon salt
½ teaspoon cream of tartar
1 teaspoon baking soda
6 quarts popped popcorn

Combine the brown sugar, corn syrup, butter, salt and cream of tartar in a saucepan. Bring to a boil, stirring frequently. Boil for 5 minutes. Remove from heat. Add the baking soda, stirring until foamy. Pour over the popcorn in a roasting pan, tossing to coat. Bake at 250 degrees for 30 minutes, stirring once. May omit the baking step if served immediately. **Yield:** 6 to 10 servings.

Eric Burger, *Colon Grange, Michigan*

Quick and Easy Caramel Corn

1 cup packed brown sugar
1/2 cup (1 stick) butter
10 to 12 large marshmallows
4 quarts popped popcorn

Bring the brown sugar and butter to a boil in a saucepan over medium heat, stirring frequently. Add the marshmallows. Cook until blended, stirring constantly. Pour over the popcorn in a large bowl, stirring until coated. **Yield:** 6 to 8 servings.

Vernon Kramer, *Walter's Butte Grange, Idaho*

Karamelled Korn

1 1/2 cups popcorn, popped
1 cup (2 sticks) butter
2 cups packed brown sugar
1/2 cup light corn syrup
1 teaspoon salt
1 teaspoon baking soda

Pour the popcorn into a roasting pan. Heat the butter in a saucepan until melted. Stir in the brown sugar, corn syrup and salt. Bring to a boil. Boil for 5 minutes. Remove from heat. Stir in the baking soda. Pour over the popcorn and toss to coat. **Yield:** 15 servings.

Sharon K. Nossaman, *Mt. Allison Grange, Colorado*

In 1984 National Grange delegates sent a telegram to President Reagan from their session requesting that he release more surplus grain to help with devastating famine in Ethiopia and Mozambique. "America has a moral duty to share our bounty with those in need," the telegram said.

Microwave Granola

3 cups rolled oats
1 cup coarsely chopped pecans
1 cup coarsely chopped walnuts
3/4 cup slivered almonds
1/2 cup shredded coconut
1/3 cup packed brown sugar
1/4 cup honey
1/4 cup vegetable oil
1 teaspoon cinnamon
1 teaspoon vanilla extract
1 cup raisins

Combine the oats, pecans, walnuts, almonds and coconut in a bowl and mix well. Combine the brown sugar, honey, oil and cinnamon in a 3-quart microwave-safe bowl and mix well. Microwave on High for 1 1/2 minutes or until the mixture comes to a boil. Stir in the vanilla. Add the oats mixture and toss to coat. Microwave on High for 6 minutes, stirring 2 to 3 times. Stir in the raisins. Let stand for 2 hours before serving, stirring twice. **Yield:** 6 cups.

Winifred Curtiss, *Pleasant Ridge Grange, Idaho*

Peanut Butter and Jelly Granola

9 cups quick-cooking oats
1 cup wheat germ
1 cup wheat bran
1 cup sliced almonds
1/2 cup sunflower seed kernels
1/2 cup pumpkin seeds
1/2 cup flax seeds
1/4 cup sesame seeds
1 teaspoon cinnamon
3/4 cup honey
3/4 cup jelly or jam
1/2 cup packed brown sugar
1/2 cup vegetable oil
1/2 cup peanut butter

Combine the oats, wheat germ, wheat bran, almonds, sunflower kernels, pumpkin seeds, flax seeds, sesame seeds and cinnamon in a large bowl and mix well. Combine the honey, jelly, brown sugar, oil and peanut butter in a saucepan and mix well. Cook just until heated through, stirring frequently. Pour over the oats mixture and toss to coat. Spoon into two 9x13-inch baking pans. Bake at 325 degrees for 25 minutes or until brown, stirring every 10 minutes. May stir in dried fruits and raisins at end of baking process if desired. **Yield:** 3 quarts.

Diane Flynn, *Maine Director of Women's Activities*

Toffee Gems

44 honey graham crackers
1/2 cup (1 stick) butter
1/2 cup (1 stick) margarine
1/2 cup sugar
1 cup chopped walnuts or pecans

Arrange the graham crackers in a single layer on a baking sheet. Combine the butter, margarine and sugar in a saucepan. Bring to a boil. Boil for 2 minutes, stirring frequently. Drizzle over the graham crackers. Sprinkle with the walnuts. Bake at 350 degrees for 10 minutes. Let stand until cool. Break apart. **Yield:** 44 servings.

Charlotte Montgomery, *New Market Grange, Maryland*

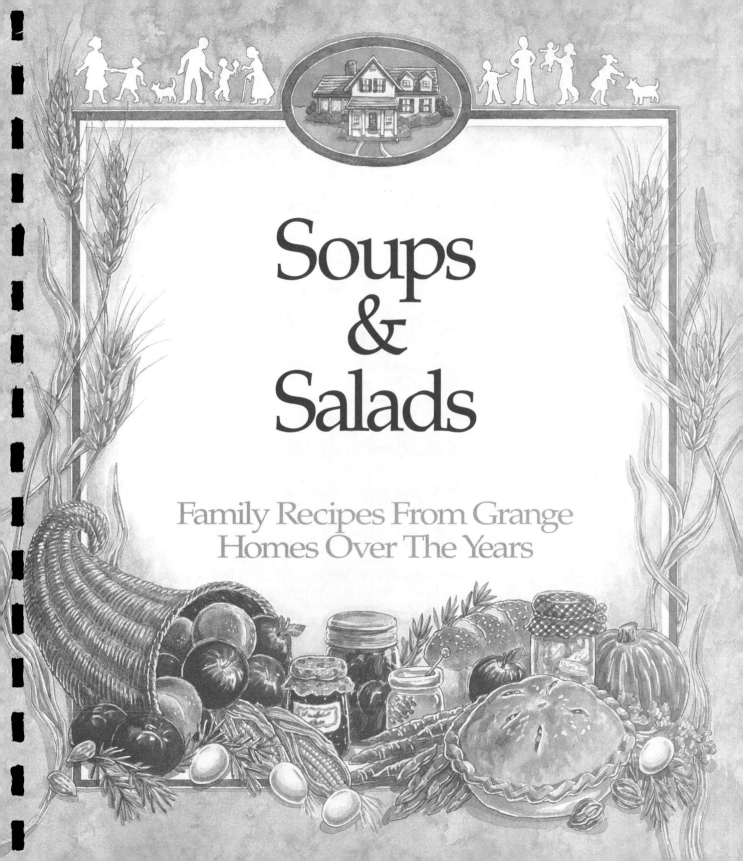

Soups & Salads

Family Recipes From Grange
Homes Over The Years

Carrot Soup

2 pounds carrots, peeled, sliced
1 medium onion, chopped
5¹/₂ cups fat-free chicken broth
2 tablespoons sugar
2 teaspoons dillweed
¹/₂ teaspoon salt
¹/₄ teaspoon pepper
1 (12-ounce) can evaporated skim milk
¹/₂ cup skim or 1% milk

Combine the carrots, onion, broth, sugar, dillweed, salt and pepper in a saucepan; cover. Bring to a boil; reduce heat. Simmer for 45 minutes or until the vegetables are tender, stirring occasionally. Process the carrot mixture in a food processor or blender until puréed. Return the purée to the saucepan. Stir in the evaporated skim milk and skim milk. Cook for 10 to 15 minutes or until heated through, stirring occasionally; do not boil. Ladle into soup bowls. **Yield:** 5 servings.

Kathy Carter, *Glastonbury Grange, Connecticut*

Chili

1¹/₂ pounds ground beef
1 (32-ounce) can tomato juice
2 (16-ounce) cans Mexican-style
    stewed tomatoes
2 (15-ounce) can chili beans
2 cups water
1 onion, chopped
1 teaspoon salt
Chili powder to taste

Brown the ground beef in a skillet, stirring until crumbly; drain. Combine the tomato juice, undrained tomatoes, undrained beans, water, onion, salt and chili powder in a saucepan and mix well. Stir in the ground beef. Bring to a boil, stirring occasionally; reduce heat. Cook until of the desired consistency, stirring occasionally. Adjust the seasonings. Ladle into chili bowls. **Yield:** 6 servings.

Rita L. Johnson, *Riverview Grange, Nebraska*

Creamy Corn Soup

2 tablespoons butter
2 tablespoons flour
1 small onion, finely chopped
1¹/₂ cups water
1 (15-ounce) can cream-style corn
1¹/₂ cups milk
4 teaspoons instant chicken bouillon
¹/₈ teaspoon salt
¹/₈ teaspoon pepper
1 tablespoon finely chopped
    fresh parsley

Heat the butter in a 3-quart saucepan over low heat until melted. Stir in the flour. Cook until smooth and bubbly, stirring constantly. Add the onion. Cook for 1 minute, stirring constantly. Stir in the water. Bring to a boil, stirring occasionally. Boil for 1 minute, stirring constantly. Add the corn, milk and bouillon granules and mix well. Bring to a boil, stirring frequently. Stir in the salt and pepper. Ladle into soup bowls. Sprinkle with the parsley. **Yield:** 6 servings.

Atsuko K. Crum, *Glade Valley Grange, Maryland*

Cheeseburger Soup

8 ounces ground beef
3/4 cup chopped onion
3/4 cup shredded carrot
3/4 cup chopped celery
1 teaspoon basil
1 teaspoon parsley flakes
1 tablespoon butter
4 cups chopped peeled potatoes
3 cups chicken broth
3 tablespoons butter
1/4 cup flour
8 ounces American cheese, shredded
1 1/2 cups milk
Salt and pepper to taste
1/4 cup sour cream

Brown the ground beef in a 4-quart saucepan, stirring until crumbly; drain. Set aside. Sauté the onion, carrot, celery, basil and parsley flakes in 1 tablespoon butter in the 4-quart saucepan for 10 to 12 minutes or until the vegetables are tender. Stir in the ground beef, potatoes and broth. Bring to a boil; reduce heat. Simmer, covered, for 12 to 14 minutes or until the potatoes are tender, stirring occasionally. Heat 3 tablespoons butter in a skillet until melted. Stir in the flour. Cook for 2 minutes, stirring constantly. Add to the potato mixture and mix well. Cook for 2 to 3 minutes, stirring constantly. Add the cheese, milk, salt and pepper and mix well. Cook over low heat until the cheese melts, stirring frequently; do not boil. Remove from heat. Stir in the sour cream. Ladle into soup bowls. **Yield:** 6 to 8 servings.

Betty Lemon, *Happy Camp Grange, California*

Gazpacho

1 cup finely chopped peeled tomato
1/2 cup finely chopped green
    bell pepper
1/2 cup finely chopped zucchini
1/2 cup finely chopped cucumber
1/4 cup finely chopped onion
2 teaspoons parsley
1 small garlic clove, minced
2 cups vegetable juice cocktail
2 tablespoons olive oil
1 teaspoon Worcestershire sauce
1/2 teaspoon salt
1/4 teaspoon pepper (optional)

Combine the tomato, green pepper, zucchini, cucumber, onion, parsley and garlic in a stainless steel or glass bowl and mix well. Add the vegetable juice cocktail, olive oil, Worcestershire sauce, salt and pepper and stir until mixed. Chill, covered, for 4 hours or longer. Ladle into chilled soup bowls. Garnish with croutons and/or sour cream. **Yield:** 4 servings.

Paul Rush, *Moosup Valley Grange, Rhode Island*

North Carolina farmers experienced the worst drought on record in the summer of 1986. They were faced with threats of livestock starvation on top of difficult economic conditions. Grange activists across the nation became concerned and organized a massive "hay lift" to assist the struggling farmers.

Ham Hock and Bean Soup

3/4 cup mixed dried small beans,
    limas and split peas
1 smoked ham hock
4 cups chicken or beef broth
2 cups cooked or fresh tomatoes
2 large carrots, chopped
1 large onion, chopped
1 potato, chopped
1 cup coarsely chopped cabbage
1/2 teaspoon pepper
Salt to taste

Sort and rinse the beans. Combine the beans with enough water to cover in a large bowl. Let stand for 8 to 10 hours; drain. Combine the beans, ham hock, broth, tomatoes, carrots, onion, potato, cabbage and pepper in a 4-quart stockpot. Bring to a boil, stirring occasionally; reduce heat. Simmer for 2 hours or until the beans are tender, stirring occasionally. Discard the bone. Season with salt. Ladle into soup bowls.
Yield: 8 to 10 servings.

Fern Lang, *Woodburn Grange, Oregon*

Lentil Stew

1 pound lentils
1 (14-ounce) can beef broth
4 broth cans water
2 cups chopped onions
3/4 cup sliced celery
5 cups chopped peeled potatoes
1 cup sliced carrot
1 (11-ounce) can tomato juice
1 teaspoon salt

Sort and rinse the lentils. Combine the lentils, broth, water, onions and celery in a 5- or 6-quart stockpot. Bring to a boil; reduce heat. Simmer for 20 minutes, stirring occasionally. Add the potatoes, carrot, tomato juice and salt and mix well. Bring to a boil over high heat; reduce heat. Simmer for 20 to 25 minutes or until the potatoes and carrot are tender, stirring occasionally. Ladle into soup bowls. **Yield:** 6 servings.

Deb Elliott, *Hookstown Grange, Pennsylvania*

Cream of Mushroom Soup

1 pound fresh mushrooms, sliced
1/2 cup finely chopped onion
2 tablespoons butter
3/4 teaspoon salt
1/8 teaspoon pepper
2 tablespoons butter
3 tablespoons flour
1 (10-ounce) can chicken broth
2 cups half-and-half
1/4 teaspoon nutmeg (optional)

Sauté the mushrooms and onion in 2 tablespoons butter in a skillet for 4 to 5 minutes. Sprinkle with the salt and pepper. Remove from heat. Heat 2 tablespoons butter in a saucepan until melted. Stir in the flour. Cook until bubbly and light brown, stirring constantly. Remove from heat. Add the broth gradually, stirring constantly. Cook for 5 minutes or until thickened, stirring constantly. Add the half-and-half gradually and mix well. Stir in the mushroom mixture. Cook just until heated through, stirring frequently; do not boil. Stir in the nutmeg. Ladle into soup bowls. **Yield:** 6 servings.

Mona R. Bowmaster, *Logan Grange, Pennsylvania*

French Onion Soup

3 large onions, thinly sliced
1/2 cup (1 stick) margarine
8 ounces fresh mushrooms, sliced
    (optional)
6 cups hot water
6 bouillon cubes
2 tablespoons Worcestershire sauce
1/2 teaspoon salt
6 slices French bread, toasted
    (optional)
8 ounces mozzarella cheese, shredded
    (optional)

Sauté the onions in the margarine in a large skillet until light brown. Combine the onions, mushrooms, hot water, bouillon cubes, Worcestershire sauce and salt in a 4-quart slow cooker and mix well. Cook, covered, on Low for 4 to 6 hours or until of the desired consistency. Ladle the soup into 6 ovenproof soup bowls. Top each serving with a slice of bread. Sprinkle with the cheese. Arrange the bowls on a baking sheet. Broil for 2 minutes or until the cheese melts. Serve immediately. **Yield:** 6 servings.

June Pinkston, *Wesley's Chapel Grange, Tennessee*

Green Pea and Lettuce Soup

2 tablespoons butter
2 heads lettuce, sliced
1 onion, chopped
4 cups chicken stock
2 cups green peas
2 potatoes, peeled, chopped
Sugar to taste

Heat the butter in a saucepan until melted. Add the lettuce and onion and mix well. Cook just until tender, stirring frequently. Stir in the stock, peas, potatoes and sugar. Simmer, covered, until the peas and potatoes are tender, stirring occasionally. Process in a blender until smooth. Reheat if desired. Ladle into soup bowls. May be frozen for future use. **Yield:** 4 to 5 servings.

Mary Nazemetz, *Raritan Valley Grange, New Jersey*

The National Grange Convention of 1997 established a new department for Community Service. The 400,000 Grange members sponsor programs and projects in their communities to benefit people of all ages, regardless of race or religion.

Cheesy Potato Soup

3 cups chopped peeled potatoes
1 cup water
¹/₂ cup chopped celery
¹/₂ cup chopped or sliced carrot
¹/₄ cup chopped onion
1 chicken bouillon cube
1 teaspoon parsley flakes
¹/₂ teaspoon salt
¹/₈ teaspoon pepper
1³/₄ cups milk
2 tablespoons flour
8 ounces Velveeta or American cheese,
    shredded
Bacon bits to taste

Combine the potatoes, water, celery, carrot, onion, bouillon cube, parsley flakes, salt and pepper in a saucepan. Simmer for 15 to 20 minutes or until the vegetables are tender-crisp, stirring occasionally. Whisk the milk and flour in a bowl until blended. Stir into the vegetable mixture. Cook until thickened, stirring frequently. Add the cheese and mix well. Cook just until the cheese melts, stirring frequently. Ladle into soup bowls. Sprinkle with bacon bits. May add additional milk for a thinner consistency. **Yield:** 6 to 8 servings.

Beverly Stewart, *Rural Valley Grange, Pennsylvania*

Potato Soup

2 pounds potatoes, peeled, chopped
¹/₂ cup chopped celery
¹/₂ cup chopped onion
¹/₃ cup shredded carrot
¹/₄ cup (¹/₂ stick) margarine
2 cups milk
¹/₂ cup flour
2 teaspoons salt
Pepper to taste
¹/₂ cup shredded sharp Cheddar cheese

Combine the potatoes, celery, onion and carrot with enough water to measure twice the depth of the vegetables in a saucepan. Cook until the vegetables are tender, stirring occasionally. Add the margarine and mix well. Stir in a mixture of the milk and flour. Add the salt and pepper and mix well. Bring to a boil, stirring occasionally. Remove from heat. Add the cheese and stir until melted. May add additional milk for a thinner consistency. Ladle into soup bowls. **Yield:** 6 to 8 servings.

Marie A. Elliott, *Hookstown Grange, Pennsylvania*

Sauerkraut Soup

1 pound summer or kielbasa sausage,
    coarsely ground
2 tablespoons flour
2 cups milk
1 cup half-and-half
6 to 12 ounces sauerkraut
1¹/₂ tablespoons lemon juice

Brown the sausage in a saucepan, stirring until crumbly. Stir in the flour. Cook until of a roux consistency, stirring constantly. Add the milk and half-and-half and mix well. Cook over medium heat until thickened, stirring occasionally. Stir in the sauerkraut and lemon juice. Cook over low heat for 5 to 10 minutes or until of the desired consistency. Ladle into soup bowls. **Yield:** 4 servings.

David Roberts, *Blanchard Grange, Idaho*

Sausage Bean Chowder

1 pound bulk pork sausage
2 (16-ounce) cans kidney beans
1 quart canned tomatoes
1 quart water
1 large onion, chopped
1 bay leaf
1 1/2 teaspoons seasoned salt
1/2 teaspoon thyme
1/2 teaspoon pepper
1/2 teaspoon garlic powder
1 1/2 cups chopped potatoes
1/2 green bell pepper, chopped

Brown the sausage in a skillet, stirring until crumbly; drain. Combine the undrained beans, undrained tomatoes, water, onion, bay leaf, seasoned salt, thyme, pepper and garlic powder in a stockpot and mix well. Stir in the sausage. Simmer, covered, for 1 hour, stirring occasionally. Add the potatoes and green pepper and mix well. Cook, covered, for 10 to 15 minutes or until the potatoes are tender. Discard the bay leaf. Ladle into soup bowls. **Yield:** 15 to 20 servings.

Betty Thompson, *First Lady, Maryland State Grange*

Seafood Chowder

1 cup scallops
2 (10-ounce) cans cream of
    shrimp soup
2 soup cans milk
1 (4-ounce) can cocktail shrimp,
    drained
1 medium onion, minced
1 cup imitation crab meat
Salt and pepper to taste
Butter or margarine to taste

Combine the scallops with just enough water to cover in a saucepan. Simmer for 5 minutes or until tender. Combine the undrained scallops, soup, milk, shrimp, onion and crab meat in a slow cooker. Cook, covered, until heated through. Season with salt and pepper. Stir in the butter. Ladle into soup bowls. **Yield:** 4 servings.

Marion T. Jones, *Daniel Webster Grange, New Hampshire*

In 1999 a new Community Recognition Program was introduced to honor police and firefighters. In the year 2000 we'll be adding a teacher to this recognition. A Fill An Empty Plate Food Drive once a month has also been added.

Winter Squash and Tomato Soup

1 large onion, chopped
2 tablespoons butter
1 small butternut squash, peeled,
    chopped
2 or 3 tomatoes, peeled, chopped
2 ribs celery, chopped
2 carrots, peeled, chopped
2 potatoes, peeled, chopped
4 cups chicken broth
1 1/2 cups half-and-half or milk
Salt and pepper to taste

Cook the onion in the butter in a saucepan for 3 minutes, stirring frequently. Add the squash, tomatoes, celery, carrots and potatoes. Cook until tender-crisp, stirring frequently. Mash the squash mixture or process in a blender until smooth. Return the mixture to the pan. Add the broth and mix well. Simmer, covered, for 35 minutes, stirring occasionally. Stir in the half-and-half, salt and pepper. Cook just until heated through, stirring constantly. Ladle into soup bowls. May substitute chopped baked acorn squash for the butternut squash. Add leftover chicken or turkey for a heartier soup.
Yield: 6 to 10 servings.

Dorothy Eich, *Geneva Community Grange, Nebraska*

Speedy Vegetable Soup

1 pound cooked beef roast
1 quart water
1 quart tomato juice
1 1/2 teaspoons garlic salt
1 teaspoon onion flakes
1 teaspoon salt
2 (16-ounce) packages frozen mixed
    vegetables
2 bouillon cubes

Chop the beef into 1/2-inch pieces. Combine the beef, water, tomato juice, garlic salt, onion flakes and salt in a saucepan. Bring to a boil, stirring occasionally. Add the mixed vegetables and bouillon cubes and mix well. Simmer for 15 minutes or until the vegetables are tender, stirring occasionally. Ladle into soup bowls. **Yield:** 6 servings.

Elsie Cornelius, *Jasper Grange, Oregon*

Cheesy Apricot Salad

2 (3-ounce) packages lemon gelatin
1 cup boiling water
1 cup apricot juice
1 1/2 cups cottage cheese
1 cup whipping cream, whipped
1 cup sliced canned apricots
1/2 cup chopped walnuts
1/2 cup maraschino cherry quarters

Dissolve the gelatin in the boiling water in a bowl and mix well. Stir in the apricot juice. Chill until partially set. Fold in the cottage cheese, whipped cream, apricots, walnuts and maraschino cherries. Spoon into a lightly oiled 1 1/2-quart mold. Chill, covered, until set. Garnish with additional apricot slices.
Yield: 8 to 12 servings.

Dolly Aylsworth, *Kuna Grange, Idaho*

Cherry Nut Salad

1 (16-ounce) can sour red cherries
1 (3-ounce) package cherry gelatin
3/4 cup sugar
1 (8-ounce) can juice-pack crushed
    pineapple
1/2 cup chopped walnuts

Bring the undrained cherries to a boil in a saucepan. Remove from heat. Add the gelatin and sugar and stir until dissolved. Stir in the undrained pineapple and walnuts. Pour into a 4-cup mold. Chill, covered, until set. **Yield:** 8 servings.

Keith Nordquest, *Mile Branch Grange, Ohio*

Cranberry Salad

3 cups cranberries, ground
1 cup sugar
1 (6-ounce) package raspberry gelatin
1 cup hot water
1 cup pineapple juice
1 cup drained crushed pineapple
2 cups chopped celery
1/2 cup walnut pieces

Combine the cranberries and sugar in a bowl and mix well. Dissolve the gelatin in the hot water in a bowl. Stir in the cranberry mixture, pineapple juice and pineapple. Add the celery and walnuts and mix well. Pour into a 9x12-inch dish or mold. Chill, covered, until set. **Yield:** 12 servings.

Sigi Turner, *Elk Plain Grange, Washington*

Through our Family Outreach Program, Grange members are working to establish or assist with child care centers. Leadership projects instituted to assist the youth of communities include purchasing playground equipment and giving scholarships toward their education.

Frog Eye Salad

1 (20-ounce) can juice-pack pineapple
   chunks
1 (20-ounce) can juice-pack crushed
   pineapple
16 ounces acini di pepe
1 cup sugar
3 tablespoons flour
3 egg yolks, lightly beaten
1/2 teaspoon salt
2 (11-ounce) cans mandarin oranges,
   drained
12 ounces whipped topping
1 (10-ounce) package marshmallows

Drain the pineapple chunks and crushed pineapple, reserving 1 3/4 cups of the juice. Cook the pasta using package directions. Rinse and drain. Combine the reserved pineapple juice, sugar, flour, egg yolks and salt in a saucepan and mix well. Cook until thickened, stirring constantly. Add the pasta and mix well. Chill, covered, for 8 to 10 hours. Fold in the pineapple chunks, crushed pineapple, mandarin oranges, whipped topping and marshmallows. Chill, covered, until serving time.
Yield: 40 servings.

Beryl Mann, *Mosherville Grange, Michigan*

LuLa's Fruit Salad

1/4 cup vinegar
1/4 cup sugar
2 eggs, lightly beaten
2 tablespoons butter
1 cup whipping cream, whipped
2 cups drained pineapple chunks
2 cups drained fruit cocktail
1 cup drained sliced peaches
1 (6-ounce) jar maraschino cherries,
   drained
2 cups miniature marshmallows
1 cup grapes

Combine the vinegar, sugar and eggs in a double boiler and mix well. Cook until thickened, stirring frequently. Stir in the butter. Let stand until cool. May be prepared to this point and stored, covered, in the refrigerator. Fold in the whipped cream. Combine the pineapple, fruit cocktail, peaches and cherries in a bowl and mix gently. Add the whipped cream mixture and mix gently. Stir in the marshmallows and grapes. Chill, covered, until serving time. **Yield:** 10 servings.

Patricia Ford, *Mayfield Grange, New York*

Orange Tapioca Salad

3 cups water
1 (4-ounce) package vanilla instant
   pudding mix
1 (3-ounce) package tapioca pudding mix
1 (3-ounce) package orange gelatin
1 (15-ounce) can mandarin oranges,
   drained
1 (8-ounce) can crushed pineapple,
   drained
8 ounces frozen whipped topping,
   thawed

Bring the water to a boil in a saucepan. Whisk in the pudding mixes and gelatin. Bring to a boil, stirring constantly. Boil for 1 minute. Remove from heat. Let stand until cool. Fold in the mandarin oranges, pineapple and whipped topping. Spoon into a serving bowl. Chill, covered, for 2 hours or longer.
Yield: 12 to 14 servings.

Leona Bailey, *Eureka Grange, New York*

Pistachio Nut Salad

12 ounces whipped topping
1 (4-ounce) package pistachio
 instant pudding mix
1 (20-ounce) can pineapple tidbits,
 drained
1 (20-ounce) can fruit cocktail,
 drained
1 (20-ounce) can mandarin oranges,
 drained
2 cups miniature marshmallows
1 cup flaked coconut
1/2 cup chopped pistachios

Combine the whipped topping and pudding mix in a bowl and mix well. Stir in the pineapple, fruit cocktail, mandarin oranges, marshmallows, coconut and pistachios. Chill, covered, for 8 to 10 hours. **Yield:** 12 servings.

Zella Ferrando, *Glastonbury Grange, Connecticut*

Pretzel Salad

1 (6-ounce) package strawberry
 gelatin
2 cups boiling water
1/2 cup cold water
2 (10-ounce) packages frozen
 strawberries, partially thawed
3/4 cup (1 1/2 sticks) margarine,
 softened
3 tablespoons sugar
2 cups coarsely crushed pretzels
8 ounces cream cheese, softened
3/4 cup confectioners' sugar
8 ounces whipped topping

Dissolve the gelatin in the boiling water in a large bowl. Stir in the cold water. Stir in the undrained strawberries. Let stand until cool; do not chill. Beat the margarine and sugar in a mixer bowl until creamy. Stir in the pretzels. Press the pretzel mixture over the bottom of a 9x13-inch baking pan. Bake at 350 degrees for 10 minutes. Let stand until cool. Beat the cream cheese and confectioners' sugar in a mixer bowl until blended. Fold in the whipped topping. Spread over the baked layer. Chill until set. Spread with the strawberry mixture. Chill, covered, for 8 to 10 hours. **Yield:** 15 servings.

Eileen Parrish, *Bell Township Grange, Pennsylvania*

Granges are helping the homeless, working on highway safety improvements, working with community beautification projects, supporting community libraries—the list goes on and on. Community Service is the heartbeat of the Grange.

Frosted Raspberry Salad

1 (6-ounce) package raspberry gelatin
1 1/2 cups boiling water
1 (16-ounce) can cranberry sauce
1 (15-ounce) can juice-pack crushed
    pineapple
8 ounces cream cheese, softened
1/4 cup sugar
1 cup sour cream
1/2 cup chopped pecans

Dissolve the gelatin in the boiling water in a bowl. Whisk in the cranberry sauce until smooth. Stir in the undrained pineapple. Spoon into a lightly oiled 9x13-inch dish. Chill until set. Beat the cream cheese and sugar in a mixer bowl until smooth. Stir in the sour cream and pecans. Spread over the prepared layer. Chill, covered, until set. **Yield:** 15 servings.

Emalee Colver, *Director of Junior Activities, National Grange*

Ribbon Salad

1 (6-ounce) package any flavor gelatin
1 (3-ounce) package lemon gelatin
1 cup hot water
1/2 cup miniature marshmallows
8 ounces cream cheese
1 (20-ounce) can juice-pack crushed
    pineapple
1 cup whipping cream, whipped
1/2 to 1 cup mayonnaise
1 (6-ounce) package any flavor gelatin

Prepare the desired flavor of gelatin using package directions. Pour into a 10x14-inch dish or three 1-quart bowls. Chill until partially set. Dissolve the lemon gelatin in the hot water in a double boiler. Add the marshmallows. Cook over simmering water until blended, stirring frequently. Remove from heat. Add the cream cheese. Beat until smooth. Stir in the undrained pineapple. Cool slightly. Fold in the whipped cream and mayonnaise. Chill, covered, until thickened. Spread over the prepared layer. Chill until almost set. Prepare the desired flavor of gelatin using package directions. Chill until of a syrupy consistency. Pour over the prepared layers. Chill, covered, until set. **Yield:** 15 to 20 servings.

Betty Lawrence, *Wisconsin Director of Women's Activities*

Corned Beef Salad

1 (12-ounce) can corned beef
1 cup chopped celery
2 tablespoons chopped onion
2 tablespoons chopped sweet pickle
2 tablespoons chopped green bell
    pepper (optional)
2 tablespoons chopped black or green
    olives (optional)
1 (3-ounce) package lemon gelatin
1 1/2 cups boiling water
1 cup mayonnaise

Mash the corned beef in a bowl with a fork. Stir in the celery, onion, sweet pickle, green pepper and black olives. Dissolve the gelatin in the boiling water in a large bowl. Stir in the corned beef mixture. Let stand until cool. Fold in the mayonnaise. Spoon into a mold, 8x8-inch dish or loaf pan. Chill, covered, until set. Invert onto a lettuce-lined serving platter. **Yield:** 8 to 10 servings.

Norma J. Shaw, *Centre Grange, Delaware*

English Walnut and Chicken Salad

24 English walnuts
1 onion slice
Sprig of parsley
1 to 2 cups chicken broth
2 cups chopped cooked chicken
2 cups chopped celery
1/2 onion, finely chopped
1 cup French salad dressing
1 cup mayonnaise
8 lettuce cups

Parboil the walnuts, 1 onion slice and parsley in the chicken broth in a saucepan until the skins on the walnuts are loosened; drain. Discard the skins from the walnuts. Combine the walnuts, chicken, celery and finely chopped onion in a bowl and mix well. Stir in the French salad dressing. Chill, covered, for 1 hour or longer. Stir in the mayonnaise just before serving. Spoon into lettuce cups. **Yield:** 8 servings.

Diane Froemke, *Washington Director of Women's Activities*

Indonesian Salad

7 cups chopped cooked turkey
    or chicken
2 tablespoons lime juice (optional)
2 cups raisins
2 cups dry roasted peanuts
2 cups chopped celery
2 cups chopped green bell pepper
1 cup flaked coconut
1 cup mayonnaise
1 cup yogurt
1/2 cup minced onion
3 tablespoons chopped chutney
2 teaspoons lemon juice
1 teaspoon curry powder

Combine the turkey and lime juice in a bowl and mix well. Marinate, covered, in the refrigerator for 8 to 10 hours. Combine the turkey, raisins, peanuts, celery, green pepper and coconut in a bowl and mix well. Chill, covered, until serving time. Combine the mayonnaise, yogurt, onion, chutney, lemon juice and curry powder in a bowl and mix well. Chill, covered, for 4 hours or longer. Stir the chutney dressing into the turkey mixture just before serving or serve on the side.
Yield: 10 to 12 servings.

Cindy Greer, *Marvel Grange, Colorado*

One of the largest needlework contests in the country has been co-sponsored by National Grange and Coats & Clark for more than forty years. Participation is open to everyone—Grange members and the public. Men, young people, and children (as well as women) take part and receive awards for accomplishments.

Taco Salad

1 pound ground beef
1 1/2 cups Western salad dressing,
  or to taste
1 envelope taco seasoning mix
1 head lettuce, torn into bite-size pieces
4 tomatoes, chopped
1 onion, chopped
8 ounces Cheddar cheese, shredded
1 (5-ounce) package tortilla chips

Brown the ground beef in a skillet, stirring until crumbly; drain. Combine the salad dressing and seasoning mix in a bowl and mix well. Stir in the ground beef. Chill, covered, in the refrigerator. Toss the lettuce, tomatoes, onion and cheese in a bowl. Chill, covered, in the refrigerator. Layer the lettuce mixture, ground beef mixture and tortilla chips alternately in a bowl until all of the ingredients are used. Toss just before serving. **Yield:** 10 servings.

Donna West, *Flora Grange, Illinois*

Bean Salad

1 (16-ounce) can cut green beans,
  drained
1 (16-ounce) can yellow wax beans,
  drained
1 (16-ounce) can garbanzo beans,
  drained
1 (16-ounce) can dark red kidney
  beans, drained
1 (16-ounce) can black beans, drained
1 cup finely chopped onion
1 whole dill pickle, finely chopped
1 green bell pepper, finely chopped
1 (2-ounce) jar sliced pimento, drained
1 cup dark vinegar
1 cup water
1 tablespoon canola oil

Combine the beans in a 14-cup container and mix gently. Stir in the onion, dill pickle, green pepper and pimento. Bring the vinegar and water to a boil in a saucepan. Stir in the canola oil. Pour over the bean mixture, tossing gently to coat. Chill, covered, until serving time. **Yield:** 31 servings.

Kathryn Cree, *Montana Co-Director of Women's Activities*

Beet Salad

2 (16-ounce) cans julienned beets
2 (8-ounce) cans juice-pack crushed
  pineapple
1 cup sugar
1/2 cup vinegar
2 (3-ounce) packages lemon gelatin

Drain the beets, reserving the liquid. Drain the pineapple, reserving the juice. Combine 2 cups of the reserved liquids, sugar and vinegar in a measuring cup. Add water to measure 3 cups. Pour into a saucepan. Bring to a boil, stirring occasionally. Remove from heat. Add the gelatin, stirring until dissolved. Let stand until cool. Stir in the beets and pineapple. Pour into a 9x13-inch dish. Chill, covered, until set. Garnish with sliced kiwifruit. **Yield:** 15 servings.

Flo Carter, *Texas Director of Women's Activities*

Broccoli Salad

1 large bunch broccoli, cut into
    bite-size pieces
1¹/₂ cups red grape halves
1 cup chopped celery
Chopped mixed nuts to taste
Chopped red onion (optional)
1 cup mayonnaise
¹/₃ cup sugar
1 tablespoon vinegar
8 ounces bacon, crisp-fried, crumbled

Combine the broccoli, grapes, celery, nuts and onion in a bowl and mix well. Stir in a mixture of the mayonnaise, sugar and vinegar. Add the bacon just before serving. **Yield:** 8 servings.

Jessie Butt, *Fairfield Grange, Wisconsin*

Sunday Broccoli Salad

1 bunch broccoli, cut into bite-size
    pieces
³/₄ cup chopped onion
8 ounces Colby cheese, cubed
¹/₂ cup mayonnaise-type salad dressing
¹/₂ cup mayonnaise
8 slices bacon, crisp-fried, crumbled

Combine the broccoli, onion and cheese in a bowl and mix well. Stir in a mixture of the salad dressing and mayonnaise. Sprinkle with the bacon. **Yield:** 6 servings.

Becky Ledoux, *David Crockett Grange, Texas*

The Stuffed Toy contest (sponsored by Fairfield Processing, Inc.) has resulted in an average of eighteen thousand toys being made for children in each of the twenty-three years the contest has been in existence. Every toy is donated to a child in need. Many of the toys made for "loving" are given to police departments, fire companies, and ambulance services to be used to comfort any child involved in a frightening situation.

Twigs and Raisin Salad

2 or 3 large bunches broccoli, cut into
    bite-size pieces
1/2 to 1 cup raisins
1/4 to 1 cup chopped white or red onion
10 slices crisp-fried bacon, crumbled
1 cup sunflower seed kernels
1 cup mayonnaise
3 tablespoons sugar
2 tablespoons vinegar

Combine the broccoli, raisins, onion, bacon and sunflower seed kernels in a bowl and mix well. Stir in a mixture of the mayonnaise, sugar and vinegar. **Yield:** 12 servings.

Harriet Mullen, *Little Beaver Grange, Wyoming*

Fresh Cauliflower Salad

4 cups sliced fresh cauliflower
1/2 cup chopped green bell pepper
1/2 cup chopped onion
2/3 cup sour cream
3 tablespoons mayonnaise
1 teaspoon dry mustard
1 teaspoon sugar
1 teaspoon dillweed
1/8 teaspoon hot pepper sauce
1 medium tomato, sliced

Toss the cauliflower, green pepper and onion in a bowl. Combine the sour cream, mayonnaise, dry mustard, sugar, dillweed and hot pepper sauce in a bowl and mix well. Add to the cauliflower mixture, stirring gently until mixed. Chill, covered, for several hours. Add the tomato just before serving. **Yield:** 6 servings.

Louise Goodell, *Middleton Grange, Idaho*

Cool Cucumber Pasta

8 ounces penne
2 medium cucumbers, thinly sliced
1 medium onion, thinly sliced
1 tablespoon vegetable oil
1 1/2 cups sugar
1 cup water
3/4 cup vinegar
1 tablespoon prepared mustard
1 tablespoon parsley flakes
1 teaspoon salt
1 teaspoon pepper
1/2 teaspoon garlic salt

Cook the pasta using package directions; drain. Rinse with cold water and drain. Combine the pasta, cucumbers, onion and oil in a bowl and mix well. Combine the sugar, water, vinegar, prepared mustard, parsley flakes, salt, pepper and garlic salt in a bowl and mix well. Add to the pasta mixture and toss to coat. Chill, covered, for 3 to 4 hours, stirring occasionally. **Yield:** 8 to 10 servings.

Norma J. Peck, *Centre Grange, Delaware*

Sauerkraut Salad

1 quart sauerkraut, drained, rinsed
2 cups chopped celery
1 cup chopped green bell pepper
1 cup chopped onion
1 (2-ounce) jar chopped pimento,
    drained
1¹/₂ cups sugar
¹/₂ cup vinegar
1 teaspoon salt

Combine the sauerkraut, celery, green pepper, onion and pimento in a bowl and mix well. Whisk the sugar, vinegar and salt in a bowl. Add to the sauerkraut mixture and mix well. Spoon into a jar with a tight-fitting lid. Chill for 8 to 10 hours, shaking and turning the jar several times. **Yield:** 8 servings.

Barbara Moberg, *Pickford Grange, Michigan*

Seven-Layer Salad

1 head lettuce, torn into bite-size pieces
¹/₂ cup chopped celery
¹/₂ cup chopped green bell pepper
1 small onion, chopped
¹/₂ cup shredded carrot
1 (10-ounce) package frozen peas
2 cups mayonnaise
2 tablespoons sugar
4 ounces Cheddar cheese, shredded
2 to 4 slices crisp-fried bacon, crumbled

Layer the lettuce, celery, green pepper, onion, carrot and peas in the order listed in a 9x13-inch dish. Spread with the mayonnaise, sealing to the edges. Sprinkle with the sugar, cheese and bacon. Chill, tightly covered, for 8 to 10 hours. **Yield:** 15 servings.

Elizabeth P. Green, *Northumberland Grange, Pennsylvania*

Our Grange Women's Activities committees work closely with shelters. Packages are made up for those in need. Cloth bags are filled with personal items to be given to women and children who have been forced to flee from an abusive situation at home.

Spinach Salad

3/4 cup sugar
1/2 cup catsup
1/2 cup vinegar
1 teaspoon Worcestershire sauce
1 cup salad oil
1 (16-ounce) package fresh spinach,
    trimmed, torn into bite-size pieces
8 ounces bacon, crisp-fried, crumbled
2 medium onions, chopped
2 hard-cooked eggs, chopped

Combine the sugar, catsup, vinegar and Worcestershire sauce in a saucepan and mix well. Cook over low heat until the sugar dissolves, stirring frequently; do not boil. Stir in the oil. Let stand until cool. Toss the spinach, bacon, onions and eggs in a bowl. Add the dressing and toss to coat. **Yield:** 6 servings.

Dorothy Airgood, *Mountain Grange, Pennsylvania*

Sweet-and-Sour Salad

4 medium cucumbers, chopped
4 medium tomatoes, chopped
1 small purple onion, finely chopped
1 cup cider vinegar
1/2 cup sugar, or to taste
1 tablespoon dillweed
1/4 cup mayonnaise

Combine the cucumbers, tomatoes and onion in a bowl and mix gently. Stir in a mixture of the vinegar, sugar and dillweed. Chill, covered, for 4 hours or longer. Stir in the mayonnaise just before serving. **Yield:** 6 to 8 servings.

Betty Crumley, *David Crockett Grange, Texas*

Sweet-and-Sour Veggies

3 cups cauliflorets
3 cups broccoli florets
2 medium carrots, thinly sliced
1 medium zucchini, cut into quarters,
    thinly sliced
Thinly sliced onion to taste
3/4 cup cider vinegar
1/4 cup sugar
1/2 teaspoon salt
2 tablespoons vegetable oil

Toss the cauliflorets, broccoli florets, carrots, zucchini and onion in a bowl. Bring the vinegar, sugar and salt to a boil in a saucepan, stirring frequently. Remove from heat. Stir in the oil. Pour over the vegetable mixture and toss gently to coat. Chill, covered, for 8 to 10 hours. **Yield:** 12 to 14 servings.

Ruth W. Speer, *N. Washington Grange, Pennsylvania*

Three P Salad

1 cup Spanish peanuts
1 (15-ounce) can small June peas
1/2 cup chopped sweet pickles
1 tablespoon (about) mayonnaise

Remove the skins from the peanuts if desired. Combine the peanuts, peas and sweet pickles in a bowl and mix well. Add the mayonnaise, stirring until the mixture adheres. Chill, covered, until serving time. Do not prepare more than 2 hours in advance as the peanuts become soggy. **Yield:** 6 servings.

Cecil Thomas, *Colonial Grange, South Carolina*

Marinated Vegetables

2 small bunches broccoli
Florets of 1 small head cauliflower
1 pound carrots, thinly sliced
1 onion, thinly sliced, separated into
    rings
1 green bell pepper, julienned
3 to 4 ribs celery, chopped
2 cups vinegar
2 cups sugar
1 cup salad oil
1 envelope ranch salad dressing mix

Separate the broccoli into bite-size florets, reserving the stems. Peel and slice the stems. Combine the broccoli, sliced broccoli stems, cauliflorets, carrots, onion, green pepper and celery in a bowl and mix gently. Whisk the vinegar, sugar, oil and dressing mix in a bowl. Pour over the broccoli mixture and toss to coat. Chill, covered, for 8 to 10 hours, stirring occasionally. May store, covered, in the refrigerator for several days. **Yield:** 12 servings.

Pearl Buell, *Master, Wyoming State Grange*

In addition to the major national contests, each State Director of Women's Activities carries on contests at the state level. There are baking and cooking contests, canning and dried fruit competitions, craft categories, and subjects that are of interest in each local area.

Veggie Mandarin Salad

2/3 cup salad oil
6 tablespoons tarragon vinegar
6 tablespoons sugar
1 teaspoon Tabasco sauce
3/4 teaspoon salt
3/4 teaspoon pepper
1 head lettuce, chopped
1 cup chopped celery
1 cup drained mandarin oranges
1/2 cup almond slivers, toasted
4 green onions, chopped
2 tablespoons chopped fresh parsley

Combine the oil, tarragon vinegar, sugar, Tabasco sauce, salt and pepper in a jar with a tight-fitting lid; seal tightly. Shake to mix. Chill in the refrigerator. Toss the lettuce, celery, mandarin oranges, almonds, green onions and parsley in a salad bowl. Add the chilled dressing just before serving and toss to mix. **Yield:** 12 servings.

Louise Rigor, *Evergreen Grange, Oregon*

Rice Salad

3 cups cooked rice, cooled
1 teaspoon dry mustard
Salt and pepper to taste
1 (6-ounce) can large black olives, drained, chopped
1 (4-ounce) jar sliced pimentos, drained
8 gherkins, finely chopped
4 hard-cooked eggs, chopped
Mayonnaise to taste

Combine the rice, dry mustard, salt and pepper in a bowl. Stir in the olives, pimentos, pickles and eggs. Add just enough mayonnaise until the mixture adheres and mix well. Chill, covered, until serving time. **Yield:** 24 servings.

Amy Whitcomb, *Taghhannuck Grange, Connecticut*

Salad Dressing à la Tomato

1 cup salad oil
1/2 cup vinegar
1/4 cup water
2 envelopes Italian salad dressing mix
1 (16-ounce) can stewed Italian tomatoes

Combine the oil, vinegar, water and dressing mix in a blender container. Pulse until thoroughly mixed. Add the undrained tomatoes. Pulse just until the tomatoes are broken up; do not overprocess. **Yield:** 10 (1/4-cup) servings.

Marilynn Rasp, *Rainbow Valley Grange, California*

The Main Course

Family Recipes From Grange
Homes Over The Years

Smothered Steak

1 1/2 pounds beef chuck steak,
    cut into strips
1/3 cup flour
1 teaspoon salt
1/4 teaspoon pepper
1 (16-ounce) can tomatoes
1 (10-ounce) package frozen
    French-style green beans (optional)
1 (4-ounce) can mushrooms, drained
1 large onion, sliced
1 or 2 green bell peppers, sliced
3 tablespoons soy sauce
2 tablespoons molasses (optional)

Combine the steak strips, flour, salt and pepper in a slow cooker and stir until the beef is coated. Add the undrained tomatoes, green beans, mushrooms, onion, green peppers, soy sauce and molasses and mix well. Cook, covered, on High for 1 hour. Reduce the heat to Low. Cook for 8 hours longer. Serve with hot cooked rice. May cook on High for 6 hours total instead of reducing heat to Low. **Yield:** 6 servings.

Joyce A. Chase, *Moosup Valley Grange, Rhode Island*

Barbecued Beef

20 pounds beef round, cut into
    2-inch cubes
Salt and pepper to taste
Bacon drippings
6 cups catsup
4 cups chopped celery
4 cups water
8 small onions, chopped
1 cup packed brown sugar
1 cup lemon juice
3 tablespoons plus 1 teaspoon
    Worcestershire sauce
3 tablespoons salt
2 teaspoons pepper
1 teaspoon prepared mustard

Season the beef with salt and pepper to taste. Brown the beef in batches in the bacon drippings in a large skillet; drain. Combine the catsup, celery, water, onions, brown sugar, lemon juice, Worcestershire sauce, 3 tablespoons salt, 2 teaspoons pepper and prepared mustard in a stockpot and mix well. Simmer for 30 minutes, stirring occasionally. Add the beef and mix well. Simmer for 2 hours or until the beef is tender, stirring occasionally. May bake, covered, in several baking pans at 325 degrees until the beef is tender. **Yield:** 48 servings.

Norman Tooker, *Gatekeeper, National Grange*

Beef Stroganoff

8 ounces medium noodles
1/4 cup chopped onion
2 tablespoons vegetable oil
1 1/2 pounds round steak, tenderized,
    cut into bite-size pieces
1 cup mushrooms
3/4 cup sour cream

Cook the noodles using package directions; drain. Cover to keep warm. Sauté the onion in the oil in a skillet. Stir in the beef. Sauté for 5 minutes or until the beef is brown on both sides. Stir in the mushrooms and sour cream. Cook just until heated through, stirring occasionally. Serve with the noodles. **Yield:** 6 servings.

Jeanne Davies, *Overseer, National Grange*

Old-Fashioned Beef Stroganoff

4 (4-ounce) cans mushrooms
1 (1/2-inch thick) round steak
3 tablespoons flour
2 tablespoons vegetable oil
1 (10-ounce) can tomato soup
1 tablespoon Worcestershire sauce
8 drops of Tabasco sauce
1/2 teaspoon salt
1/2 teaspoon pepper
2 cups sour cream

Drain the mushrooms, reserving the liquid. Cut the steak into 3/4-inch cubes. Combine the steak and flour in a sealable plastic bag and seal tightly. Toss to coat. Brown the steak in the oil in a skillet; drain. Stir in the mushrooms. Add a mixture of the reserved liquid and tomato soup and mix well. Stir in the Worcestershire sauce, Tabasco sauce, salt and pepper. Add the sour cream and mix well; cover. Bring to a simmer. Remove from heat. Serve over hot cooked spaghetti or rice.
Yield: 6 servings.

Jeaneen Harra, *Morning Grange, Kansas*

Savory Meal in a Skillet

1 (1-pound) round steak
1/4 cup flour
Salt and pepper to taste
1/4 cup vegetable oil
1 onion, thinly sliced
4 potatoes, cut into quarters
4 carrots cut into quarters
1 (10-ounce) can golden mushroom soup
1 tablespoon steak sauce

Tenderize the steak with commercial meat tenderizer or pound with a meat mallet. Cut the steak into 4 equal portions. Coat the steak with a mixture of the flour, salt and pepper. Brown on both sides in the oil in a 10-inch skillet. Layer the onion over the steak. Arrange the potatoes and carrots around and on the steak. Spoon a mixture of the soup and steak sauce over the steak and vegetables; cover. Bring to a boil; reduce heat. Simmer for 45 minutes or until the beef is tender, stirring twice.
Yield: 4 servings.

Linda J. Skeen, *Trinity Grange, North Carolina*

Many hospitals are given hundreds of baby caps knitted or crocheted with love by the women of the Grange. Some hats are for newborns, but most are very tiny and made for premature babies.

Pepper Steak

1 (1-pound) round steak
1 tablespoon paprika
3 garlic cloves, minced
2 tablespoons butter or margarine
1 (14-ounce) can beef broth
3/4 cup sliced onion, separated into rings
1 green bell pepper, sliced
4 ounces fresh mushrooms (optional)
1/4 cup water
1/4 cup soy sauce
2 tablespoons cornstarch
1 (16-ounce) can stewed tomatoes,
    drained

Pound the steak on a hard surface with a meat mallet to tenderize. Cut into strips. Sprinkle with the paprika. Cook the steak and garlic in the butter in a skillet until the steak is brown on both sides, stirring frequently. Add the broth. Cook for 30 minutes, stirring occasionally. Stir in the onion, green pepper and mushrooms. Cook, covered, for 5 minutes. Stir in a mixture of the water, soy sauce and cornstarch. Cook until thickened, stirring constantly. Add the tomatoes and mix well. Cook until heated through, stirring frequently. Serve over hot cooked rice. May substitute venison for the round steak. **Yield:** 4 servings.

Audrey Planer, *New Jersey Director of Women's Activities*

Swiss Steak

2 pounds boneless round or sirloin steak
1/2 cup flour
2 to 3 tablespoons vegetable oil
Salt and pepper to taste
Garlic powder to taste
2 or 3 carrots, chopped
2 or 3 ribs celery, chopped
1 onion, chopped
2 (15-ounce) cans tomatoes

Cut the steak into bite-size pieces. Coat with the flour. Brown the steak in the oil in a skillet; drain. Season with salt, pepper, garlic powder and any other desired seasonings. Combine the carrots, celery, onion and undrained tomatoes in a saucepan. Cook until the vegetables are tender-crisp, stirring occasionally. Spread the bottom of a greased 10x10-inch baking dish with a thin layer of the vegetable mixture. Layer with the steak. Top with the remaining vegetable mixture. Bake, covered, for 2 to 3 hours or until the steak is tender. **Yield:** 6 to 8 servings.

Sandra Ault, *Kuna Grange, Idaho*

Best-Ever Corned Beef

1 (4- to 5-pound) corned beef brisket
2 cups apple juice
2 large garlic cloves
1 bay leaf
1/2 teaspoon peppercorns
2 teaspoons ground cloves
3/4 cup packed dark brown sugar

Combine the brisket, apple juice, garlic, bay leaf, peppercorns and cloves with enough water to cover in a saucepan. Bring to a boil; reduce heat. Stir in the brown sugar. Simmer, covered, for 4 hours or until the brisket is tender, stirring occasionally. Remove the brisket to a serving platter, reserving the pan juices. Discard the bay leaf. Thicken the juices as desired for gravy. Serve with boiled potatoes and your favorite boiled vegetables. **Yield:** 10 to 12 servings.

Roger Johnson, *Livingston Grange, New Jersey*

Reuben Casserole

1 (10-ounce) can cream of chicken soup
3/4 cup sour cream
8 ounces wide noodles, cooked, drained
1 can corned beef, thinly sliced
6 slices Old English cheese
1 (14-ounce) can sauerkraut, drained
6 slices Swiss cheese
Crushed potato chips

Mix the soup and sour cream in a bowl. Layer half the noodles, half the corned beef, Old English cheese, sauerkraut and half the soup mixture in a buttered 3-quart baking dish. Top with the remaining noodles, remaining corned beef, Swiss cheese and remaining soup mixture. Sprinkle with potato chips. Bake at 350 degrees for 35 minutes. **Yield:** 10 servings.

Alaire Freeman, *Wyoming Director of Women's Activities*

Beef Biscuit Bake

1 pound ground beef
1/2 onion, chopped
2 (10-ounce) cans cream of
    mushroom soup
2 cups frozen mixed vegetables
1 cup milk
1/2 teaspoon garlic powder
2 cups baking mix
1 cup milk
Chopped fresh parsley to taste

Brown the ground beef with the onion in a skillet, stirring until the ground beef is crumbly; drain. Stir in the soup, mixed vegetables, 1 cup milk and garlic powder. Spoon into a 9x13-inch baking pan. Combine the baking mix and 1 cup milk in a bowl and mix well. Spoon over the prepared layer. Sprinkle with parsley. Bake at 450 degrees for 27 to 30 minutes or until light brown. **Yield:** 6 servings.

Mary Jo Kubichek, *Sheffield Star Grange, Ohio*

The health and safety of our members and friends is a vital concern to our Women's Activities committees. Programs and workshops on these subjects are held in many Granges.

Mexican Corn Bread Casserole

1½ pounds ground beef
1 cup chopped onion
3 (6-ounce) packages corn bread mix
1 (17-ounce) can cream-style corn
1 (12-ounce) jar hot or mild picante
  sauce
8 to 10 ounces shredded Cheddar cheese

Preheat the oven to 400 degrees. Brown the ground beef with the onion in a skillet, stirring until the ground beef is crumbly; drain. Prepare the corn bread mix using package directions. Stir in the corn. Spoon half the corn bread batter into a greased 9x13-inch baking pan. Spread with the ground beef mixture. Spoon the picante sauce over the prepared layers and sprinkle with the cheese. Top with the remaining corn bread batter. Reduce the oven temperature to 375 degrees. Bake for 1 hour or until golden brown. **Yield:** 8 to 10 servings.

Kathryn Skeen, *Kenna Grange, West Virginia*

Enchilada Casserole

2 pounds lean ground beef
½ cup chopped onion
1 teaspoon salt
1 teaspoon cumin
¼ teaspoon garlic powder
1 (10-ounce) can cream of chicken soup
1 (10-ounce) can cream of
  mushroom soup
1 (2-ounce) can chopped green chiles
½ cup enchilada sauce
12 corn tortillas, cut into quarters
1 pound Cheddar cheese, shredded

Brown the ground beef with the onion, salt, cumin and garlic powder in a skillet, stirring until the ground beef is crumbly and the onion is tender; drain. Stir in the soups, chiles and enchilada sauce. Cook just until heated through, stirring frequently. Layer the tortillas and ground beef mixture alternately in a 9x13-inch baking pan sprayed with nonstick cooking spray until all of the ingredients are used, ending with the ground beef mixture. Sprinkle with the cheese. Bake at 325 degrees for 30 minutes. **Yield:** 9 servings.

Barbara Knight, *Pomona, National Grange*

Hamburger Casserole

1 pound ground beef
½ onion, chopped
2 cups shredded Cheddar cheese
1 (10-ounce) can cream of
  mushroom soup
¼ cup milk
Salt and pepper to taste
1 (16-ounce) package frozen Tater Tots

Brown the ground beef with the onion in a skillet, stirring until the ground beef is crumbly; drain. Stir in the cheese, soup, milk, salt and pepper. Spoon into a greased baking dish. Top with the Tater Tots. Bake at 350 degrees for 30 minutes or until bubbly. May substitute cream of chicken soup or cream of celery soup for the cream of mushroom soup. Add leftover green beans or corn if desired. **Yield:** 4 servings.

Oleta Ball, *Idaho Director of Women's Activities*

Hamburger Broccoli Quiche

1¹/2 pounds ground beef
¹/2 cup chopped onion
1 to 2 tablespoons butter
¹/2 cup milk
¹/2 cup mayonnaise
2 eggs
1 tablespoon flour
1¹/2 cups shredded Cheddar cheese
¹/2 cup chopped steamed broccoli
1 unbaked (9-inch) pie shell

Brown the ground beef in a large skillet, stirring until crumbly; drain. Sauté the onion in the butter in a skillet until tender. Whisk the milk, mayonnaise, eggs and flour in a large bowl until blended. Stir in the ground beef, onion, cheese and broccoli. Spoon into the pie shell. Bake at 350 degrees for 40 minutes. **Yield:** 8 servings.

Fae Snyder, *Priestess Annalist, National Grange*

Microwave Meatballs

1 pound ground beef
¹/2 cup dry bread crumbs
¹/4 cup finely chopped onion
¹/4 cup milk
1 egg, lightly beaten
1 teaspoon Worcestershire sauce
1 teaspoon pepper
³/4 teaspoon salt
¹/4 teaspoon garlic powder

Combine the ground beef, bread crumbs and onion in a bowl and mix well. Stir in the milk, egg, Worcestershire sauce, pepper, salt and garlic powder. Shape into 1¹/2-inch meatballs. Arrange the meatballs in a single layer in an 8x12-inch microwave-safe dish sprayed with nonstick cooking spray. Microwave, covered loosely, on High for 3 minutes; turn the meatballs. Microwave, covered, for 5 to 7 minutes or until the meatballs are cooked through. Let stand for 3 minutes; drain. **Yield:** 4 to 6 servings.

Jenny Grobusky, *Bounty Land Grange, South Carolina*

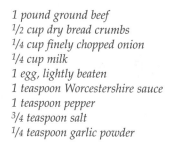

The Grange quilting contests have contributed to a revival of the good old quilting parties. The ladies (often with participation from the men) get together to make quilts to enter into competition or to use as fund-raisers for the Grange treasury.

Saturday Night Special

1 pound ground beef
1/2 cup chopped onion
1 (16-ouncea) can whole kernel corn, drained
1 (10-ounce) can cream of mushroom soup
1 cup sour cream
1 (2-ounce) jar chopped pimento
1 teaspoon salt
1/8 teaspoon pepper
1 large tomato, thinly sliced

Combine the ground beef and onion in a microwave-safe dish. Microwave on High for 5 minutes or until the ground beef is cooked through and the onion is tender; drain. Stir in the corn, soup, sour cream, pimento, salt and pepper. Microwave, covered with waxed paper, on High for 5 minutes. Top with the tomato slices. Microwave on High for 3 minutes or just until the tomatoes are tender. Let stand for 3 minutes.
Yield: 5 to 6 servings.

Mary R. Buffington, *Kennett Grange, Pennsylvania*

Potato Lasagna

2 pounds ground beef
Salt and pepper to taste
2 large jars meatless spaghetti sauce
1 pound mozzarella cheese, shredded
1 pound sharp Cheddar cheese, shredded
5 pounds potatoes, peeled, thinly sliced
2 cups cottage cheese
1 pound canned or fresh mushrooms, sliced
2 large onions, chopped

Brown the ground beef in a skillet, stirring until crumbly; drain. Season with salt, pepper and any other desired seasonings. Reserve about 1 to 2 cups of the spaghetti sauce and about 1 cup each of the mozzarella cheese and Cheddar cheese. Layer the potatoes, ground beef, remaining spaghetti sauce, cottage cheese, remaining mozzarella cheese, remaining Cheddar cheese, mushrooms and onions alternately in a large baking pan until all of the ingredients are used, ending with the potatoes. Drizzle with the reserved spaghetti sauce and sprinkle with the reserved mozzarella cheese and Cheddar cheese. Bake at 350 degrees until the potatoes are tender. **Yield:** 8 to 12 servings.

Clyde Berry, *Lecturer, National Grange*

Taco Bake

1 pound ground beef
1 small onion, chopped
3/4 cup water
1 envelope taco seasoning mix
1 (15-ounce) can tomato sauce
8 ounces shell macaroni, cooked, drained
1 (4-ounce) can chopped green chiles
2 cups shredded Cheddar cheese

Brown the ground beef with the onion in a skillet over medium heat, stirring until the ground beef is crumbly; drain. Stir in the water, seasoning mix and tomato sauce. Bring to a boil; reduce heat. Simmer for 20 minutes, stirring occasionally. Stir in the macaroni, chiles and 1 1/2 cups of the cheese. Spoon into a greased 1 1/2-quart baking dish. Sprinkle with the remaining 1/2 cup cheese. Bake at 350 degrees for 30 minutes.
Yield: 6 servings.

Nathalie Heath, *First Lady, Florida State Grange*

Frankfurter Bake

12 to 16 ounces noodles
1/4 cup (1/2 stick) butter or margarine
2 tablespoons flour
1/2 teaspoon salt
1 cup milk
1 cup grated Parmesan cheese
1 (16-ounce) package frankfurters, sliced
1/4 cup packed brown sugar
1/4 cup mayonnaise
2 tablespoons prepared mustard

Cook the noodles using package directions; drain. Heat the butter in a saucepan until melted. Add the flour and salt and mix well. Add the milk gradually, stirring constantly. Cook until thickened, stirring constantly. Stir in the cheese. Add the noodles and mix gently. Spoon into a greased 8x12-inch baking dish. Combine the frankfurters, brown sugar, mayonnaise and prepared mustard in a bowl and mix well. Spoon over the noodle mixture. Bake at 350 degrees for 25 minutes or until bubbly. **Yield:** 6 servings.

Maureen Heritage, *Stewartsville Grange, New Jersey*

Ground Lamb Casserole

8 medium onions, sliced
1 bunch celery, chopped
2 green bell peppers, chopped
Vegetable oil
1 1/2 pounds ground lamb or ground beef
3 (10-ounce) cans tomato soup
1 large package noodles, cooked, drained
2 tablespoons butter
1 pound sharp Cheddar cheese, shredded

Sauté the onions, celery and green peppers in a small amount of oil in a skillet until tender; drain. Brown the lamb in a skillet, stirring until crumbly; drain. Combine the sautéed vegetables, lamb, soup, noodles, butter and cheese in a large bowl and mix well. Spoon into a 5-quart baking dish. Bake at 350 degrees for 1 1/2 hours. **Yield:** 15 to 20 servings.

Neva Woolley, *Villenova Grange, New York*

A friendly competition takes place among the states to see which state's Grange can make the most toys in a year. Pennsylvania and Washington have consistently been the top toy makers, but in 1998, Michigan broke all the records with more than 11,000 made for children.

Barbecued Pork

1 (6-pound) pork roast, coarsely chopped
6 onions, chopped or grated
1 large bunch celery, chopped or grated
3 1/2 cups tomato juice
1 cup each catsup and vinegar
7 tablespoons brown sugar
7 tablespoons Worcestershire sauce
3 1/2 tablespoons paprika
3 1/2 teaspoons each salt and dry mustard
1 teaspoon chili powder
1/2 teaspoon cayenne pepper

Brown the pork in a large roasting pan until cooked through, stirring frequently. Add the onions, celery, tomato juice, catsup, vinegar, brown sugar, Worcestershire sauce, paprika, salt, dry mustard, chili powder and cayenne pepper and mix well. Cook until the vegetables are tender and the barbecue is of the desired consistency, stirring occasionally. Spoon onto sandwich buns.
Yield: 40 servings.

Robert Brown, *Master, Michigan State Grange*

Hot Pork Sandwiches

1 (3-pound) pork roast
2 ribs celery, cut into halves
2 carrots, cut into halves
1 medium onion
1 cup water
3 tablespoons catsup
2 tablespoons sugar
2 tablespoons cornstarch
2 tablespoons prepared mustard
Salt to taste

Cook the pork, celery, carrots and onion in the water in a stockpot over medium heat until the pork is cooked through. Transfer the pork to a platter, reserving broth and vegetables. Cool slightly. Shred the pork, discarding the bones and excess fat. Strain the vegetables, reserving the broth. Mash the vegetables in a bowl. Mix the catsup, sugar, cornstarch, mustard and salt in the stockpot. Stir in the pork, mashed vegetables and reserved broth. Cook until thickened, adding additional water if needed for the desired consistency. Serve on buns.
Yield: 24 sandwiches.

Helen Shoemaker, *First Lady, Ohio State Grange*

Tangy Pork Chops

1 beef bouillon cube
3 to 4 tablespoons hot water
4 (1/2-inch thick) pork chops
1/2 teaspoon salt (optional)
1/8 teaspoon pepper
1 (15-ounce) can stewed tomatoes
2 medium onions, chopped
2 ribs celery, chopped
1 large green bell pepper, sliced
1/2 cup catsup
2 tablespoons vinegar
2 tablespoons brown sugar
2 tablespoons Worcestershire sauce
1 tablespoon lemon juice
2 tablespoons each cornstarch and water

Dissolve the bouillon cube in the hot water in a bowl. Sprinkle the pork chops with the salt and pepper. Place in a slow cooker. Add the undrained tomatoes, onions, celery and green pepper. Combine the catsup, vinegar, brown sugar, Worcestershire sauce, lemon juice and bouillon in a bowl and mix well. Spoon over the vegetables. Cook, covered, on Low for 5 to 6 hours or until the pork chops are cooked through. Stir in a mixture of the cornstarch and 2 tablespoons water. Cook, covered, on High for 30 minutes longer or until thickened. Serve over hot cooked rice.
Yield: 4 servings.

Susan Tau, *Hayfield Grange, Pennsylvania*

Fabulous Ham and Cheese Soufflé

16 slices white sandwich bread, crusts
   trimmed
1 pound cooked ham, cubed
1 pound sharp Cheddar cheese, shredded
1 1/2 cups shredded Swiss cheese
3 cups milk
6 eggs
1/2 teaspoon onion salt
1/2 teaspoon dry mustard
3 cups crushed cornflakes
1/2 cup (1 stick) butter or margarine,
   melted

Cut the bread into 1-inch cubes. Layer half the bread cubes, ham, Cheddar cheese, Swiss cheese and remaining bread cubes in a greased 9x13-inch baking dish. Whisk the milk, eggs, onion salt and dry mustard in a bowl until blended. Pour over the prepared layers. Chill, covered, for 8 to 10 hours if desired. Sprinkle with a mixture of the cornflakes and butter. Bake at 375 degrees for 40 minutes. **Yield:** 12 to 15 servings.

Cleora C. Morton, *Alpha Grange, Idaho*

Ham Loaf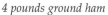

4 pounds ground ham
2 pounds ground lean pork
1 pound ground chuck
1 (18-ounce) package Wheaties, crushed
3 cups milk
7 eggs, beaten
1 large onion, chopped
1 tablespoon salt
2 teaspoons pepper
Prepared mustard
Brown sugar

Combine the ground ham, ground pork, ground chuck, cereal, milk, eggs, onion, salt and pepper in a bowl and mix well. Pack the ground ham mixture into 4 loaf pans. Bake at 350 degrees for 1 hour. Mix the desired amount of prepared mustard and brown sugar in a bowl until of a glaze consistency. Spread over the tops of the loaves. Bake for 30 minutes longer. Cool in pans on a wire rack for 30 minutes before serving. **Yield:** 40 servings.

Pat West, *Director of Community Service, National Grange*

   The National Grange supports the work being done in Elk River, Minnesota, at the home of our primary founder, Oliver Hudson Kelley. The farm there was the home of Mr. Kelley at the time our fraternity was organized. Operated by the Minnesota Historical Society, the attraction invites visitors (especially groups of school children) to a "living history farm," with interpreters dressed in period 1870 clothing performing the tasks of the mid 19th century and presenting a program of interest and education to all. The Junior Grange and the women's department carry on continuing projects at the farm.

King Ranch Chicken Casserole

1 (3-pound) chicken
1 medium onion
3 ribs celery
2 teaspoons salt
1 (10-ounce) can cream of chicken soup
1 (10-ounce) can tomatoes with
    green chiles
1/2 teaspoon salt
2 cups shredded Cheddar cheese
12 corn tortillas, cut into 1/2-inch strips
1 cup chopped onion

Combine the chicken with enough water to cover in a saucepan. Add the whole onion, celery and 2 teaspoons salt. Cook, covered, until the chicken is cooked through. Cool slightly. Drain, reserving the chicken and 1 1/3 cups of the broth. Discard the vegetables. Chop the chicken, discarding the skin and bones. Combine the reserved broth, soup, undrained tomatoes and 1/2 teaspoon salt in a saucepan and mix well. Cook just until heated through, stirring frequently. Reserve 2/3 cup of the cheese. Layer the chicken, tortillas, remaining cheese, chopped onion and tomato mixture 1/2 at a time in a 4-quart baking dish. Sprinkle with the reserved cheese. Bake at 350 degrees for 50 minutes. **Yield:** 6 servings.

Stacy Graschel, *David Crockett Grange, Texas*

Poppy Seed Chicken

2 pounds chicken pieces
1 (10-ounce) can cream of chicken soup
1 cup sour cream
1 sleeve butter crackers, crushed
2 tablespoons poppy seeds
1/2 cup (1 stick) margarine, melted

Combine the chicken with enough water to cover in a stockpot. Cook until the chicken is tender; drain. Chop the chicken, discarding the skin and bones. Combine the chicken, soup and sour cream in a bowl and mix well. Spoon into a 9x9-inch baking dish. Sprinkle with a mixture of the cracker crumbs and poppy seeds. Drizzle with the margarine. Bake at 375 degrees for 1 hour or until bubbly. **Yield:** 8 servings.

Gretchen Kralj, *Scrubgrass Grange, Pennsylvania*

Sweet-and-Sour Chicken

2 1/2 to 3 pounds chicken pieces
1 (20-ounce) can crushed pineapple
1 (10-ounce) can tomato soup
1 cup catsup
2 tablespoons Worcestershire sauce
2 tablespoons brown sugar
2 teaspoons soy sauce

Arrange the chicken in a 9x13-inch baking dish. Combine the undrained pineapple, soup, catsup, Worcestershire sauce, brown sugar and soy sauce in a bowl and mix well. Spoon over the chicken. Bake at 375 degrees for 1 hour or until the chicken is tender. **Yield:** 4 to 6 servings.

Sue Scranton, *Rundell's Grange, Pennsylvania*

Chicken Olé

4 boneless skinless chicken breasts,
    cooked
1 (10-ounce) can cream of chicken soup
1 (10-ounce) can cream of
    mushroom soup
2 cans green chile salsa
1 cup milk
1 onion, grated or minced
2 to 3 tablespoons chicken broth
12 corn tortillas, cut into 1-inch strips
8 ounces Cheddar cheese, shredded

Cut the chicken into bite-size pieces. Combine the soups, salsa, milk and onion in a bowl and mix well. Pour the broth into a greased 9x13-inch baking dish. Layer the tortillas, chicken and soup mixture $1/2$ at a time in the prepared baking dish. Sprinkle with the cheese. Chill, covered, for 24 hours. Bake at 300 degrees for 1 to $1^1/2$ hours or until bubbly. **Yield:** 8 to 10 servings.

Loretta Hooper, *Millville Grange, California*

Easy Chicken Divan

2 (10-ounce) packages frozen broccoli
3 boneless skinless chicken breasts,
    cooked, chopped
1 (10-ounce) can cream of
    mushroom soup
1 cup mayonnaise-type salad dressing
2 teaspoons lemon juice
Shredded Cheddar cheese
Shredded mozzarella cheese
Crushed potato chips (optional)

Cook the broccoli using package directions; drain. Arrange the broccoli in a 9x13-inch baking pan. Layer with the chicken. Combine the soup, salad dressing and lemon juice in a bowl and mix well. Spread over the chicken. Sprinkle with Cheddar cheese and mozzarella cheese. Top with potato chips. Bake at 350 degrees for 35 to 40 minutes or until bubbly.
Yield: 6 servings.

Bob Scranton, *Rundell's Grange, Pennsylvania*

The National Grange joins hands with the American Red Cross and the Salvation Army. We unite in helping others.

Old-Fashioned Chicken Potpie

3 cups chopped potatoes
1 cup chopped carrot
1 (6-ounce) package frozen peas
Chicken stock
1/4 cup (1/2 stick) butter
1 cup milk
1/4 cup plus 1 tablespoon flour
2 cups chicken stock
3 cups chopped cooked chicken
1/2 to 1 teaspoon salt
Pepper to taste
Salt to taste
1 1/2 cups flour
1 1/2 teaspoons baking powder
1/2 teaspoon salt
5 tablespoons shortening
1/2 cup plus 1 tablespoon milk

Combine the potatoes, carrot and peas with enough chicken stock to cover in a saucepan. Cook until the vegetables are tender; drain. Heat the butter in a saucepan until melted. Process 1 cup milk and 1/4 cup plus 1 tablespoon flour in a blender until blended. Stir 2 cups stock into the butter. Add the milk mixture gradually, stirring constantly. Cook over medium heat until thickened, stirring constantly. Add the vegetables, chicken, 1/2 to 1 teaspoon salt and pepper. Spoon into a large baking dish. Sprinkle with pepper and salt to taste. Combine 1 1/2 cups flour, baking powder and 1/2 teaspoon salt in a bowl and mix well. Cut in the shortening until crumbly. Add 1/2 cup plus 1 tablespoon milk gradually, stirring constantly until a soft dough forms. Knead the dough on a lightly floured surface for 30 seconds and roll to the size required to cover the chicken mixture. Cover the top with the pastry; cut slits. Bake at 450 degrees for 25 minutes. **Yield:** 8 servings.

Mary C. Lantz, *Glade Valley Grange, Maryland*

Deviled Clams

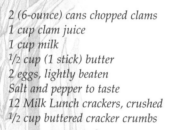

2 (6-ounce) cans chopped clams
1 cup clam juice
1 cup milk
1/2 cup (1 stick) butter
2 eggs, lightly beaten
Salt and pepper to taste
12 Milk Lunch crackers, crushed
1/2 cup buttered cracker crumbs

Bring the undrained clams and clam juice to a boil in a saucepan. Stir in the milk, butter, eggs, salt and pepper. Add the 12 crushed crackers and mix well. Cook until thickened, stirring frequently. Spoon into an 8x8-inch baking dish. Sprinkle with 1/2 cup buttered crumbs. Bake at 400 degrees or broil until brown on top. **Yield:** 6 servings.

Gertrude Prelli, *Riverton Grange, Connecticut*

Clam and Eggplant Delicious

1 small onion, minced
Vegetable oil
1 large eggplant, peeled, chopped
Salt to taste
1 (6-ounce) can minced clams
3/4 cup chopped tomato or tomato sauce

Sauté the onion in oil in a saucepan until light brown. Add the eggplant. Sauté until brown. Add a small amount of hot water and salt. Cook, covered, over low heat for several minutes, stirring occasionally. Stir in the undrained clams and tomatoes. Cook until thickened, stirring frequently. **Yield:** 2 to 3 servings.

Joy Beatie, *California Director of Women's Activities*

Crab Cakes

1 pound crab meat, flaked
1/2 cup Italian-style bread crumbs
2 eggs, lightly beaten
1/2 teaspoon baking powder
1/2 teaspoon prepared mustard
1/8 teaspoon red pepper
Salt to taste
Vegetable oil for frying

Combine the crab meat, bread crumbs, eggs, baking powder, prepared mustard, red pepper and salt in a bowl and mix well. Shape the crab meat mixture into 8 patties. Fry in the oil in a skillet until brown on both sides, turning once; drain. **Yield:** 8 crab cakes.

Shirley L. Millman, *Henlopen Grange, Delaware*

The Grange was the first organization to give women equal status with men. There are sixteen officers in each Grange unit. Women may hold any of those offices, but four of those offices are held exclusively by women.

Crab Supreme

1 cup chopped celery
8 slices bread, cubed
1 pound crab meat, flaked
1 onion, chopped
1/2 cup chopped green bell pepper
1/2 teaspoon salt
1/8 teaspoon Tabasco sauce
1/2 cup mayonnaise
2 cups milk
4 eggs, beaten
1 cup cream of mushroom soup
Grated cheese

Combine the celery with enough water to cover in a saucepan. Simmer for 10 minutes; drain. Arrange half the bread cubes in a baking dish. Combine the crab meat, celery, onion, green pepper, salt and Tabasco sauce in a bowl and mix well. Stir in the mayonnaise. Spoon over the bread cubes. Top with the remaining bread cubes. Whisk the milk and eggs in a bowl until blended. Pour over the prepared layers. Chill, covered, for 4 to 10 hours. Spread with the soup. Sprinkle with cheese. Bake at 325 degrees for 1 1/4 hours. **Yield:** 12 to 15 servings.

Betty Thompson, *First Lady, Maryland State Grange*

Nut Crab Puff

1 (6-ounce) can crab meat, drained, flaked
1 cup shredded Cheddar cheese
8 ounces cream cheese, softened, cubed
1/4 cup chopped green onions
1 (3-ounce) jar macadamia nuts, broken into pieces
2 cups milk
1 cup baking mix
4 eggs
3/4 teaspoon salt

Combine the crab meat, Cheddar cheese, cream cheese and green onions in a bowl and mix well. Spoon into a 9x9-inch baking dish. Sprinkle with the macadamia nuts. Combine the milk, baking mix, eggs and salt in a mixer bowl. Beat at medium speed for 1 minute. Pour over the prepared layer. Bake at 400 degrees for 35 to 40 minutes or until a knife inserted in the center comes out clean. Let stand for 5 minutes before serving. **Yield:** 8 servings.

Diane Schlagel, *Homestead Grange, Colorado*

Baked Scalloped Oysters

1 pint oysters
2 cups cracker crumbs
1/2 cup (1 stick) butter or margarine, melted
1/4 teaspoon pepper
Milk or cream
1/2 teaspoon salt
1/4 to 1 teaspoon Worcestershire sauce

Drain the oysters, reserving the liquor. Toss the cracker crumbs with the butter in a bowl. Layer 1/3 of the cracker crumbs and 1/2 of the oysters in a buttered 8-inch round baking pan. Sprinkle with half the pepper. Top with half the remaining cracker crumbs, remaining oysters and remaining pepper. Combine the reserved oyster liquor with enough milk to measure 1 cup. Stir in the salt and Worcestershire sauce. Pour over the prepared layers. Top with the remaining cracker crumbs. Bake at 350 degrees for 40 minutes. **Yield:** 4 servings.

Mary Jane Shepard, *Shenango Township Grange, Pennsylvania*

Baked Salmon Puff

3 tablespoons chopped celery
2 1/2 tablespoons chopped fresh parsley
2 tablespoons butter
2 cups drained canned salmon, bones
    removed, flaked
2 cups mashed potatoes
1 tablespoon lemon juice
1 1/2 teaspoons minced chives
1 teaspoon minced onion
1 teaspoon salt
1/8 teaspoon pepper
3 egg yolks
3 egg whites, stiffly beaten

Cook the celery and parsley in the butter in a skillet for
3 minutes. Combine the celery mixture, salmon, potatoes,
lemon juice, chives, onion, salt and pepper in a mixer bowl and
mix well. Add the egg yolks. Beat until light, scraping the bowl
occasionally. Fold in the egg whites. Spoon into a 2-quart baking
dish. Bake at 350 degrees for 1 hour and 10 minutes. Serve with
peas and grilled cheese sandwiches. **Yield:** 4 servings.

Caroline M. Reilly, *Blair County Pomona, Pennsylvania*

South Texas Tuna Casserole

6 ounces medium noodles, cooked,
    drained
1 (9-ounce) can tuna, drained
1 cup chopped celery
1/4 cup chopped onion
1/4 cup chopped green bell pepper
1/4 cup chopped pimentos
1 teaspoon salt
1/2 cup mayonnaise
1 (10-ounce) can cream of celery soup
1/2 cup milk
1 cup shredded Cheddar cheese
1/2 cup slivered almonds

Combine the noodles, tuna, celery, onion, green pepper,
pimentos and salt in a bowl and mix gently. Stir in the
mayonnaise. Combine the soup and milk in a saucepan and
mix well. Cook just until heated through, stirring frequently.
Add the cheese. Cook until the cheese melts, stirring constantly.
Stir into the noodle mixture. Spoon into an ungreased 1 1/2-quart
baking dish. Sprinkle with the almonds. Bake at 350 degrees for
20 minutes or until bubbly. **Yield:** 6 to 8 servings.

Florence Wuest, *David Crockett Grange, Texas*

*The first lecturer of the National Grange was John R. Thompson (1867–1892). The only woman
to serve as National Lecturer was Mary R. Buffington of Pennsylvania (1987–1997).*

Breakfast Sausage Casserole

2 pounds hot sausage
1 medium onion, chopped
2 (10-ounce) cans cream of celery soup
2 cups shredded Cheddar cheese
8 to 10 eggs, beaten
2 cups crisp rice cereal

Brown the sausage and onion in a skillet, stirring until the sausage is crumbly; drain. Stir in the soup, cheese and eggs. Pour half the sausage mixture into a greased 9x13-inch baking pan. Sprinkle with 1 cup of the cereal and press gently. Top with the remaining sausage mixture and remaining 1 cup cereal. Press lightly. Bake at 350 degrees for 40 minutes. **Yield:** 15 servings.

Cordelia Dunn, *Tennessee Director of Women's Activities*

Escalloped Eggs

2 tablespoons butter
3 tablespoons flour
2 cups milk
1 tablespoon chopped fresh parsley or green onions
1 teaspoon salt
$^1/_8$ teaspoon pepper
6 hard-cooked eggs, sliced
Buttered bread crumbs

Heat the butter in a saucepan until melted. Stir in the flour until blended. Add the milk gradually, stirring constantly. Cook until thickened, stirring constantly. Stir in the parsley, salt and pepper. Remove from heat. Layer the eggs and sauce $^1/_2$ at a time in a greased 1-quart baking dish. Sprinkle with bread crumbs. Bake at 350 degrees for 25 minutes. **Yield:** 6 servings.

Marilyn La Tourette, *Enterprise Grange, Pennsylvania*

Overnight Breakfast Omelet

6 slices bread, cubed
1 pound bacon, crisp-fried, crumbled
2 cups milk
8 eggs, lightly beaten
1 cup shredded sharp Cheddar cheese
1 teaspoon salt
1 teaspoon dry mustard
Shredded sharp Cheddar cheese

Layer the bread and bacon in the order listed in a 9x13-inch baking pan. Whisk the milk, eggs, 1 cup cheese, salt and dry mustard in a bowl. Pour over the prepared layers. Sprinkle with additional cheese. Chill, covered, for 12 hours. Bake at 350 degrees for 35 minutes. May substitute cooked crumbled sausage or ham for the bacon. **Yield:** 6 to 8 servings.

Dolores Basinger, *Pleasant Valley Grange, Pennsylvania*

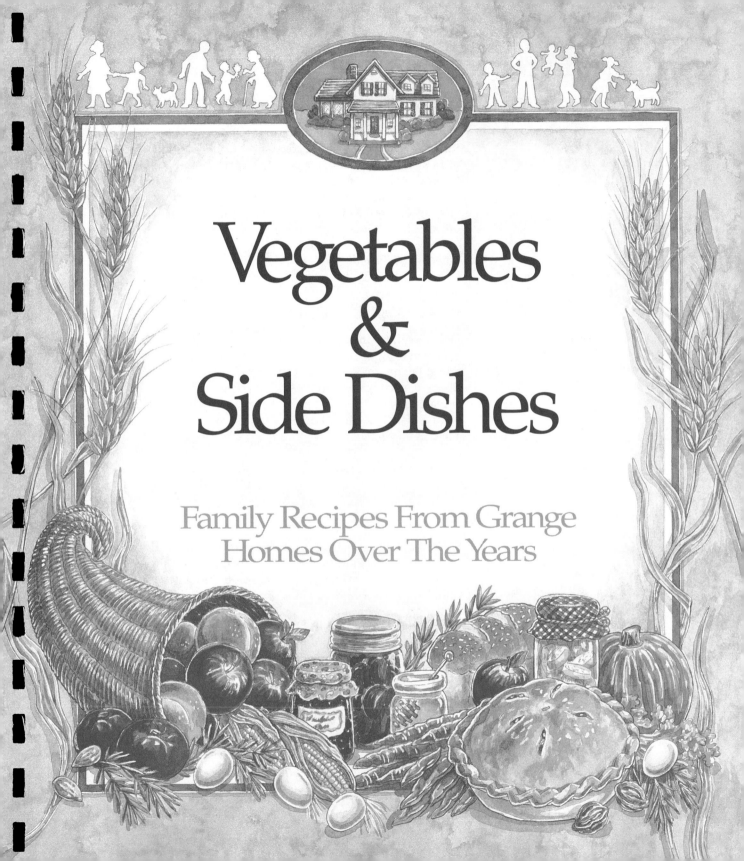

Vegetables & Side Dishes

Family Recipes From Grange
Homes Over The Years

Creamy Asparagus Casserole

2 pounds fresh asparagus, cut into
    1-inch pieces
1/4 cup (1/2 stick) butter or margarine
1/4 cup flour
2 cups milk or half-and-half
1/2 teaspoon salt
1/4 teaspoon pepper
6 hard-cooked eggs, sliced
1 cup shredded Cheddar cheese
1 cup bread crumbs

Combine the asparagus with just enough water to cover in a large saucepan. Cook until tender-crisp; drain. Heat the butter in a saucepan until melted. Stir in the flour until blended. Add the milk gradually, stirring constantly. Cook for 2 minutes or until thickened, stirring constantly. Stir in the salt and pepper. Layer the asparagus, eggs, cheese and sauce 1/2 at a time in a 7x11-inch baking dish. Sprinkle with the bread crumbs. Bake at 350 degrees for 30 minutes. May substitute chopped cooked broccoli for the asparagus. **Yield:** 6 to 8 servings.

Janet Nace, *Gidion Grange, Pennsylvania*

Apple Bake Beans

1/4 cup (1/2 stick) butter
2 large cooking apples, chopped
1/2 cup packed light brown sugar
1/2 cup sugar
1/2 cup catsup
1 tablespoon molasses
1 teaspoon salt
1 teaspoon cinnamon, or to taste
1 (48-ounce) jar Great Northern beans

Heat the butter in a large skillet until melted. Add the apples. Cook over low to medium heat until tender, stirring frequently. Stir in the brown sugar and sugar. Cook until the sugars dissolve, stirring constantly. Add the catsup, molasses, salt and cinnamon and mix well. Stir in the beans. Spoon into a 2-quart baking dish. Bake at 400 degrees for approximately 1 hour. **Yield:** 8 servings.

Dianne P. Warner, *Hayes Grange, Michigan*

Green Bean Casserole

1 cup chopped red bell pepper
1 cup finely chopped onion
1 tablespoon margarine
1 (10-ounce) can any flavor cream soup
1/4 cup milk
1 teaspoon teriyaki sauce
1/8 teaspoon pepper
2 (16-ounce) packages frozen green
    beans, thawed, drained
1 (8-ounce) can sliced water chestnuts,
    drained
1 cup shredded Cheddar cheese

Sauté the red pepper and onion in the margarine in a skillet until tender. Stir in the soup, milk, teriyaki sauce and pepper. Add the green beans and water chestnuts and mix well. Cook until bubbly, stirring frequently. Spoon into a 2-quart baking dish. Sprinkle with the cheese. Bake at 350 degrees for 15 minutes or until heated through. **Yield:** 6 to 8 servings.

Elaine R. Nothe, *Palmer Grange, Massachusetts*

Broccoli Casserole

1 cup instant rice
1 large onion, chopped
1/4 cup (1/2 stick) margarine
1 (10-ounce) can cream of chicken soup
8 ounces mild processed cheese, cut into
    chunks
1/2 cup evaporated milk
2 (10-ounce) packages frozen chopped
    broccoli, thawed, drained

Cook the rice using package directions. Brown the onion in the margarine in a skillet, stirring constantly. Stir in the soup, cheese and evaporated milk. Add the broccoli and mix well. Fold in the rice. Spoon into a greased 9x13-inch baking dish. Bake at 325 degrees for 1 1/4 hours. **Yield:** 10 servings.

Esther F. Russell, *Rainbow Valley Grange, California*

German-Style Red Cabbage

1 medium head red cabbage, finely
    shredded
Boiling water
3 apples, peeled, thinly sliced
3 tablespoons butter
2 teaspoons flour
1/2 cup packed brown sugar
1/3 cup vinegar
1/3 cup red wine
1 teaspoon salt
1/8 teaspoon pepper

Combine the cabbage with a small amount of boiling water in a saucepan. Cook for 10 minutes or until tender-crisp; drain. Combine the apples with enough water to cover in a saucepan. Cook until tender; drain. Heat the butter in a large skillet until melted. Stir in the cabbage and apples. Cook for several minutes, stirring frequently. Stir in the flour. Add the brown sugar, vinegar, red wine, salt and pepper and mix well. Cook over low heat for 10 minutes, stirring occasionally. **Yield:** 6 servings.

Ruth C. Lampman, *Leon Valley Grange, Texas*

For the first time in many years, the Junior Grange (for children between the ages of five and fourteen) celebrated a national net gain in membership in 1998 with the following states contributing to this milestone: California, Colorado, Connecticut, Iowa, Kansas, Montana, North Carolina, Oregon, South Carolina, Texas, Vermont, and West Virginia.

Copper Penny Carrots

2 pounds carrots, sliced
Salt to taste
1 small green bell pepper, thinly sliced
1 small onion, sliced
1 (10-ounce) can tomato soup
1 cup sugar
3/4 cup cider vinegar
1/2 cup vegetable oil
1 teaspoon prepared mustard
1 teaspoon salt
1/8 teaspoon pepper

Combine the carrots and salt to taste with enough water to cover in a saucepan. Cook until tender-crisp; drain. Rinse and drain. Layer the carrots, green pepper and onion in a large baking dish. Combine the soup, sugar, cider vinegar, oil, prepared mustard, 1 teaspoon salt and pepper in a saucepan and mix well. Bring to a boil, stirring constantly. Pour over the prepared layers. Chill, covered, for 8 to 10 hours.
Yield: 12 servings.

Elizabeth Hammett, *Colonial Grange, South Carolina*

Orange-Spiced Carrots

2 1/2 cups thinly sliced peeled carrots
3/4 cup water
1/2 cup orange juice
1 tablespoon brown sugar
1 1/2 teaspoons cornstarch
1/2 teaspoon salt
1/8 teaspoon ginger
1/8 teaspoon nutmeg
1/8 teaspoon cinnamon
Chopped fresh parsley (optional)

Combine the carrots and water in a saucepan. Cook, covered, until tender; drain. Combine the orange juice, brown sugar, cornstarch, salt, ginger, nutmeg and cinnamon in a bowl and mix well. Add to the carrots and toss gently. Cook until thickened, stirring frequently. Spoon into a serving bowl. Sprinkle with parsley. **Yield:** 4 servings.

Gene Rector, *West Oshtemo Grange, Michigan*

Iced Cauliflower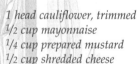

1 head cauliflower, trimmed
1/2 cup mayonnaise
1/4 cup prepared mustard
1/2 cup shredded cheese

Place the cauliflower in a microwave-safe dish. Microwave, covered tightly with plastic wrap, on High for 7 minutes. Ice the entire surface of the cauliflower with a mixture of the mayonnaise and prepared mustard. Sprinkle with the cheese. Microwave on High for 1 minute. **Yield:** 4 to 6 servings.

Elizabeth C. Johnson, *Trinity Grange, North Carolina*

Baked Corn Pudding

1 (16-ounce) can cream-style corn
1 (16-ounce) can whole kernel corn
1 (9-ounce) package corn muffin mix
1 cup sour cream
2 eggs, beaten
2 tablespoons sugar

Combine the cream-style corn, undrained whole kernel corn, muffin mix, sour cream, eggs and sugar in a bowl and mix well. Spoon into a greased 1¹/2-quart baking dish. Bake at 350 degrees for 1 hour. **Yield:** 6 servings.

Harvey Brown, *Bayard Grange, Ohio*

Sour Cream Corn Casserole

1 (16-ounce) can whole kernel corn,
    drained
1 (16-ounce) can cream-style corn
1 (8-ounce) package corn bread mix
¹/2 cup (1 stick) margarine, melted
2 eggs, lightly beaten
1 cup sòur cream

Combine the whole kernel corn, cream-style corn, corn bread mix, margarine and eggs in a bowl and mix well. Stir in the sour cream. Spoon into a greased 2-quart baking pan. Bake at 350 degrees for 1 hour. Bake at 325 degrees in a glass baking dish. **Yield:** 8 servings.

Betty H. Barett, *Chico Grange, California*

Every year a representative from each region is chosen to serve on the National Grange Youth Team. The team members plan the coming year's activities when they meet in Washington, D.C., in January. They select a theme and carry it through the entire year. The team is made up of one young couple and five male/female youth age individuals.

Farmer's Casserole

2 large potatoes, thinly sliced
1 large onion, thinly sliced
2 medium zucchini, cut into small
  chunks
4 tomatoes, coarsely chopped
2 carrots, thinly sliced
Thyme to taste
Marjoram to taste
Salt and freshly ground pepper to taste
3/4 cup dry white wine or chicken broth
2 cups shredded Cheddar cheese
1 cup fresh bread cubes
1 tablespoon butter or margarine, melted

Layer the potatoes, onion, zucchini, tomatoes and carrots in a baking dish in the order listed, sprinkling each layer lightly with thyme, marjoram, salt and pepper. Pour the white wine over the layers. Bake, covered, at 375 degrees for 1 hour; remove the cover. Sprinkle with the cheese. Toss the bread cubes and butter in a bowl. Sprinkle over the top. Bake for 15 to 20 minutes longer or until brown and bubbly. Add a layer of ground beef for a complete meal. **Yield:** 6 servings.

Susan R. Flynn, *Moosup Valley Grange, Rhode Island*

Garden Casserole

1 cup broccoli florets
1 cup cauliflorets
1 cup sliced zucchini
1 cup sliced yellow squash
1/2 cup sliced carrot
1/2 cup sliced mushrooms
1 cup shredded Cheddar or
  mozzarella cheese
2 tablespoons butter or margarine
2 tablespoons flour
2 cups milk
3/4 teaspoon parsley flakes
1/2 teaspoon garlic powder
1/2 teaspoon onion flakes
1/8 teaspoon celery salt
Salt and pepper to taste
1/2 cup grated Parmesan cheese

Steam the broccoli, cauliflower, zucchini, yellow squash, carrot and mushrooms in a steamer until tender-crisp; drain. Arrange the vegetables in a buttered baking dish. Sprinkle with the Cheddar cheese. Heat the butter in a saucepan until melted. Stir in the flour. Add the milk gradually, stirring constantly. Cook until thickened, stirring constantly. Stir in the parsley flakes, garlic powder, onion flakes, celery salt, salt and pepper. Spoon over the prepared layers. Sprinkle with the Parmesan cheese. Bake at 350 degrees for 30 minutes or until light brown and bubbly. May be assembled in advance and stored, covered, in the refrigerator. Bake at 350 degrees for 45 minutes.
Yield: 6 to 8 servings.

Doris Brady, *Azale Grange, Oregon*

Potato Casserole

6 medium potatoes, cooked, drained
2 cups shredded Cheddar cheese
2 cups sour cream
1/2 cup (1 stick) butter, melted
1/3 cup chopped green onions or chives
1/2 teaspoon salt

Cook the potatoes 1 day in advance. Store in the refrigerator. Peel and grate the potatoes. Combine the potatoes, cheese, sour cream, butter, green onions and salt in a bowl and mix well. Spoon into a 9x13-inch baking dish. Bake at 350 degrees for 30 to 35 minutes or until brown and bubbly. **Yield:** 15 servings.

Pat Bright, *Elk Creek Grange, California*

Aunt Ann's Potato Casserole

4 cups mashed cooked potatoes
1/4 cup (1/2 stick) butter, softened
1/2 teaspoon salt
1/4 teaspoon pepper
1 (28-ounce) can French-fried onions, crushed
1 cup whipping cream
1/2 teaspoon salt
2/3 cup shredded extra-sharp Cheddar cheese
Parsley flakes to taste

Combine the potatoes, butter, 1/2 teaspoon salt and pepper in a bowl and mix well. Add half the onions and mix well. Spoon into a 9x9-inch baking pan. Combine the whipping cream and 1/2 teaspoon salt in a mixer bowl. Beat until soft peaks form. Fold in the cheese. Spread over the prepared layer. Sprinkle with the remaining onions and parsley flakes. Bake at 325 degrees for 25 to 30 minutes or until light brown and heated through. Double the recipe for a larger crowd. **Yield:** 9 servings.

Joyce Meeker, *Outlook Grange, Washington*

Church Supper Potatoes

3 pounds russet potatoes, peeled, cut into 1/2-inch chunks
2 garlic cloves
6 ounces cream cheese, softened
2 tablespoons butter, softened
1 cup shredded Cheddar cheese
1/2 cup sour cream
1 (10-ounce) package frozen chopped spinach, thawed, drained
1 teaspoon garlic salt
1 teaspoon onion salt
1 cup shredded Cheddar cheese

Combine the potatoes and garlic with enough water to cover in a saucepan. Bring to a boil. Boil for 25 minutes or until the potatoes are tender; drain. Mash the potatoes, garlic, cream cheese and butter in a bowl. Stir in 1 cup Cheddar cheese and sour cream. Squeeze the excess moisture from the spinach. Add the spinach, garlic salt and onion salt to the potato mixture and mix well. Spoon into a greased 2-quart baking dish. Bake at 350 degrees for 30 to 35 minutes or until heated through. Sprinkle with 1 cup Cheddar cheese. Bake for 5 minutes longer or until the cheese melts. **Yield:** 10 to 12 servings.

Irene Jefferson, *Massachusetts Co-Director of Women's Activities*

Each state selects an outstanding male, female, and young couple to represent their state at the National Convention. Each ambassador attends the convention as a guest. All financing for this program has been raised through donations by individuals and Granges nationwide.

Hash Brown Casserole

1 (32-ounce) package frozen hash brown
    potatoes
2 cups shredded medium Cheddar cheese
2 cups sour cream
1 (10-ounce) can cream of mushroom
    soup
1/2 cup chopped onion
1/4 teaspoon salt
1/8 teaspoon pepper
2 cups crushed cornflakes
1/2 cup (1 stick) butter or margarine,
    melted

Combine the hash brown potatoes, cheese, sour cream, soup, onion, salt and pepper in a bowl and mix well. Spoon into a 9x13-inch baking dish. Sprinkle with the cornflakes. Drizzle with the butter. Bake at 350 degrees for 1 hour.
Yield: 24 servings.

Jamie Klenklen, *Ceres, National Grange*

Ranch Potatoes

4 medium baking potatoes, peeled, cut
    into 1/4-inch slices
1 cup ranch salad dressing
1 teaspoon salt
1/4 teaspoon pepper
1/3 cup Italian-style bread crumbs

Combine the potatoes, salad dressing, salt and pepper in a bowl and toss gently. Spoon into a greased 9x13-inch baking pan. Sprinkle with the bread crumbs. Bake, covered, at 375 degrees for 30 minutes; remove cover. Bake for 20 minutes longer or until the potatoes are tender. **Yield:** 6 to 8 servings.

Helen Crise, *Mendon Grange, Pennsylvania*

Ranch-Style Potatoes

8 to 10 medium potatoes, peeled, coarsely
    chopped
1 (10-ounce) can any flavor cream soup
1 1/4 cups milk
1 cup shredded sharp Cheddar cheese
1 envelope ranch salad dressing mix
Pepper to taste
1/4 cup shredded sharp Cheddar cheese
6 slices crisp-fried bacon, crumbled

Combine the potatoes with enough water to cover in a saucepan. Bring to a boil. Boil for 10 minutes; drain. Spoon the potatoes into a 9x13-inch baking dish. Combine the soup, milk, 1 cup cheese, dressing mix and pepper in a bowl and mix well. Spoon over the potatoes. Sprinkle with 1/4 cup cheese and bacon. Bake at 350 degrees for 30 minutes. **Yield:** 10 servings.

Myrtle Stanley, *Methuen Grange, Massachusetts*

Banana Squash

3 cups mashed cooked banana squash
1 cup sugar
1/4 cup (1/2 stick) margarine, melted
1 egg, beaten
2 teaspoons lemon juice
1 teaspoon cinnamon
1 teaspoon salt
1/2 cup packed brown sugar
1/4 cup flour
1/4 cup (1/2 stick) margarine, softened
1/2 cup chopped pecans

Combine the squash, sugar, 1/4 cup melted margarine, egg, lemon juice, cinnamon and salt in a bowl and mix well. Spoon into a 10x10-inch baking pan. Combine the brown sugar, flour and 1/4 cup margarine in a bowl, stirring until crumbly. Stir in the pecans. Sprinkle over the top. Bake at 350 degrees for 45 minutes. **Yield:** 12 to 15 servings.

Mildred Millisor, *Rush Creek Grange, Ohio*

Summer Squash Casserole

6 to 8 cups sliced or chopped squash
1 cup grated carrot
1/4 cup sliced or chopped onion
1/2 cup water
1 (10-ounce) can cream of chicken soup
1 cup sour cream
1 (6-ounce) package stove-top stuffing
    mix
1/2 cup (1 stick) butter, softened

Combine the squash, carrot, onion and water in a saucepan. Cook for 5 minutes. Stir in the soup and sour cream. Combine the stuffing mix and butter in a bowl and mix well. Layer half the stuffing mix, vegetable mixture and remaining stuffing mix in a 2-quart baking dish. Bake at 350 degrees for 25 to 30 minutes or until brown and bubbly. May substitute cream of celery soup for the cream of chicken soup.
Yield: 8 to 10 servings.

Burley Whitten, *Edgemere Grange, Idaho*

In 1998 and 1999, Grange members from across the United States went bowling for a good cause the first Saturday in March. The total funds raised in the first two years exceeded $23,000 for Mother Voices (AIDS Awareness) and the National Juvenile Diabetes Association.

Green Tomatoes Parmesan

1 egg, beaten
Milk
1 tablespoon vegetable oil
6 large green tomatoes, cut into 1/2-inch
    slices
1/2 cup flour
1/4 cup vegetable oil
1 garlic clove, minced
Salt to taste
1/2 cup grated Parmesan cheese
1/2 cup shredded mozzarella cheese
2 (8-ounce) cans tomato sauce

Whisk the egg, milk and 1 tablespoon oil in a bowl until blended. Coat the tomato slices with the flour. Dip the slices in the egg mixture. Heat 1/4 cup oil and garlic in a skillet. Add the tomato slices. Cook until brown on both sides, sprinkling with salt during the browning process; drain. Layer the tomatoes, Parmesan cheese and mozzarella cheese 1/2 at a time in a 8x11-inch baking dish. Pour the tomato sauce over the top. Bake at 350 degrees for 45 minutes. **Yield:** 8 servings.

Linda Brown, *Bayard Grange, Ohio*

Turnip Casserole

1 medium turnip, peeled, chopped
1 medium potato, peeled, chopped
1 medium onion, cut into wedges
Butter or margarine, softened
1/2 cup milk
1 egg
1/2 cup sugar
1/4 cup flour
1/2 teaspoon ginger
Crushed potato chips
2 tablespoons butter or margarine

Combine the turnip, potato and onion with enough water to cover in a saucepan. Cook until the vegetables are tender; drain. Mash the vegetables with the desired amount of softened butter in a bowl. Whisk the milk and egg in a bowl until blended. Add the sugar, flour and ginger, stirring until smooth. Stir into the vegetable mixture. Spoon into a buttered baking dish. Sprinkle with potato chips. Dot with 2 tablespoons butter. Bake at 350 degrees for 1 hour. **Yield:** 8 servings.

Phyllis R. Bierce, *Riverton Grange, Connecticut*

Zippy Zucchini

1 cup baking mix
1/2 cup grated Parmesan cheese
1 teaspoon salt
1/2 cup vegetable oil
4 eggs, beaten
4 small zucchini, thinly sliced
1/2 cup chopped onion
Chopped fresh tomato (optional)
Chopped green bell pepper (optional)

Combine the baking mix, cheese and salt in a bowl and mix well. Stir in the oil and eggs. Add the zucchini, onion, tomato and green pepper and mix gently. Spoon into a greased 9x13-inch baking dish. Bake at 350 degrees for 30 minutes. **Yield:** 6 servings.

Ida Norris, *Olanta Grange, Pennsylvania*

Hot Lettuce

Chopped cooked ham
$^1/_2$ cup vinegar
3 eggs
2 cups light cream
2 heads lettuce, shredded

Fry the ham in a skillet until crisp; drain. Add the vinegar and mix well. Set aside. Whisk the eggs in a bowl. Add the light cream and whisk until blended. Stir into the ham mixture. Bring to a boil over low heat, stirring constantly until thickened. Add the lettuce or pour over the lettuce in a bowl and toss to mix; the lettuce will wilt. Serve with boiled potatoes. **Yield:** 8 to 10 servings.

Bernice Maze, *Lawrenceville Grange, New Jersey*

Noodle Kugel

8 ounces noodles
$^1/_2$ cup (1 stick) butter or margarine, melted
3 egg yolks, beaten
2 tablespoons sugar
2 cups cottage cheese
1 cup sour cream
3 egg whites
1 cup cornflakes
3 tablespoons butter or margarine

Cook the noodles using package directions; drain. Stir in $^1/_2$ cup butter. Whisk the egg yolks and sugar in a bowl. Fold into the noodle mixture. Fold in the cottage cheese and sour cream. Beat the egg whites in a mixer bowl until stiff peaks form. Fold into the noodle mixture. Spoon into a 9x13-inch baking pan. Sprinkle with the cornflakes. Dot with 3 tablespoons butter. Bake at 350 degrees for 45 minutes. May be prepared 1 day in advance and stored, covered, in the refrigerator. Increase the baking time by 10 to 15 minutes. **Yield:** 12 to 15 servings.

Lila Tooker, *Elkhorn V.E. Grange, Nebraska*

The first Juvenile Grange (for children ages five to fourteen) was organized at San Sabo, Texas, in August of 1888. The name was later changed to Junior Grange. Having meetings and projects for the children at the same time as the adults meet, makes the Grange a truly family-oriented organization with programs to interest everyone from the youngest to the oldest member of the family.

Noodle Pudding

8 ounces wide noodles
2 apples, thinly sliced
1 cup golden raisins
3/4 cup sugar
2 eggs, beaten
1/4 teaspoon cinnamon
2 tablespoons butter

Cook the noodles using package directions for 10 minutes or until al dente; drain. Combine the noodles, apples, raisins, sugar, eggs and cinnamon in a bowl and mix gently. Spoon into an 8x8-inch baking pan. Dot with the butter. Bake at 400 degrees for 35 minutes or until light brown. Serve hot or at room temperature. May double the recipe and bake in a 9x13-inch baking dish. **Yield:** 9 servings.

Barbara Prindle, *Taghhannuck Grange, Connecticut*

Baked Pineapple

1 (20-ounce) can juice-pack pineapple
    tidbits
1 cup shredded Cheddar cheese
1 cup sugar
2 tablespoons flour
1 cup dry bread crumbs
2 tablespoons butter

Drain the pineapple, reserving the juice. Combine the pineapple and cheese in a bowl and mix well. Spoon into an 8x8-inch baking dish. Combine the reserved juice, sugar and flour in a saucepan and mix well. Cook just until blended, stirring constantly. Spoon over the pineapple mixture. Sprinkle with the bread crumbs and dot with the butter. Bake at 350 degrees for 20 to 25 minutes or until light brown. **Yield:** 12 servings.

Phyllis Tooker, *Elkhorn V.E. Grange, Nebraska*

Spinach Quiche

1 (10-ounce) package frozen chopped
    spinach, thawed, drained
10 ounces Monterey Jack cheese, cubed
1 unbaked (9-inch) pie shell
1 cup milk
1 cup flour
1/2 cup (1 stick) butter, sliced
2 eggs
2 teaspoons baking powder
Garlic to taste
Salt and pepper to taste

Squeeze the excess moisture from the spinach. Arrange the cheese in the pie shell. Whisk the milk, flour, butter, eggs, baking powder, garlic, salt and pepper in a bowl until blended. Stir in the spinach. Pour into the prepared pie shell. Bake at 325 degrees for 1 hour. **Yield:** 6 servings.

Tracy Taylor, *Legislative Department, National Grange*

Tomato Basil Tart

1/2 cup shredded mozzarella cheese
1 unbaked (9-inch) pie shell
4 or 5 Roma tomatoes, sliced
1 cup loosely packed fresh basil leaves
4 garlic cloves, minced
1 cup shredded mozzarella cheese
1/2 cup mayonnaise
1/4 cup grated Parmesan cheese

Spread 1/2 cup mozzarella cheese over the bottom of the pie shell. Layer the tomatoes, basil and garlic over the cheese. Combine 1 cup mozzarella cheese, mayonnaise and Parmesan cheese in a bowl and mix well. Spread over the prepared layers. Bake at 375 degrees for 35 to 40 minutes or until brown and bubbly. **Yield:** 8 servings.

Peg Brown, *First Lady, Michigan State Grange*

Beet Pickles

4 cups packed brown sugar
4 cups vinegar
4 cups water
2 teaspoons salt
1 peck small beets, cooked, peeled

Combine the brown sugar, vinegar, water and salt in a stockpot and mix well. Bring to a boil, stirring occasionally. Add the beets and mix gently. Simmer for 15 minutes, stirring occasionally. Pack the beets into hot sterilized pint jars. Ladle the hot syrup over the beets, leaving 1/2 inch headspace; seal with 2-piece lids. **Yield:** 12 to 13 pints.

John M. Pepau, *Stratford Grange, New Hampshire*

The National Junior Grange Merit Badge program was begun in 1970 with sixteen colorful felt badges. There were additions of badges and bars over the years. On January 1, 1995, the Merit Badge program was revised, changing to button-type metal pin badges. Badges are available on a rotating basis; some badges are retired and new badges are added every year.

Bread and Butter Pickles

4 quarts sliced zucchini
1 quart sliced onions
2 green bell peppers, sliced
3 garlic cloves, chopped
1/3 cup salt
5 cups sugar
3 cups white vinegar
2 tablespoons mustard seeds
1 1/2 teaspoons celery seeds
1 1/2 teaspoons turmeric

Combine the zucchini, onions, green peppers, garlic and salt in a large bowl and mix well. Cover with 3 trays of ice cubes. Let stand for 3 hours; drain. Spoon the zucchini mixture into a stockpot. Add the sugar, vinegar, mustard seeds, celery seeds and turmeric and mix well. Bring to a boil, stirring occasionally; decrease heat to low. Ladle the zucchini mixture into hot sterilized pint jars, leaving 1/2 inch headspace; seal with 2-piece lids. Process in a boiling water bath for 5 minutes if desired. Chill before serving for a crisp pickle. **Yield:** 7 pints.

Jean Accornero, *Glastonbury Grange, Connecticut*

Freezer Pickles

7 cups sliced unpeeled cucumbers
1 medium onion, sliced
2 tablespoons canning salt
2 cups sugar
1 cup cider vinegar
1 teaspoon celery seeds

Combine the cucumbers, onion and salt with enough water to cover in a large bowl. Let stand for 8 to 10 hours in a cool place; drain. Pack the cucumber mixture into freezer containers, leaving 1 inch headspace. Combine the sugar, vinegar and celery seeds in a bowl and mix well. Ladle over the cucumber mixture; cover. Freeze for several weeks before serving.
Yield: 3 pints.

Loeta Wales, *Azalea Grange, Oregon*

Golden Glow Pickles

4 pounds yellow or green cucumbers,
    peeled
6 large onions, chopped
3 green bell peppers, chopped
3 red bell peppers, chopped
1/2 cup salt
2 cups vinegar
2 cups packed brown sugar
2 cups sugar
1 tablespoon celery seeds
1 teaspoon turmeric
1 teaspoon mustard seeds

Discard the seeds and pulp of the cucumbers. Chop the firm white inner rind. Combine the cucumbers, onions, green peppers and red peppers in a large bowl and mix well. Stir in the salt. Let stand for 8 to 10 hours; drain. Rinse in cold water and drain. Transfer the cucumber mixture to a stockpot. Combine the vinegar, brown sugar, sugar, celery seeds, turmeric and mustard seeds in a bowl and mix well. Add to the cucumber mixture and mix well. Cook over low heat for 20 minutes or until the cucumbers are tender but not mushy. Pack the cucumber mixture into hot sterilized quart jars. Add the hot liquid, leaving 1/2 inch headspace; seal with 2-piece lids.
Yield: 3 quarts.

Judy L. Snyder, *Penn Grange, Pennsylvania*

Catherine's Pickles

4 quarts cucumbers or zucchini, sliced
1¹/₂ cups sliced onions
¹/₂ cup noniodized salt
5 cups sugar
5 cups vinegar
2 tablespoons mustard seeds
1¹/₂ teaspoons turmeric
1¹/₂ teaspoons celery seeds
¹/₂ teaspoon ground cloves
1 large red or green bell pepper, sliced

Combine the cucumbers, onions and salt in a large bowl and mix well. Cover with ice cubes. Let stand for 3 to 4 hours; drain. Combine the sugar, vinegar, mustard seeds, turmeric, celery seeds and cloves in a stockpot and mix well. Stir in cucumber mixture and red pepper. Bring to a boil, stirring occasionally. Boil for 5 minutes, stirring occasionally. Pack the cucumber mixture into hot sterilized pint jars. Add the boiling liquid, leaving ¹/₂ inch headspace; seal with 2-piece lids. **Yield:** 6 to 7 pints.

Doris Sherman, *Chippewa Grange, Pennsylvania*

Pickled Eggs and Beets

1¹/₄ cups sugar
1 cup white vinegar
¹/₄ teaspoon salt
¹/₈ teaspoon cinnamon
1 (16-ounce) can beets
Sliced onion (optional)
12 to 14 hard-cooked eggs

Combine the sugar, vinegar, salt and cinnamon in a saucepan and mix well. Add the undrained beets and sliced onion and mix well. Bring to a boil, stirring occasionally. Pour over the eggs in a bowl and mix gently. Chill, covered, until serving time. **Yield:** 12 to 14 servings.

Mary Bibel, *Mendon Grange, Pennsylvania*

Junior Grangers are involved in a program called "Stop the Violence." Members take part in programs and workshops teaching alternatives to violence. An emphasis is placed on building self-esteem in children, respecting others, and teaching conflict resolution skills.

Pickled Strawberries

4 quarts ripe strawberries
Cinnamon to taste
Cloves to taste
2 1/2 cups sugar
1 cup white vinegar

Layer the strawberries in a 1-gallon glass jar until all of the strawberries are used, sprinkling each layer with cinnamon and cloves. Bring the sugar and vinegar to a boil in a saucepan, stirring occasionally; skim. Pour over the strawberries. Let stand, covered, at room temperature for 8 to 10 hours. Drain the syrup into a saucepan. Bring to a boil, stirring occasionally. Pour over the strawberries. Let stand, covered, at room temperature for 8 to 10 hours. Transfer the strawberries and syrup to a saucepan. Bring to a boil. Boil for 20 minutes. Pack the strawberries into hot sterilized pint jars. Ladle the hot syrup over the strawberries, leaving 1/2 inch headspace; seal with 2-piece lids. **Yield:** 4 pints.

Lisa Heuschkel, *Jacinto Grange, California*

Fruit Chutney

1 (20-ounce) can crushed pineapple
1 pound dried apricots, chopped
1 pound golden raisins
1 pound fresh cranberries
2 cups chopped apples
1 cup each orange juice and sugar
1 cup packed brown sugar
1 cup whiskey or rum (optional)
1/2 cup white vinegar
Ground pulp and zest of 1 orange
1 teaspoon cinnamon
1/2 teaspoon ground cloves
1/2 teaspoon each nutmeg and allspice

Combine the undrained pineapple, apricots, raisins, cranberries, apples, orange juice, sugar, brown sugar, whiskey, vinegar, orange, cinnamon, cloves, nutmeg and allspice in a stockpot and mix well. Simmer for 1 hour, stirring occasionally. Ladle into hot sterilized jars, leaving 1/2 inch headspace; seal with 2-piece lids. **Yield:** 10 to 12 pints.

Douglas A. Bonsall, *Perry Valley Grange, Pennsylvania*

Sweet Relish

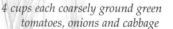

4 cups each coarsely ground green
   tomatoes, onions and cabbage
12 green bell peppers, coarsely ground
6 red bell peppers, coarsely ground
1/2 cup salt
6 cups sugar
4 cups vinegar
2 cups water
2 tablespoons mustard seeds
1 tablespoon celery seeds
1 1/2 teaspoons turmeric

Mix the green tomatoes, onions, cabbage, green peppers and red peppers in a bowl and. Sprinkle with the salt. Let stand at room temperature for 8 to 10 hours; drain. Rinse and drain. Transfer the vegetable mixture to a stockpot. Stir in a mixture of the sugar, vinegar, water, mustard seeds, celery seeds and turmeric. Bring to a boil; reduce heat. Simmer for 2 to 3 minutes, stirring frequently. Pack the relish into hot sterilized pint jars, leaving 1/2 inch headspace. Seal with 2-piece lids. **Yield:** 8 pints.

Albert B. Tomlinson, *Colonial Grange, South Carolina*

Zucchini Relish

10 cups ground seeded zucchini
4 cups ground onions
2 red bell peppers, ground
2 green bell peppers, ground
5 tablespoons canning salt
5 cups sugar
2 1/2 cups cider vinegar
1 tablespoon cornstarch
1 tablespoon nutmeg
1 tablespoon turmeric
2 teaspoons celery seeds
1 teaspoon pepper

Combine the zucchini, onions, red peppers and green peppers in a large bowl and mix well. Stir in the salt. Let stand at room temperature for 3 to 10 hours; drain. Rinse and drain. Combine the sugar, vinegar, cornstarch, nutmeg, turmeric, celery seeds and pepper in a stockpot and mix well. Cook over low heat until mixed, stirring constantly. Add the zucchini mixture and mix well. Bring to a boil; reduce heat. Simmer for 30 minutes, stirring occasionally. Ladle into hot sterilized pint jars, leaving 1/2 inch headspace. Seal with 2-piece lids. Process in a boiling water bath for 10 minutes. **Yield:** 6 pints.

Carolee Barrett, *New Hampshire Director of Women's Activities*

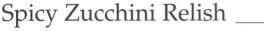

Spicy Zucchini Relish

10 cups chopped unpeeled zucchini
4 cups chopped onions
1 large red bell pepper, chopped
1 large green bell pepper, chopped
3 tablespoons canning salt
3 1/2 cups sugar
3 cups vinegar
1 (4-ounce) can chopped green chiles
   (optional)
4 teaspoons celery seeds
1 tablespoon turmeric
1 teaspoon pepper
1/2 teaspoon nutmeg

Combine the zucchini, onions, red pepper, green pepper and salt in a large bowl and mix well. Chill, covered, for 8 to 10 hours; drain. Rinse and drain. Combine the sugar, vinegar, chiles, celery seeds, turmeric, pepper and nutmeg in a stockpot and mix well. Bring to a boil. Stir in the zucchini mixture. Simmer for 10 minutes, stirring occasionally. Ladle into hot sterilized pint jars, leaving 1/4 inch headspace. Seal with 2-piece lids. Process in a boiling water bath for 10 minutes. **Yield:** 5 pints.

Verno Shorthill, *Indian Creek Grange, Kansas*

Junior Grangers are involved in an environmental program called "Our Earth Needs You." Study and projects are completed in beautification, recycling, composting, conservation, and pollution control.

Beet Jelly

12 to 14 large beets, coarsely chopped
1/4 cup lemon juice
1 envelope pectin
6 cups sugar

Combine the beets with enough water to cover in a large saucepan. Cook until tender. Drain, reserving 4 cups of the liquid. Discard the beets or save for another use. Combine the reserved liquid, lemon juice and pectin in a stockpot. Bring to a boil, stirring occasionally. Add the sugar and mix well. Boil for 5 minutes, stirring occasionally; skim. Ladle into hot sterilized jelly jars, leaving 1/4 inch headspace. Let stand until cool. Seal with paraffin. **Yield:** 4 jelly jars.

Ruby Resner, *Evergreen Grange, Oregon*

Banana Butter

3 cups mashed ripe bananas
1/2 cup lemon juice
5 cups sugar
1/2 teaspoon butter
1 pouch liquid pectin

Combine the bananas and lemon juice in a large saucepan and mix well. Stir in the sugar. Add the butter and mix well. Bring to a boil, stirring frequently. Stir in the pectin. Bring to a boil. Boil for 1 minute. Remove from heat; skim. Ladle into hot sterilized jelly jars, leaving 1/4 inch headspace. Seal with 2-piece lids. Process in a boiling water bath for 10 minutes.
Yield: 3 to 4 jelly jars.

Edwina Ward, *Brandywine Grange, Maryland*

Rhubarb Jam

5 cups finely chopped rhubarb
1 cup water
5 cups sugar
1 (21-ounce) can cherry pie filling
2 (3-ounce) packages cherry, strawberry
  or raspberry gelatin

Combine the rhubarb and water in a saucepan. Cook until tender. Stir in the sugar. Cook for 2 minutes, stirring occasionally. Add the pie filling and mix well. Cook for 6 minutes, stirring frequently. Remove from heat. Add the gelatin, stirring until dissolved. Ladle into hot sterilized jelly jars, leaving 1/4 inch headspace. Seal with 2-piece lids. Store in the refrigerator.
Yield: 5 to 6 jelly jars.

Madge M. Durm, *Lake Hubert Grange, Minnesota*

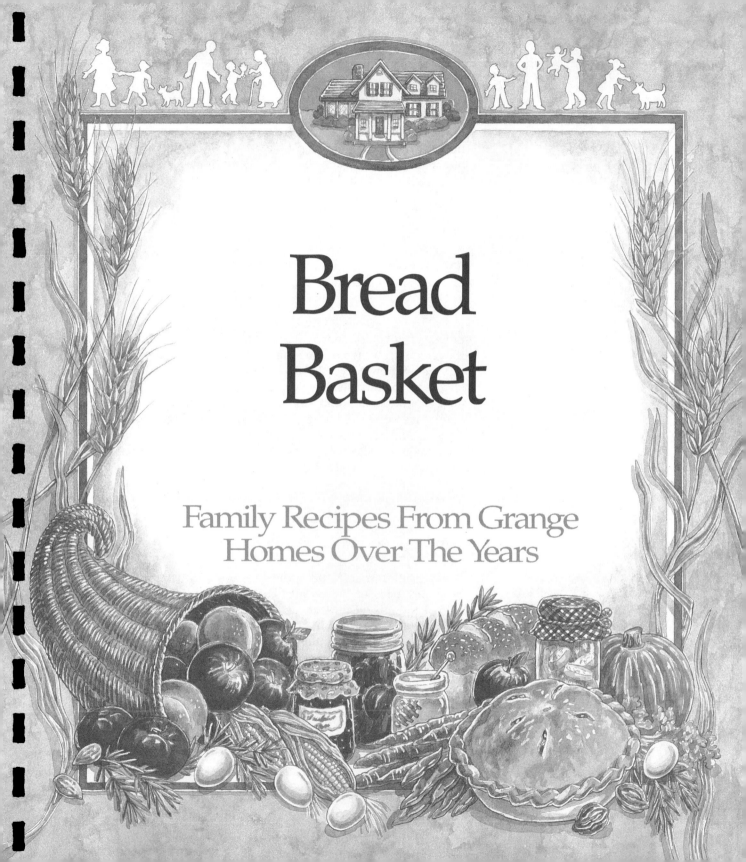

Bread Basket

Family Recipes From Grange
Homes Over The Years

Baking Powder Biscuits

2 cups flour
2 tablespoons sugar
4 teaspoons baking powder
1/2 teaspoon cream of tartar
1/2 teaspoon salt
1/2 cup shortening
2/3 cup milk
1 egg

Sift the flour, sugar, baking powder, cream of tartar and salt into a bowl and mix well. Cut in the shortening until crumbly. Add the milk and egg and mix well. Knead the dough on a lightly floured surface several times. Roll 1/2 inch thick; cut with a biscuit cutter. Arrange the biscuits on a baking sheet. Bake at 450 degrees for 10 to 15 minutes or until light brown. **Yield:** 12 biscuits.

Irene Lee, *Freeman Lake Grange, Idaho*

Everlasting Biscuits

1 cake yeast or 1 envelope dry yeast
1/3 cup cold water
1 quart milk
6 cups flour
2 teaspoons salt
2 teaspoons baking powder
1 teaspoon baking soda
1 cup mashed potatoes
3/4 cup shortening or lard
3/4 cup sugar
Flour

Soften the yeast in the cold water in a bowl. Scald the milk in a saucepan. Cool slightly. Combine the flour, salt, baking powder and baking soda in a bowl and mix well. Combine the potatoes, shortening, sugar and warm milk in a bowl and mix well. Stir in the yeast mixture. Stir in the flour mixture; should be the consistency of a sponge. Let rise for 2 hours. Add enough additional flour to make a stiff dough and mix well. Chill, covered, for 24 hours. Roll the dough on a lightly floured surface; cut with a biscuit cutter. Arrange the biscuits on a greased baking sheet. Let rise until light. Bake at 400 degrees until light brown. **Yield:** 3 dozen biscuits.

Thelma B. Tate, *Mt. Allison Grange, Colorado*

Blueberry Coffee Cake

2 cups fresh or frozen blueberries
5 tablespoons sugar
2 teaspoons cinnamon
3 cups flour
2 cups sugar
1 tablespoon baking powder
1 teaspoon salt
1 cup vegetable oil
1/4 cup orange juice
4 eggs, lightly beaten
1 teaspoon vanilla extract

Toss the blueberries, 5 tablespoons sugar and cinnamon in a bowl. Sift the flour, 2 cups sugar, baking powder and salt into a bowl and mix well. Make a well in the center of the flour mixture. Add the oil, orange juice, eggs and vanilla and mix well. Spread 1/3 of the batter in a greased and floured bundt pan. Layer the blueberries and remaining batter 1/2 at a time in the prepared pan. Bake at 350 degrees for 45 to 60 minutes or until light brown. Cover with foil during the end of the baking process to prevent overbrowning if needed. Remove to a wire rack to cool. Serve warm or at room temperature. If serving at room temperature, sprinkle with confectioners' sugar if desired. **Yield:** 12 servings.

Gloria Ballantine, *Hawks Mountain Grange, Vermont*

Easter Morn Coffee Cake

3 cups flour
1¹/2 teaspoons baking powder
1¹/2 teaspoons baking soda
1 teaspoon salt
1¹/2 cups sugar
¹/2 cup (1 stick) butter or margarine,
    softened
3 eggs
1¹/2 teaspoons vanilla extract
2 cups sour cream
¹/2 cup chopped nuts
¹/4 cup sugar
1 teaspoon cinnamon

Sift the flour, baking powder, baking soda and salt together. Beat 1¹/2 cups sugar, butter, eggs and vanilla in a mixer bowl until creamy, scraping the bowl occasionally. Add the dry ingredients alternately with the sour cream, beating well after each addition. Beat for 2 to 3 minutes. Combine the nuts, ¹/4 cup sugar and cinnamon in a bowl and mix well. Stir half the nut mixture into the batter. Spoon the batter into a greased and floured tube pan. Sprinkle with the remaining nut mixture. Bake at 350 degrees for 40 to 50 minutes or until light brown. Cool in pan for several minutes. Remove to a wire rack to cool completely.
Yield: 14 to 16 servings.

Marie A. Robidoux, *Chepachet Grange, Rhode Island*

Jewish Coffee Cake

2 cups flour
1 teaspoon baking powder
1 teaspoon baking soda
¹/4 teaspoon salt
1 cup sugar
¹/2 cup (1 stick) butter or margarine,
    softened
2 eggs
1 cup sour cream
1 teaspoon almond extract
¹/2 cup chopped walnuts
¹/4 cup sugar
1 teaspoon cinnamon

Sift the flour, baking powder, baking soda and salt together. Beat 1 cup sugar and butter in a mixer bowl until creamy, scraping the bowl occasionally. Beat in the eggs. Add the dry ingredients alternately with the sour cream, beating well after each addition. Beat in the flavoring. Combine the walnuts, ¹/4 cup sugar and cinnamon in a bowl and mix well. Layer the batter and walnut mixture ¹/2 at a time in a greased tube pan; swirl with a knife. Bake at 350 degrees for 45 to 60 minutes or until a wooden pick inserted near the center comes out clean. **Yield:** 10 servings.

Kathryn E. Ruff, *Glastonbury Grange, Connecticut*

Members of the Junior Grange participate in many Community Service projects. One suggested by National Grange is the "Stuff-A-Stocking" project. Members make and decorate a very large Christmas stocking and stuff it with gifts and useful items to give to a family in need.

Sour Cream Coffee Cake

2 cups flour
1 teaspoon baking powder
1 teaspoon baking soda
1/2 teaspoon salt
1 cup sugar
1/2 cup (1 stick) margarine, softened
1 cup sour cream
2 eggs
1 1/2 teaspoons vanilla extract
3/4 cup packed brown sugar
1/2 cup chopped nuts
1 teaspoon cinnamon

Sift the flour, baking powder, baking soda and salt together. Beat 1 cup sugar and margarine in a mixer bowl until creamy, scraping the bowl occasionally. Add the sour cream, eggs and vanilla and mix well. Stir in the dry ingredients. Combine the brown sugar, nuts and cinnamon in a bowl and mix well. Layer the batter and nut mixture 1/2 at a time in a greased and floured tube pan. Bake at 350 degrees for 40 minutes. Cool in pan for several minutes. Remove to a wire rack to cool completely. **Yield:** 16 servings.

Helen Halbert, *Butternut Valley Grange, New York*

Monkey Bread

3/4 cup packed brown sugar
3/4 cup chopped walnuts (optional)
1/2 teaspoon cinnamon
4 (10-count) cans buttermilk biscuits
3/4 cup (1 1/2 sticks) butter or margarine
1/2 cup packed brown sugar
1/2 teaspoon cinnamon

Combine 3/4 cup brown sugar, walnuts and 1/2 teaspoon cinnamon in a bowl and mix well. Cut each biscuit into halves. Roll each half into a ball. Coat with the brown sugar mixture. Layer the balls in a greased bundt pan. Combine the butter, 1/2 cup brown sugar and 1/2 teaspoon cinnamon in a saucepan. Cook over low heat until blended, stirring occasionally. Drizzle over the prepared layers. Bake at 350 degrees for 40 to 45 minutes. Cool in pan for several minutes. Remove to a wire rack to cool. Serve warm or at room temperature. To serve break the bread into pieces; do not cut. **Yield:** 16 servings.

Marcia J. Pauls, *Bayside Grange, Maine*

Streusel Coffee Cake

1/4 cup (1/2 stick) butter, chilled
1 (2-layer) package yellow cake mix
3/4 cup packed brown sugar
3/4 cup chopped walnuts
3 eggs
1 1/2 cups sour cream

Cut the butter into 2/3 cup of the cake mix until crumbly. Stir in the brown sugar and walnuts. Whisk the eggs in a bowl until blended. Stir in the sour cream. Add the remaining cake mix and mix well. Layer the batter and walnut mixture 1/2 at a time in a 9x13-inch baking pan. Bake at 350 degrees for 40 to 45 minutes or until the coffee cake tests done. **Yield:** 12 to 16 servings.

Emily Russell, *Goshen Grange, Oregon*

Sunburst Coffee Cakes

1/2 cup shredded coconut, toasted
1/2 cup sugar
2 teaspoons grated orange zest
3 1/2 cups flour
1/4 cup sugar
1 envelope dry yeast
1 teaspoon salt
1 cup milk
1/4 cup (1/2 stick) butter or margarine
1 egg
2 tablespoons butter, melted
2 cups sifted confectioners' sugar
2 to 3 tablespoons orange juice
1 teaspoon grated orange zest

Combine the coconut, 1/2 cup sugar and 2 teaspoons zest in a bowl and mix well. Combine 1 1/2 cups of the flour, 1/4 cup sugar, yeast and salt in a mixer bowl. Heat the milk and 1/4 cup butter to 120 to 130 degrees in a saucepan, stirring occasionally. Add the milk mixture gradually to the flour mixture, beating at low speed until blended. Beat at medium speed for 2 minutes. Add the egg and 1/2 cup of the flour. Beat for 2 minutes, scraping the bowl occasionally. Add the remaining 1 1/2 cups flour and stir until a firm dough forms. Let rest, covered with a tea towel, for 15 minutes. Knead the dough on a lightly floured surface for 1 minute or until no longer sticky, adding additional flour if needed. Divide the dough into 2 portions. Roll each portion with a floured rolling pin into a 12-inch circle on a lightly floured surface. Brush with 2 tablespoons butter. Sprinkle with the coconut mixture. Cut each circle into 12 wedges. Roll wedges up from wide end. Arrange point side down in two greased 9-inch round baking pans. Curve the ends gently to form crescents. Let rise, covered, in a warm place for 45 minutes or until doubled in bulk. Bake at 375 degrees for 20 minutes or until golden brown. Remove to a wire rack. Cool for 10 minutes. Drizzle the warm coffee cakes with a mixture of the confectioners' sugar, orange juice and 1 teaspoon zest.
Yield: 24 servings.

Lucille Groves, *Lake Grange, Indiana*

There are an estimated 300 deaths and 23,500 injuries to children under age 20 on U.S. farms and ranches every year. Junior Granges participate in the "Farm Safety 4 Just Kids" program. Their mission is to prevent farm-related childhood injuries, health risks, and fatalities. More than one-fourth of childhood agricultural injuries are incurred by children who do not live on farms, so it is important that this program reach urban children also.

Cinnamon Twists

1 cup sour milk
3 tablespoons sugar
2 tablespoons shortening
1 teaspoon salt
1/8 teaspoon baking soda
1 egg, lightly beaten
1 cake yeast
3 cups sifted flour
1/3 cup melted butter
1/2 cup packed brown sugar
1 tablespoon cinnamon

Bring the sour milk to a boil in a saucepan. Remove from heat. Stir in the sugar, shortening, salt and baking soda. Let stand until lukewarm. Add the egg and yeast, stirring until the yeast dissolves. Stir in the flour. Knead on a lightly floured surface for a few seconds. Let rest for several minutes. Roll the dough into a long and narrow rectangle, 1/4 inch thick. Brush with the butter. Sprinkle with the brown sugar and cinnamon. Fold over to enclose the filling. Cut into narrow strips and twist each strip. Arrange the twists on a greased baking sheet. Let rise in a warm place for 1 hour. Bake at 375 degrees for 15 minutes. Remove to a wire rack. Spread the warm twists with confectioners' sugar frosting. **Yield:** 12 to 15 twists.

Linda Faye Anderson, *Macleay Grange, Oregon*

Company Corn Bread

1 cup flour
3/4 cup cornmeal
2 tablespoons sugar
1 tablespoon baking powder
3/4 teaspoon salt
1 cup milk
1/4 cup shortening, melted, or
    vegetable oil
2 eggs, beaten

Heat a cast-iron skillet in a 400-degree oven for 3 minutes. Combine the flour, cornmeal, sugar, baking powder and salt in a bowl and mix well. Whisk the milk, shortening and eggs in a bowl until blended. Add to the dry ingredients and stir just until moistened. Spoon into the preheated skillet. Bake at 400 degrees for 20 minutes. May bake in a round baking pan; do not preheat the pan. **Yield:** 6 to 8 servings.

Virginia K. Sloop, *Corriher Grange, North Carolina*

Doughnuts

1 cup flour
1 tablespoon baking powder
1/2 teaspoon salt
Nutmeg to taste
Cinnamon to taste
Ginger to taste
1 cup milk
3/4 cup sugar
2 eggs
Flour
Vegetable oil for frying

Combine 1 cup flour, baking powder, salt, nutmeg, cinnamon and ginger in a bowl and mix well. Whisk the milk, sugar and eggs in a bowl until mixed. Add to the flour mixture and mix well. Add enough additional flour to make an easily handled but soft dough. Roll dough on a lightly floured surface; cut with a doughnut cutter. Fry the doughnuts in oil in a skillet until brown on both sides; drain. **Yield:** 6 to 8 doughnuts.

Claudia Boucher, *Wattannick Grange, New Hampshire*

Allison's Doughnuts

6 envelopes dry yeast
6 to 8 tablespoons lukewarm water
1 cup shortening
1 tablespoon salt
1 cup sugar
2 eggs (optional)
1 quart warm water
7 to 8 cups flour
Shortening or vegetable oil for frying

Dissolve the yeast in lukewarm water in a bowl and mix well. Combine 1 cup shortening and salt in a mixer bowl. Add the sugar. Beat until creamy, scraping the bowl occasionally. Add the eggs and beat until blended. Add half the warm water, stirring until the shortening and sugar dissolve. Stir in the remaining warm water. Add the yeast mixture and mix well. Add enough flour until of a sponge consistency and mix well. Add the remaining flour, stirring until a stiff dough forms; dough should not be as stiff as bread dough. Let rise in a warm place for 1 hour or until doubled in bulk. Roll on a lightly floured surface; cut with a doughnut cutter. Let rise in a warm place for 30 minutes. Fry the doughnuts in shortening in a skillet until brown on both sides; drain. Drizzle with a mixture of confectioners' sugar, water and vanilla or sprinkle with cinnamon and sugar. **Yield:** 80 doughnuts.

Shirley Engler, *Mt. Allison Grange, Colorado*

Banana Bread

1 cup sugar
1/2 cup (1 stick) margarine, softened
1 cup mashed ripe banana
2 eggs
1/3 cup milk
1 teaspoon vinegar or lemon juice
    (optional)
1 teaspoon baking soda
1/2 teaspoon salt
2 cups flour
1/2 cup chopped nuts (optional)

Beat the sugar and margarine in a mixer bowl until creamy. Add the banana and eggs and mix well. Combine the milk and vinegar in a bowl and mix well. Stir in the baking soda and salt. Add to the creamed mixture and beat until blended. Beat in the flour. Fold in the nuts. Spoon into a greased 5x9-inch loaf pan. Bake at 350 degrees for 1 hour. Cool in pan for 10 minutes. Remove to a wire rack to cool completely. **Yield:** 1 loaf.

Shanda Phelps, *Mt. Allison Grange, Colorado*

Deaf Activities began in 1970 as the health project of the National Grange.

Banana Apple Bread

1¼ cups sifted flour
¾ teaspoon baking soda
1 cup sugar
½ cup applesauce
2 eggs
1 large banana, mashed

Sift the flour and baking soda together. Beat the sugar and applesauce in a mixer bowl until creamy. Add the eggs 1 at a time, beating well after each addition. Stir in the banana. Add the flour mixture and mix well. Spoon into a greased 9x9-inch baking pan. Bake at 350 degrees for 35 to 40 minutes or until light brown. **Yield:** 9 servings.

Susan J. Cox, *Hawks Mountain Grange, Vermont*

Banana Date Nut Bread

2 cups flour
1 teaspoon baking soda
½ teaspoon salt
½ cup (1 stick) butter, softened
1 cup sugar
1 cup mashed banana
2 eggs
⅓ cup milk
2 tablespoons lemon juice
¾ cup chopped nuts
⅓ cup chopped dates

Sift the flour, baking soda and salt together. Beat the butter in a mixer bowl until creamy. Add the sugar gradually, beating constantly until blended. Add the banana and eggs and mix well. Mix the milk and lemon juice in a measuring cup. Fold in the flour mixture alternately with the milk mixture. Fold in the nuts and dates. Spoon the batter into a 5x9-inch loaf pan lined with greased waxed paper. Bake at 350 degrees for 55 to 60 minutes or until the loaf tests done. Cool in pan for 10 minutes. Remove to a wire rack to cool completely. **Yield:** 1 loaf.

Roberta K. Morrow, *Narcisse Grange, Washington*

Banana Honey Bread

2 cups flour
1 teaspoon baking powder
½ teaspoon baking soda
½ teaspoon salt
2 cups mashed ripe bananas
1½ cups Wheat Bran cereal
⅔ cup honey
½ cup (1 stick) butter or margarine, softened
2 eggs
½ cup chopped nuts (optional)

Coat the bottom and sides of a 5x9-inch loaf pan with butter. Sprinkle with flour; tap pan to remove excess flour. Combine 2 cups flour, baking powder, baking soda and salt in a bowl and mix well. Mash the bananas and cereal together in a bowl. Let stand for 3 to 5 minutes. Beat the honey and butter in a mixer bowl until blended. Add the eggs and beat until smooth. Stir in the banana mixture. Add the flour mixture and mix well. Fold in the nuts. Spoon the batter into the prepared pan. Bake at 350 degrees for 1 hour or until a wooden pick inserted in the center comes out clean. Cool in pan for 10 minutes. Invert onto a wire rack to cool completely. **Yield:** 1 loaf.

Betty Langston, *Sturgis Grange, Michigan*

Blueberry Loaf Bread

2/3 cup flour
1/4 cup sugar
1/2 teaspoon baking powder
1/4 teaspoon baking soda
1/8 teaspoon salt
1/4 cup plus 2 tablespoons plain nonfat
   yogurt
1 egg white, beaten
2 teaspoons vegetable oil
1/2 teaspoon vanilla extract
1/3 cup fresh or thawed frozen
   blueberries

Combine the flour, sugar, baking powder, baking soda and salt in a bowl and mix well. Make a well in the center of the flour mixture. Combine the yogurt, egg white, oil and vanilla in a bowl and mix well. Add to the well and stir just until moistened. Fold in the blueberries. Spoon the batter into a greased 5x9-inch loaf pan. Bake at 350 degrees for 35 to 40 minutes or until a wooden pick inserted in the center comes out clean. Invert onto a wire rack immediately. Let stand until cool. **Yield:** 1 loaf.

Priscilla Meyers, *Winthrop Grange, New Hampshire*

First Place Coconut Bread

3 cups flour
2 teaspoons baking powder
1/2 teaspoon baking soda
1/2 teaspoon salt
2 cups sugar
1 cup vegetable oil
1 cup buttermilk
4 eggs, lightly beaten
2 teaspoons coconut extract
1 cup shredded coconut
1 cup chopped walnuts

Combine the flour, baking powder, baking soda and salt in a bowl and mix well. Combine the sugar, oil, buttermilk, eggs and flavoring in a bowl and mix until smooth. Add the flour mixture and stir just until moistened. Fold in the coconut and walnuts. Spoon the batter into 2 greased and floured 5x9-inch loaf pans. Bake at 325 degrees for 1 hour or until the loaves test done. Cool in pans for 10 minutes. Remove to a wire rack to cool completely. **Yield:** 2 loaves.

Jodi Waller, *Weissert Grange, Nebraska*

In 1976 the National Grange developed and produced the world's first sign language songbook, "Lift Up Your Hands," which combined music, words, and signs.

Cranberry Bread

2¹/₃ cups sifted flour
1 cup sugar
1¹/₂ teaspoons baking powder
¹/₂ teaspoon salt
³/₄ cup orange juice
1 egg, lightly beaten
2 tablespoons vegetable oil or melted
    shortening
2 cups cranberries, cut into halves
¹/₂ cup chopped walnuts

Combine the flour, sugar, baking powder and salt in a bowl and mix well. Add the orange juice, egg and oil and stir just until moistened. Fold in the cranberries and walnuts. Spoon into a greased 5x9-inch loaf pan. Bake at 350 degrees for 50 minutes. Cool in pan for 10 minutes. Remove to a wire rack to cool completely. Serve with cream cheese. **Yield:** 1 loaf.

Lois Evankow, *Lyme Grange, Connecticut*

Date Nut Bread

1¹/₂ cups boiling water
1¹/₂ cups raisins
1¹/₂ cups chopped dates
¹/₄ cup (¹/₂ stick) butter
2¹/₄ teaspoons baking soda
2²/₃ cups flour
1¹/₂ cups sugar
³/₄ teaspoon salt
3 eggs, lightly beaten
1¹/₂ teaspoons vanilla extract
³/₄ cup chopped walnuts

Pour the boiling water over the raisins, dates, butter and baking soda in a bowl and mix well. Mix the flour, sugar and salt in a bowl. Stir in the raisin mixture. Add the eggs, vanilla and walnuts and mix well. Spoon the batter into 2 oiled 5x9-inch loaf pans. Bake at 350 degrees for 50 to 60 minutes or until the loaves test done. Cool in pans for 10 minutes. Remove to wire racks to cool completely. **Yield:** 2 loaves.

Mary Creighton, *Robertsville Grange, Ohio*

Irish Bread

2¹/₂ cups flour
2 teaspoons baking powder
1 teaspoon salt
¹/₂ teaspoon baking soda
¹/₂ cup sugar
¹/₄ cup (¹/₂ stick) butter or margarine,
    softened
1¹/₂ cups buttermilk
1 egg
1 cup raisins

Sift the flour, baking powder, salt and baking soda together. Beat the sugar and butter in a mixer bowl until creamy. Add the buttermilk and egg and beat until blended. Add the dry ingredients and mix well. Fold in the raisins. Spoon into a 5x9-inch loaf pan lined with foil. Bake at 375 degrees for 30 minutes. Reduce the oven temperature to 325 degrees. Bake for 30 minutes longer or until the loaf sounds hollow when lightly tapped. Cool in pan for 10 minutes. Remove to a wire rack to cool completely. **Yield:** 1 loaf.

Florence E. Klimas, *Raritan Valley Grange, New Jersey*

Lemon Bread

1 cup sugar
1/2 cup (1 stick) butter or margarine,
    softened
1 1/2 cups flour
1/2 cup milk
2 eggs
1 teaspoon baking powder
1/4 teaspoon salt
Grated zest of 1 lemon
1/2 cup chopped nuts (optional)
1/2 cup sugar
Juice of 1 lemon

Beat 1 cup sugar and butter in a mixer bowl until creamy. Add the flour, milk, eggs, baking powder, salt and lemon zest and beat until blended. Stir in the nuts. Spoon the batter into a lightly greased 5x9-inch loaf pan. Bake at 375 degrees for 55 to 60 minutes or until the loaf tests done. Drizzle the top of the bread with a mixture of 1/2 cup sugar and lemon juice just before removing the loaf from the oven. May bake in 2 lightly greased miniature loaf pans for 45 to 50 minutes. **Yield:** 1 loaf.

Muriel A. Brooks, *Albright Grange, New York*

Quick Molasses Brown Bread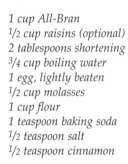

1 cup All-Bran
1/2 cup raisins (optional)
2 tablespoons shortening
3/4 cup boiling water
1 egg, lightly beaten
1/2 cup molasses
1 cup flour
1 teaspoon baking soda
1/2 teaspoon salt
1/2 teaspoon cinnamon

Combine the cereal, raisins and shortening in a bowl. Add the boiling water, stirring until the shortening melts. Cool slightly. Stir in the egg. Add the molasses and mix well. Stir in a mixture of the flour, baking soda, salt and cinnamon just until moistened. Spoon into a 5x9-inch loaf pan. Bake at 350 degrees for 45 minutes or until the loaf tests done. Cool in pan for several minutes. Remove to a wire rack to cool completely. May substitute any ready-to-eat bran for the All-Bran. **Yield:** 1 loaf.

Norma Slade, *Moravia Grange, New York*

In 1981 the Deaf Activities Department developed "The Sound and Hearing Teaching Packet" which continues to be distributed to fourth, fifth, and sixth grade classrooms.

Poppy Seed Bread

3 cups flour
3 cups sugar
1¹/2 tablespoons poppy seeds
1¹/2 teaspoons baking powder
1¹/2 cups milk
1 cup plus 2 tablespoons vegetable oil
3 eggs
1¹/2 teaspoons vanilla extract
1¹/2 teaspoons almond extract
1¹/2 teaspoons butter flavoring
¹/4 cup orange juice
¹/2 teaspoon vanilla extract
¹/2 teaspoon almond extract
¹/2 teaspoon butter flavoring

Combine the flour, 2¹/4 cups of the sugar, poppy seeds and baking powder in a mixer bowl and mix well. Add the milk, oil, eggs and 1¹/2 teaspoons each vanilla, almond and butter flavorings. Beat for 1 to 2 minutes, scraping the bowl occasionally. Spoon the batter into two 5x9-inch loaf pans. Bake at 350 degrees for 1 hour. Cool in pans for 5 minutes. Combine the remaining ³/4 cup sugar, orange juice and ¹/2 teaspoon each vanilla, almond and butter flavorings in a bowl and mix well. Drizzle over the tops of the loaves. **Yield:** 2 loaves.

Terri Denkman, *Iowa Director of Women's Activities*

Pork and Bean Bread

2 cups flour
1 teaspoon cinnamon
¹/2 teaspoon baking powder
¹/2 teaspoon baking soda
1 (16-ounce) can pork and beans, drained
2 cups sugar
1 cup vegetable oil
3 eggs
1 cup raisins
1 teaspoon vanilla extract

Grease and flour the bottom of a 5x9-inch loaf pan. Mix the flour, cinnamon, baking powder and baking soda in a bowl. Beat the pork and beans, sugar, oil and eggs in a mixer bowl until smooth, scraping the bowl occasionally. Add the flour mixture and mix just until moistened. Fold in the raisins and vanilla. Spoon into the prepared pan. Bake at 350 degrees for 20 minutes or until the loaf tests done. Cool in pan for 5 minutes. Remove to a wire rack to cool completely. **Yield:** 1 loaf.

Eileen W. Mitchell, *Morris Grange, Connecticut*

Prune Bread

2 cups boiling water
1 (16-ounce) package dried prunes
¹/4 cup vegetable oil
1 teaspoon baking soda
2 eggs, lightly beaten
2 cups flour
1 cup sugar
1 cup packed brown sugar
2 teaspoons baking powder
¹/2 teaspoon salt

Pour the boiling water over the prunes in a heatproof bowl. Stir in the oil and baking soda. Let stand for 8 to 10 hours. Drain, reserving the prunes and liquid. Chop the prunes. Combine the reserved liquid, prunes and eggs in a bowl and mix well. Stir in a mixture of the flour, sugar, brown sugar, baking powder and salt. Spoon the batter into a 5x9-inch loaf pan. Bake at 350 degrees for 1 hour. Cool in pan for 10 minutes. Remove to a wire rack to cool completely. May freeze for future use. **Yield:** 1 loaf.

Carol R. Garnett, *Imnaha Grange, Oregon*

Low-Cal Pumpkin Bread

1 (8-ounce) can pumpkin
2/3 cup nonfat dry milk powder
2 ounces cornmeal
2 eggs, lightly beaten
3 envelopes artificial sweetener
2 teaspoons cinnamon
1 teaspoon vanilla extract
1 teaspoon butter flavoring
1/2 teaspoon nutmeg

Combine the pumpkin, milk powder, cornmeal, eggs, artificial sweetener, cinnamon, flavorings and nutmeg in a bowl and mix well. Spoon into a miniature loaf pan sprayed with nonstick cooking spray. Bake at 350 degrees for 45 minutes or until the loaf tests done. Cool in pan for 10 minutes. Remove to a wire rack to cool completely. **Yield:** 2 servings.

Nola Boucher Poole, *Wattannick Grange, New Hampshire*

Strawberry Bread

3 cups flour
2 cups sugar
1 teaspoon cinnamon
1 teaspoon salt
1 teaspoon baking soda
2 cups mashed strawberries
1¼ cups vegetable oil
4 eggs, lightly beaten
1½ cups chopped pecans

Combine the flour, sugar, cinnamon, salt and baking soda in a bowl and mix well. Make a well in the center of the flour mixture. Add the strawberries, oil and eggs and mix just until moistened. Fold in the pecans. Spoon into 3 greased and floured loaf pans. Bake at 300 degrees for 1 hour. Cool in pans for 10 minutes. Remove to a wire rack to cool completely. **Yield:** 3 loaves.

Inez H. Koehler, *Poteet Grange, Texas*

In 1987 the Deaf Activities Department released the new hearing protection slide show "Listen to the Wind." It is also available on video.

Wickford Bread

3 cups flour
1 1/2 to 2 cups sugar
2 teaspoons cinnamon
1 teaspoon baking powder
1 teaspoon baking soda
1 teaspoon salt
4 eggs
1 to 1 1/3 cups vegetable oil
2 cups shredded carrots
Raisins to taste
Chopped nuts to taste

Combine the flour, sugar, cinnamon, baking powder, baking soda and salt in a bowl and mix well. Whisk the eggs in a bowl until blended. Whisk in the oil. Stir into the flour mixture. Add the carrots, raisins and nuts and mix well. Spoon into 3 greased 4x5-inch loaf pans. Bake at 350 degrees for 40 to 45 minutes or until the loaves test done. Cool in pans for 10 minutes. Remove to a wire rack to cool completely. May bake in 2 greased 4x8-inch loaf pans. **Yield:** 3 loaves.

Patricia C. Salisbury, *Richmond Grange, Rhode Island*

Zucchini Bread

3 cups flour
1 teaspoon baking soda
1 teaspoon cinnamon
1/2 teaspoon baking powder
1/2 teaspoon salt
1/2 teaspoon ground cloves
1 1/2 cups sugar
1 cup (2 sticks) butter, melted
1/2 cup packed brown sugar
2 cups grated peeled zucchini
3 eggs, lightly beaten
1 1/2 teaspoons vanilla extract
1 cup raisins
1/2 cup chopped pecans (optional)

Combine the flour, baking soda, cinnamon, baking powder, salt and cloves in a bowl and mix well. Combine the sugar, butter and brown sugar in a bowl and mix well. Stir in the zucchini, eggs and vanilla. Add the flour mixture and mix well. Fold in the raisins and pecans. Spoon the batter into 2 greased and floured loaf pans. Bake at 350 degrees for 50 to 60 minutes or until the loaves test done. Cool in pans for 10 minutes. Remove to a wire rack to cool completely. **Yield:** 2 loaves.

Hulda Hall, *Cheshire Grange, Connecticut*

Mom's Zucchini Bread

3 cups flour
1 tablespoon cinnamon
1 teaspoon salt
1 teaspoon baking soda
1/2 teaspoon baking powder
1 1/2 to 2 cups sugar
1 cup vegetable oil
3 eggs, beaten
1 tablespoon vanilla extract
2 cups grated unpeeled zucchini
1/2 cup chopped nuts or raisins

Combine the flour, cinnamon, salt, baking soda and baking powder in a bowl and mix well. Beat the sugar, oil, eggs and vanilla in a mixer bowl until blended. Add the flour mixture and mix well. Stir in the zucchini and nuts. Spoon into a greased 5x9-inch loaf pan. Bake at 325 degrees for 1 hour. Cool in pan for 10 minutes. Remove to a wire rack to cool completely. **Yield:** 1 loaf.

Eunice F. Walker, *Mont Calm Grange, New Hampshire*

Pineapple Zucchini Bread

1 (20-ounce) can crushed pineapple
3 cups flour
2 teaspoons baking soda
1¹/₂ teaspoons cinnamon
1 teaspoon salt
³/₄ teaspoon nutmeg
¹/₂ teaspoon baking powder
3 eggs
2 cups sugar
1 cup vegetable oil
2 teaspoons vanilla extract
2 cups shredded zucchini
1 cup coarsely chopped nuts
¹/₂ cup raisins

Drain the pineapple. Combine the flour, baking soda, cinnamon, salt, nutmeg and baking powder in a bowl and mix well. Beat the eggs in a mixer bowl until blended. Add the sugar, oil and vanilla. Beat until thick and foamy. Stir in the pineapple and zucchini. Add the flour mixture and mix well. Stir in the nuts and raisins. Spoon the batter into 2 greased and floured 5x9-inch loaf pans. Bake at 350 degrees for 1 hour. Cool in pans for 10 minutes. Remove to a wire rack to cool completely. **Yield:** 2 loaves.

Betty Richard, *Delaware Director of Women's Activities*

Holiday Pineapple Zucchini Bread

3 cups flour
2 teaspoons baking soda
1¹/₂ teaspoons cinnamon
1 teaspoon salt
³/₄ teaspoon nutmeg
¹/₂ teaspoon baking powder
3 eggs
2 cups sugar
1 cup vegetable oil
2 teaspoons vanilla extract
2 cups shredded zucchini
1 (15-ounce) can crushed pineapple,
    drained
1 cup chopped walnuts

Combine the flour, baking soda, cinnamon, salt, nutmeg and baking powder in a bowl and mix well. Beat the eggs in a bowl with a rotary beater until blended. Add the sugar, oil and vanilla. Beat until thick and foamy. Stir in the zucchini and pineapple. Add the flour mixture and mix well. Fold in the walnuts. Spoon the batter into 2 greased and floured 5x9-inch loaf pans. Bake at 350 degrees for 1 hour or until the loaves test done. Cool in pans for 10 minutes. Remove to a wire rack to cool completely. **Yield:** 2 loaves.

Lillian C. Wood, *Taconic Grange, Vermont*

In 1989 the Deaf Activities Department established an Intern Scholarship Program at Gallaudet University, the only liberal arts university for deaf students in the world.

Spiced Apple Muffins

2 cups sifted flour
1/2 cup sugar
4 teaspoons baking powder
1/2 teaspoon cinnamon
1 cup milk
1/4 cup (1/2 stick) butter, melted
1 egg, beaten
1 cup chopped apple
2 tablespoons sugar (optional)
1/2 teaspoon cinnamon (optional)

Sift the flour, 1/2 cup sugar, baking powder and 1/2 teaspoon cinnamon together. Combine the milk, butter and egg in a bowl and mix well. Stir in the flour mixture. Fold in the apple. Spoon the batter into greased muffin cups. Sprinkle with a mixture of 2 tablespoons sugar and 1/2 teaspoon cinnamon. Bake at 400 degrees for 20 to 25 minutes or until the muffins test done. Cool in pan for 10 minutes. Remove to a wire rack to cool completely. **Yield:** 2 dozen muffins.

David C. Settle, *Colonial Grange, South Carolina*

Applesauce Spice Muffins

2 1/2 cups flour
1 sleeve graham crackers, crushed
1 tablespoon cinnamon
2 teaspoons baking soda
1/2 teaspoon allspice
1 cup (2 sticks) margarine, softened
1 cup sugar
1/2 cup packed brown sugar
2 eggs
1 3/4 cups applesauce
1 teaspoon vanilla extract
1 cup chopped walnuts
1 cup raisins

Combine the flour, graham cracker crumbs, cinnamon, baking soda and allspice in a bowl and mix well. Beat the margarine, sugar and brown sugar in a mixer bowl until creamy. Add the eggs and beat until blended. Add the applesauce and vanilla and mix well. Stir in the flour mixture. Fold in the walnuts and raisins. Fill greased or paper-lined muffin cups 2/3 full. Bake at 350 degrees for 20 minutes. Cool in pan for 10 minutes. Remove to a wire rack to cool completely. **Yield:** 2 dozen muffins.

Sheila F. Rainey, *Crown Point Grange, New Hampshire*

Banana Bran Muffins

1 1/2 cups flour
1 teaspoon baking powder
1 teaspoon baking soda
1/2 teaspoon salt
2 cups All-Bran
1/2 cup chopped walnuts
1 cup buttermilk
1/2 cup packed dark brown sugar
1/4 cup (1/2 stick) margarine, melted
2 eggs, lightly beaten
1 cup mashed ripe bananas

Sift the flour, baking powder, baking soda and salt into a bowl and mix well. Stir in a mixture of the cereal and walnuts. Combine the buttermilk, brown sugar, margarine and eggs in a bowl and mix well. Stir in the bananas. Add to the flour mixture and stir just until moistened. Fill greased or paper-lined muffin cups 3/4 full. Bake at 400 degrees for 15 minutes or until the muffins test done. Cool in pan for 10 minutes. Remove to a wire rack to cool completely. **Yield:** 18 muffins.

Isabelle J. Lewis, *Pine Lake Grange, Indiana*

Banana Crumb Muffins

1¹/₂ cups flour
1 teaspoon baking soda
1 teaspoon baking powder
¹/₂ teaspoon salt
3 large ripe bananas, mashed
³/₄ cup sugar
¹/₃ cup butter or margarine, softened
1 egg, lightly beaten
¹/₃ cup packed brown sugar
1 tablespoon flour
¹/₈ teaspoon cinnamon
1 tablespoon butter or margarine

Combine 1¹/₂ cups flour, baking soda, baking powder and salt in a bowl and mix well. Combine the bananas, sugar, ¹/₃ cup butter and egg in a bowl and mix well. Add to the dry ingredients and mix just until moistened. Fill greased or paper-lined muffin cups ³/₄ full. Mix the brown sugar, 1 tablespoon flour and cinnamon in a bowl. Cut in 1 tablespoon butter until crumbly. Sprinkle over the tops of the muffins. Bake at 350 degrees for 18 to 20 minutes or until the muffins test done. Cool in pan for 10 minutes. Remove to a wire rack to cool completely. **Yield:** 1 dozen muffins.

Lucille Voshell, *Touchet Grange, Washington*

Banana Nut Muffins

2 cups sugar
1 cup shortening
4 eggs
4 cups flour
2 cups mashed ripe bananas
2 teaspoons baking soda
1 cup chopped pecans
1 teaspoon vanilla extract

Beat the sugar, shortening and eggs in a mixer bowl until creamy. Add the flour, bananas and baking soda and beat until blended. Stir in the pecans and vanilla. Fill paper-lined muffin cups ²/₃ full. Bake at 325 degrees for 45 to 60 minutes or until muffins test done. Cool in pan for 10 minutes. Remove to a wire rack to cool completely. **Yield:** 2 dozen muffins.

Blye Engel Dollahite, *Blanco Valley Grange, Texas*

In 1990 the Deaf Activities Department initiated for the first time interpreting The Seventh Degree of the Order of Patrons of Husbandry and the Convocation in sign language.

Bran Muffins

1 cup boiling water
1¼ cups All-Bran
1 cup raisins
2½ cups flour
2½ teaspoons baking soda
½ teaspoon salt
1½ cups sugar
½ cup (1 stick) butter, softened
2 eggs
2 cups buttermilk
1¾ cups 40% Bran Flakes
1 cup chopped pecans

Pour the boiling water over the All-Bran in a heatproof bowl. Combine the raisins with enough hot water to cover in a bowl. Sift the flour, baking soda and salt together. Beat the sugar and butter in a mixer bowl until creamy. Beat in the eggs 1 at a time. Add the dry ingredients alternately with the buttermilk, mixing well after each addition. Stir the drained raisins, All-Bran, Bran Flakes and pecans into the batter. Chill, covered, for 8 to 10 hours. Fill greased muffin cups ²/₃ full. Bake at 350 degrees for 25 to 30 minutes or until the muffins test done. Remove to a wire rack to cool completely. May store the batter, covered, in the refrigerator for up to 6 weeks. The batter does not have to be chilled before baking. **Yield:** 28 muffins.

Margaret Faggard, *Poteet Grange, Texas*

English Muffins

1 envelope dry yeast
¼ cup lukewarm water
3 cups flour
2 tablespoons sugar
1½ teaspoons salt
1 cup milk, scalded, cooled
3 tablespoons shortening
1 egg, lightly beaten
1 cup flour
Cornmeal

Dissolve the yeast in the lukewarm water. Mix the yeast mixture and next 6 ingredients in a bowl. Knead on a hard surface until smooth using 1 cup flour. Place the dough in a bowl. Let rise, covered with a tea towel, in a warm place until doubled in bulk. Punch the dough down. Let rest for 1 minute. Roll the dough ½ inch thick on a lightly floured surface. Cut into 12 equal portions or 12 rounds with a biscuit cutter. Arrange on a baking sheet sprinkled with cornmeal. Sprinkle the tops with additional cornmeal. Let rise, covered, in a warm place for 20 minutes. Bake on a medium-hot griddle for 6 to 8 minutes per side, turning once; turn gently. **Yield:** 12 muffins.

Debbie Sassman, *Victory Grange, Colorado*

Poppy Seed Muffins

2 cups flour
1 tablespoon poppy seeds
½ teaspoon salt
¼ teaspoon baking soda
1 cup sugar
½ cup (1 stick) butter, softened
2 eggs
1 cup plain yogurt
1 teaspoon vanilla extract

Mix the first 4 ingredients in a bowl. Beat the sugar and butter in a mixer bowl until creamy. Add the eggs 1 at a time, beating well after each addition. Beat in the yogurt and vanilla. Add the flour mixture and mix just until moistened. Fill greased muffin cups ²/₃ full. Bake at 400 degrees for 15 to 20 minutes or until the muffins test done. Cool in pan for 10 minutes. Remove to a wire rack to cool completely. **Yield:** 9 to 12 muffins.

Leta Ann Rinker, *Klondike-Piney Grange, Wyoming*

Sour Cream Chocolate Chip Muffins

1½ cups flour
⅔ cup sugar
¾ teaspoon baking powder
¾ teaspoon baking soda
¼ teaspoon salt
1 cup sour cream
5 tablespoons butter or
    margarine, melted
1 egg, lightly beaten
1 teaspoon vanilla extract
¾ cup mint or semisweet
    chocolate chips

Combine the flour, sugar, baking powder, baking soda and salt in a bowl and mix well. Combine the sour cream, butter, egg and vanilla in a bowl and mix well. Add to the flour mixture and stir just until moistened. Fold in the chocolate chips. Fill greased or paper-lined muffin cups ¾ full. Bake at 350 degrees for 18 to 20 minutes or until the muffins test done. Cool in pan for 10 minutes. Remove to a wire rack to cool completely. May substitute blueberries for the chocolate chips.
Yield: 1 dozen muffins.

Nancy West, *Ballenger Grange, Maryland*

Sugarless Muffins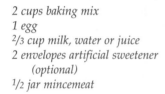

2 cups baking mix
1 egg
⅔ cup milk, water or juice
2 envelopes artificial sweetener
    (optional)
½ jar mincemeat

Combine the baking mix, egg, milk, artificial sweetener and mincemeat in a bowl and mix well. Fill muffins cups ⅔ full. Bake at 400 degrees for 20 minutes. Cool in pan for 10 minutes. Remove to a wire rack to cool completely. May substitute orange marmalade, cinnamon and raisins, dates and nuts, blueberries or cranberries and nuts for the mincemeat.
Yield: 8 large or 12 medium muffins.

Patricia McNeal, *Newington Grange, Connecticut*

In 1998 the Deaf Activities Department encouraged all the Grange states to initiate the passage of infant hearing screening legislation.

Silver Dollar Pancakes

1/2 cup flour
1 teaspoon baking powder
1/2 teaspoon salt
1 cup buttermilk
1 tablespoon vegetable oil
1 egg
1 teaspoon baking soda
1/4 cup quick-cooking oats
2 tablespoons yellow cornmeal

Sift the flour, baking powder and salt together. Whisk the buttermilk, oil, egg and baking soda in a bowl until blended. Add the oats and cornmeal and mix well. Stir in the flour mixture. Add additional buttermilk if desired for a thinner consistency. Heat an electric skillet to 380 degrees. Drop the batter by tablespoonfuls into the hot skillet. Bake until brown on both sides, turning once. May bake in a nonstick skillet on top of the stove. **Yield:** 2 to 4 servings.

Rebecca Winter, *Home Grange, Michigan*

Irish Scones

2 1/2 cups flour
1/4 cup rolled oats
2 tablespoons sugar
1 teaspoon baking soda
1 teaspoon cream of tartar
1/2 teaspoon salt
1/4 cup (1/2 stick) butter or margarine, chilled
1/2 cup raisins
1 cup buttermilk

Combine the flour, oats, sugar, baking soda, cream of tartar and salt in a bowl and mix well. Cut in the butter until crumbly. Stir in the raisins. Add the buttermilk and mix just until moistened. Pat the dough 3/4 inch thick on a lightly floured surface; cut with a biscuit cutter. Arrange on an ungreased baking sheet. Bake at 400 degrees for 10 to 15 minutes or until golden brown. Serve hot with butter and jam. **Yield:** 1 dozen scones.

Elsie Dunn, *Donalds Grange, South Carolina*

Cinnamon Raisin Scones

3 cups flour
3/4 cup sugar
3 tablespoons baking powder
1 tablespoon cinnamon
1 teaspoon salt
3/4 cup raisins
1 1/2 to 2 cups whipping cream, heated
Cinnamon and sugar to taste

Combine the flour, 3/4 cup sugar, baking powder, 1 tablespoon cinnamon and salt in a bowl and mix well. Add the raisins, stirring until coated. Add 1 1/2 cups of the whipping cream. Mix with a fork until the dough is soft and the mixture adheres; this may require using some or all of the remaining 1/2 cup whipping cream. Shape the dough into 12 equal balls. Press each ball lightly to form a thick circle. Dip the top into a mixture of cinnamon and sugar to taste. Arrange 1 1/2 inches apart on a lightly greased baking sheet. Bake at 425 degrees for 15 to 18 minutes or until light brown. **Yield:** 12 large scones.

Ida Snow, *Taconic Grange, Vermont*

Apricot Daisy Bread

3 to 3¹/2 cups flour
2 tablespoons sugar
1 teaspoon salt
1 envelope dry yeast
³/4 cup milk
¹/4 cup (¹/2 stick) margarine
2 eggs, lightly beaten
¹/2 cup apricot preserves
2 tablespoons chopped nuts
1 cup confectioners' sugar
1¹/2 tablespoons milk
¹/4 teaspoon vanilla extract

Combine 1¹/2 cups of the flour, sugar, salt and yeast in a bowl and mix well. Combine ³/4 cup milk and margarine in a saucepan. Heat to 120 to 130 degrees, stirring occasionally. Stir into the flour mixture. Add the eggs and mix well. Add enough of the remaining flour to make a soft dough. Shape the dough into a ball. Place in a greased bowl, turning to coat the surface. Let rise, covered, in a warm place for 1¹/4 hours or until doubled in bulk. Punch the dough down. Roll the dough into a 14-inch circle on a greased baking sheet. Place a beverage tumbler in the center of the circle. Make 4 cuts at equal intervals from outer edge of the circle to the tumbler. Cut each portion into 5 strips in the same manner, making 20 strips total. Twist 2 strips together and continue around the circle, making 10 twists. Remove the tumbler. Remove 1 twist. Coil and place in the center. Coil the remaining twists toward the center to form a daisy design. Let rise, covered, for 45 minutes or until doubled in bulk. Bake at 375 degrees for 20 to 25 minutes. Spread the preserves over the top. Sprinkle with the nuts. Drizzle with a mixture of the confectioners' sugar, 1¹/2 tablespoons milk and vanilla.
Yield: 12 to 16 servings.

Meribethe Groves, *Lake Grange, Indiana*

"Lift Up Your Hands" songbook was developed to introduce the hearing world to signing and to show the joy of communicating with persons who are deaf. (Deaf Activities Department)

Pizza Bread

1 envelope dry yeast
1 1/2 cups lukewarm water
1 (8-ounce) jar spaghetti sauce
3 tablespoons olive oil
1 tablespoon sugar
1 tablespoon grated Parmesan cheese
1 1/2 teaspoons garlic salt
1/2 teaspoon basil
1/2 teaspoon oregano
6 3/4 to 7 cups flour

Dissolve the yeast in the lukewarm water in a large bowl and mix well. Stir in the spaghetti sauce, olive oil, sugar, cheese, garlic salt, basil and oregano. Add the flour gradually, stirring constantly until a stiff dough forms. Knead on a lightly floured surface for 3 to 5 minutes or until smooth. Place the dough in a greased bowl, turning to coat the surface. Let rise, covered, in a warm place for 1 hour or until doubled in bulk. Divide the dough into 3 equal portions. Shape each portion into a loaf on a greased baking sheet. Let rise, covered, in a warm place for 45 minutes or until doubled in bulk. Bake at 375 degrees for 30 to 35 minutes or until the loaves test done. **Yield:** 3 loaves.

Mary Syphrit, *Brady Grange, Pennsylvania*

Shredded Wheat Bread

3 shredded wheat biscuits
1/3 cup dark molasses
2 tablespoons lard
1 teaspoon salt
2 3/4 cups boiling water
1 cake yeast, crumbled
5 cups bread flour

Combine the wheat biscuits, molasses, lard and salt in a bowl. Add the boiling water and mix well. Let stand until lukewarm. Stir in the yeast. Add the bread flour and mix well. Let rise in a warm place until doubled in bulk. Punch the dough down. Shape into a loaf in a loaf pan. Let rise in a warm place until doubled in bulk. Bake at 400 degrees for 1 hour. **Yield:** 1 loaf.

Ted Beebe, *Norwich Grange, Connecticut*

White Bread

2 envelopes dry yeast
1/4 cup sugar
6 cups warm water
18 cups flour
2 teaspoons salt
1/2 cup shortening
1/4 teaspoon vinegar

Dissolve the yeast and 1 tablespoon of the sugar in 1 cup of the warm water in a bowl. Place the flour in a large bowl. Make a well in the center of the flour. Combine the remaining 3 tablespoons sugar, remaining 5 cups warm water and salt in a bowl and stir until the sugar and salt dissolve. Add the yeast mixture, sugar mixture, shortening and vinegar to the well and mix well. Place the dough in a greased bowl, turning to coat the surface. Let rise, covered with a tea towel, in a warm place for 1 1/2 hours or until doubled in bulk. Punch the dough down. Let rise in a warm place for 1 hour. Divide the dough into 5 equal portions. Shape each portion into a loaf in a 4x9-inch loaf pan. Let rise, covered with tea towels, in a warm place until doubled in bulk. Bake at 400 degrees for 1 hour or until brown. **Yield:** 5 loaves.

George McCurdy, *Boot Jack Grange, Pennsylvania*

Whole Wheat Bread

1 envelope dry yeast
1/2 cup lukewarm water
2 cups milk, scalded
2 cups graham or whole wheat flour
3/4 cup packed brown sugar or 1/2 cup
   sorghum
6 tablespoons shortening
1 egg, beaten
1 tablespoon salt
4 to 5 cups sifted all-purpose flour

Soften the yeast in the lukewarm water and mix well. Combine the milk, graham flour, brown sugar and shortening in a mixer bowl and mix until blended. Cool slightly. Add the yeast mixture, egg and salt. Beat until blended. Add 2 cups of the all-purpose flour and mix well. Add enough of the remaining all-purpose flour gradually to form an easily handled dough, beating constantly. Knead on a lightly floured surface for 5 minutes. Place in a bowl. Let rise, covered, in a warm place for 8 to 10 hours. Divide the dough into 2 equal portions. Shape each portion into a loaf in a loaf pan. Let rise in a warm place for 1 hour or until doubled in bulk. Bake at 350 degrees for 50 to 60 minutes or until the loaves test done. **Yield:** 2 loaves.

Glee Call, *Custer Center Grange, Nebraska*

No-Knead Whole Wheat Bread

1 1/2 teaspoons butter, softened
4 teaspoons dry yeast
2/3 cup lukewarm water
2 teaspoons honey
5 cups whole wheat flour
3 tablespoons unsulphured molasses
2/3 cup lukewarm water
1/3 cup wheat germ
1 1/2 teaspoons salt
1 1/3 cups lukewarm water
1 tablespoon unhulled sesame seeds

Coat the bottom and sides of a 5x9-inch loaf pan with the butter, making sure the corners are well coated. Sprinkle the yeast over 2/3 cup lukewarm water. Stir in the honey. Set aside. Spread the whole wheat flour in a baking pan. Heat in a 250-degree oven for 20 minutes or until warm. Combine the molasses and 2/3 cup lukewarm water in a bowl. Stir in the yeast mixture. Add to the heated flour in a bowl and mix well. Stir in the wheat germ and salt. Add 1 1/3 cups lukewarm water and mix well; the dough will be sticky. Transfer the dough to the prepared pan; do not knead. Smooth the dough in the pan with a spatula rinsed with cold water. Sprinkle with the sesame seeds. Let rise in a warm draft-free place until the dough is even with the top edge of the pan. Bake at 400 degrees for 30 to 40 minutes or until brown. Cool in pan for 10 minutes. Remove to a wire rack to cool completely. **Yield:** 1 loaf.

Betty Huff, *Ada Grange, Oregon*

The National Grange stands for social and educational development of rural life.

All-Bran Rolls

2 envelopes dry yeast
1 cup lukewarm water
1 cup boiling water
1 cup All-Bran
3/4 cup vegetable oil
3/4 cup sugar
2 eggs, lightly beaten
2 teaspoons salt
6 cups (about) flour

Soften the yeast in 1 cup lukewarm water. Combine the boiling water, All-Bran and oil in a heatproof bowl and mix well. Let stand until cool. Combine the yeast mixture, sugar, eggs and salt in a bowl and mix well. Stir into the bran mixture. Add enough flour to make a soft dough and mix well. Shape into a ball. Place the dough in a bowl. Let rise, covered, in a warm place until doubled in bulk. Shape into rolls of the desired shape. Arrange on a baking sheet. Let rise until doubled in bulk. Bake at 350 degrees for 20 minutes. **Yield:** 3 dozen rolls.

Bayonne Birkenholz, *Sugar Grove Grange, Iowa*

Autumn Gold Dinner Rolls

1 envelope dry yeast
3/4 cup lukewarm water
1/2 cup lukewarm mashed
    butternut squash
1/2 cup flour
1/3 cup combination of half shortening
    and half margarine
2 1/2 tablespoons sugar
1/2 teaspoon salt
1 egg
3 cups (about) flour
Margarine, softened

Dissolve the yeast in the lukewarm water in a mixer bowl and mix well. Add the next 6 ingredients. Beat until smooth. Add 3 cups flour gradually, beating constantly until an easily handled dough is formed. Knead on a lightly floured surface for 5 minutes. Place in a greased bowl, turning to coat the surface. Chill, covered for 8 to 10 hours. Knead the dough lightly 2 hours before baking time. Divide the dough into 2 equal portions. Roll each portion into a 1/4-inch-thick circle on a lightly floured surface. Cut each circle into 12 wedges. Roll each wedge up from the wide end. Arrange point side down on a greased baking sheet. Let rise until doubled in bulk. Bake at 350 degrees for 18 minutes. Brush the warm rolls lightly with softened margarine. **Yield:** 2 dozen rolls.

Mildred Morgan, *Millers Run Grange, Pennsylvania*

Butterhorns

1 cake yeast
1 cup lukewarm water
1/2 cup (1 stick) margarine, melted
1/2 cup sugar
3 eggs, beaten
1 teaspoon salt
4 1/2 cups flour
Margarine, melted

Dissolve the yeast in the lukewarm water in a bowl. Stir in 1/2 cup margarine, sugar, eggs and salt. Add the flour and mix well. Chill, covered, for 4 to 10 hours. Divide the dough into 3 equal portions. Roll each portion into a 1/4-inch-thick circle on a lightly floured surface. Brush with additional melted margarine. Cut each circle into 16 wedges. Roll each wedge from the wide end. Arrange point side down on a greased baking sheet. Let rise in a warm place for 4 hours. Bake at 400 degrees for 7 to 10 minutes or until golden brown. **Yield:** 4 dozen rolls.

Lillian E. Davis, *Florida Grange, Colorado*

Old-Fashioned Butterhorns

2 cakes yeast or 2 envelopes dry yeast
1 cup lukewarm milk
1 cup lukewarm water
3/4 cup shortening
3/4 cup sugar
1 teaspoon salt
2 eggs
8 cups (about) flour

Dissolve the yeast in a mixture of the lukewarm milk and lukewarm water in a bowl and mix well. Beat the shortening, sugar and salt in a mixer bowl until creamy. Add the yeast mixture and eggs and beat until blended. Add 3 cups of the flour. Beat until blended. Let rest for 15 minutes. Add enough of the remaining flour gradually to make a soft dough and mix well. Knead on a lightly floured surface until smooth. Let rise in a warm place for 45 minutes or until doubled in bulk. Roll the dough into a circle. Cut into 12 wedges. Roll the wedges from the wide end. Arrange point side down on a greased baking sheet. Let rise in a warm place until doubled in bulk. Bake at 350 degrees for 8 to 12 minutes or until light brown. **Yield:** 1 dozen rolls.

Harriet B. Sawyer, *Scott Valley Grange, California*

Cinnamon Ring

2 cups milk, scalded
2 envelopes dry yeast or 2 cakes yeast
3/4 cup (1 1/2 sticks) butter, softened
1/2 cup sugar
2 teaspoons salt
2 eggs, beaten
6 cups (about) sifted unbleached flour
Melted butter
1 cup sugar
2 teaspoons cinnamon, or to taste

Cool the milk to 110 degrees. Sprinkle the yeast over the milk. Let stand until softened. Beat 3/4 cup butter and 1/2 cup sugar in a mixer bowl until creamy. Beat in the salt. Add the yeast mixture and eggs and mix well. Add the flour gradually, mixing constantly until a soft dough forms. Knead on a lightly floured surface until smooth and elastic. Place the dough in a greased bowl, turning to coat the surface. Let rise in a warm place until doubled in bulk. Punch the dough down. Shape the dough into balls. Dip the balls in melted butter. Coat with a mixture of 1 cup sugar and cinnamon. Layer the balls in a greased angel food cake pan. Let rise in a warm place for 30 minutes. Bake at 350 degrees for 40 minutes. **Yield:** 15 servings.

Millie E. Patterson, *Crystal Grange, Washington*

The motto of the Deaf Activities Department is "to do the most, for the most people, with the resources available."

Cinnamon Rolls

2 cups lukewarm water
2 tablespoons dry yeast
2 eggs
1/4 cup sugar
3 tablespoons butter, melted
2 teaspoons salt
1 teaspoon vanilla extract
3 cups (about) flour
Melted butter
Cinnamon and sugar

Combine the lukewarm water and yeast in a bowl and mix well. Let stand, covered, for 10 minutes. Add the eggs, sugar, 3 tablespoons butter, salt, vanilla and enough flour to make an easily handled dough in the order listed and mix well. Knead the dough on a lightly floured surface until no longer sticky, adding additional flour as needed. Place in a greased bowl, turning to coat the surface. Let rise, covered, in a warm place for 1 hour or until doubled in bulk. Divide the dough into 2 equal portions. Roll each portion into an 8x16-inch rectangle on a lightly floured surface. Brush with melted butter and sprinkle with cinnamon and sugar; roll as for a jelly roll. Cut each roll into 12 slices. Arrange the slices cut side down with edges barely touching in 2 greased baking pans. Let rise, covered with a tea towel, until doubled in bulk. Bake at 350 degrees for 30 minutes. Let stand until cool. Spread with confectioners' sugar icing and sprinkle with ground nuts if desired. **Yield:** 2 dozen rolls.

Helen Oakley, *Lawsville Grange, Pennsylvania*

Cornmeal Rolls

2 cups milk
1/2 cup shortening
1/2 cup sugar
1/3 cup cornmeal
1 teaspoon salt
1 envelope dry yeast
1/4 cup lukewarm water
2 eggs, beaten
4 cups flour
Melted butter

Combine the milk, shortening, sugar, cornmeal and salt in a saucepan. Cook until thickened, stirring frequently. Cool to lukewarm. Dissolve the yeast in the lukewarm water in a bowl and mix well. Beat in the eggs. Add to the cornmeal mixture and mix well. Let rise in a warm place for 2 hours. Add the flour gradually, mixing constantly until a soft dough forms. Knead on a lightly floured surface until smooth and elastic. Place in a greased bowl, turning to coat the surface. Let rise in a warm place for 1 hour. Punch the dough down. Roll on a lightly floured surface; cut with a round cutter. Brush the rounds with melted butter and fold over. Arrange on a greased baking sheet. Let rise in a warm place for 1 hour. Bake at 375 degrees for 20 minutes. **Yield:** 16 rolls.

Luella McGinty, *Pleasant Ridge Grange, Idaho*

Hot Cross Buns

1 cup milk, scalded
2 tablespoons butter or margarine
1 envelope dry yeast
1/4 cup lukewarm water
4 cups sifted flour
1/3 cup sugar
3/4 teaspoon salt
3/4 teaspoon cinnamon
1/4 teaspoon ground cloves
1/4 teaspoon nutmeg
3/4 cup currants
1/4 cup finely chopped orange zest or
    citrus
2 eggs, beaten
1 egg yolk
2 teaspoons water
1 cup sifted confectioners' sugar
2 teaspoons lemon juice
1 teaspoon water

Combine the hot milk and butter in a bowl, stirring until the butter melts. Cool to lukewarm. Dissolve the yeast in 1/4 cup lukewarm water. Sift the flour, sugar, salt, cinnamon, cloves and nutmeg into a bowl and mix well. Stir in the currants and orange zest. Add the milk mixture, yeast mixture and eggs and mix well. Knead the dough on a lightly floured surface until smooth and elastic. Place in a greased bowl, turning to coat the surface. Let rise, covered, in a warm place for 1 1/2 hours or until doubled in bulk. Punch the dough down. Shape into 1 1/4-inch balls. Place the balls 2 inches apart on a lightly greased baking sheet. Brush with a mixture of 1 egg yolk and 2 teaspoons water. Let rise in a warm place for 30 minutes or until doubled in bulk. Bake at 400 degrees for 10 minutes or until light brown. Cool for 5 minutes. Beat the confectioners' sugar, lemon juice and 1 teaspoon water in a bowl until smooth. Drizzle over the hot buns. **Yield:** 3 dozen buns.

Jewell Kramer, *Walter's Butte Grange, Idaho*

Pumpkin Rolls

1 1/2 cups mashed cooked pumpkin
1 cup milk, scalded
1/2 cup sugar
1/4 cup (1/2 stick) butter
1 1/2 teaspoons salt
1 cake yeast or 1 envelope dry yeast
1 teaspoon sugar
1/2 cup lukewarm water
1 egg, beaten
6 cups flour

Combine the pumpkin, hot milk, 1/2 cup sugar, butter and salt in a bowl and mix well. Cool to lukewarm. Dissolve the yeast and 1 teaspoon sugar in the lukewarm water in a bowl. Add the yeast mixture and egg to the pumpkin mixture and mix well. Add the flour and mix until blended. Knead the dough on a lightly floured surface for 5 to 10 minutes or until smooth and elastic. Place in a greased bowl, turning to coat the surface. Let rise, covered, in a warm place until doubled in bulk. Punch the dough down. Let rise for 10 minutes. Shape the dough into rolls. Arrange on a baking sheet. Bake at 400 degrees for 15 minutes. May substitute mashed cooked squash for the pumpkin. **Yield:** 3 dozen rolls.

Beth Merrill, *Antrim Grange, New Hampshire*

Today, the Grange building is the only privately held property in Executive Square in Washington, D.C.

Refrigerator Rolls

3/4 cup shortening
1 cup boiling water
2 envelopes dry yeast
1/2 cup lukewarm water
2 eggs
3/4 cup (or less) sugar
2 teaspoons salt
1 cup cold water
7 1/2 cups (about) sifted flour
Melted butter

Combine the shortening and boiling water in a mixer bowl, stirring until the shortening dissolves. Dissolve the yeast in the lukewarm water in a bowl. Beat the eggs in a mixer bowl until blended. Add the sugar and salt and beat until blended. Stir in the cold water. Beat the egg mixture into the shortening mixture. Stir in the yeast mixture. Add the flour by 1/2 cupfuls until a soft dough forms, mixing well after each addition. Let rise, covered, in the refrigerator for 8 to 10 hours. Punch the dough down with floured hands. Shape the dough into cloverleaf rolls. Arrange in greased muffin cups. Bake at 425 degrees for 15 to 20 minutes or until brown. Brush the tops of the rolls with melted butter. Serve hot. **Yield:** 3 1/2 dozen rolls.

Nan H. Barmore, *Donalds Grange, South Carolina*

Sour Cream Cinnamon Rolls

1 envelope dry yeast
1/4 cup lukewarm water
1 cup sour cream, heated
3 tablespoons sugar
2 tablespoons shortening or butter
1 teaspoon salt
3 to 4 cups flour
1 egg, lightly beaten
1/8 teaspoon baking soda
Melted butter
Cinnamon and sugar
Raisins and/or chopped nuts

Dissolve the yeast in the lukewarm water in a bowl. Combine the warm sour cream, 3 tablespoons sugar, shortening and salt in a bowl and mix well. Stir in the yeast mixture. Add the flour, egg and baking soda and mix until an easily handled dough forms. Knead on a lightly floured surface for 10 minutes. Let rest, covered, for 10 minutes. Roll into a rectangle. Brush with melted butter. Sprinkle with cinnamon and sugar, raisins and/or nuts. Roll as for a jelly roll; slice. Arrange the slices cut side down on a greased baking sheet. Let rise for 1 hour or until doubled in bulk. Bake at 350 degrees for 20 minutes or until brown. Drizzle with confectioners' sugar icing. **Yield:** 1 dozen rolls.

Lillian MacFee, *Gooding Grange, Idaho*

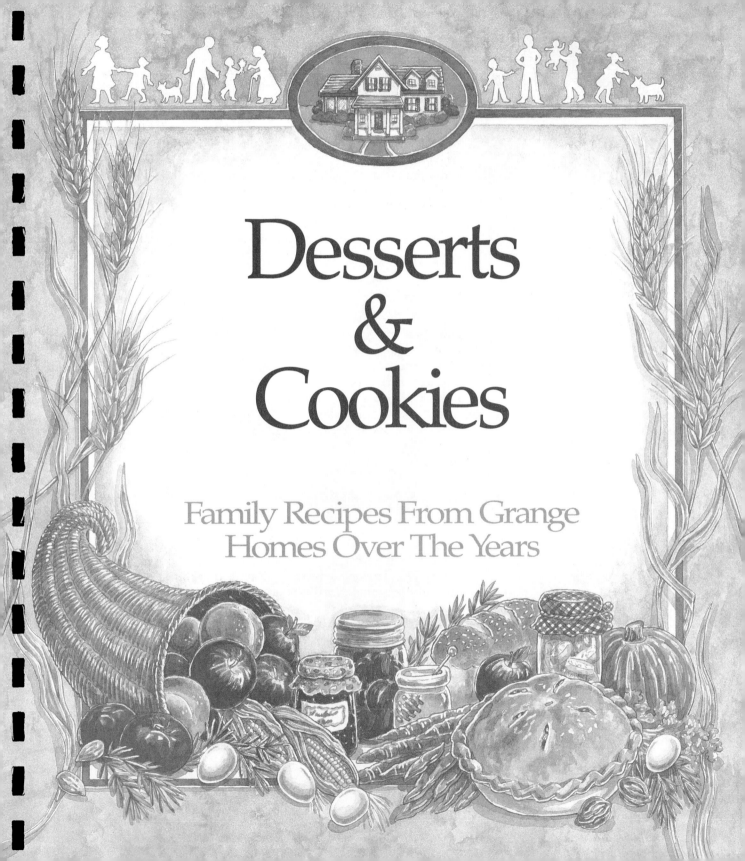

Desserts
&
Cookies

Family Recipes From Grange
Homes Over The Years

Apple Crisp

8 cups sliced peeled apples
2 tablespoons cinnamon
1 cup water
3 cups sugar
2¼ cups flour
1 cup (2 sticks) butter or margarine

Arrange the apples in a buttered 9x13-inch baking pan. Sprinkle with the cinnamon. Pour the water over the top. Combine the sugar and flour in a bowl and mix well. Cut in the butter with a fork or pastry blender until crumbly. Sprinkle the crumb mixture over the apples. Bake at 350 degrees for 30 to 40 minutes or until the apples are tender and the topping is light brown. Serve warm topped with ice cream. **Yield:** 12 to 15 servings.

Pat VanLare, *New York Co-Director of Women's Activities*

Zucchini Crisp

6 to 8 cups thickly sliced seeded peeled zucchini
²⁄₃ cup lemon juice
1 cup sugar
½ teaspoon cinnamon
¼ teaspoon nutmeg
1½ cups flour
¾ cup sugar
½ teaspoon salt
½ cup plus 2 tablespoons (1¼ sticks) butter or margarine

Combine the zucchini and lemon juice in a saucepan. Cook until tender, stirring occasionally. Stir in 1 cup sugar, cinnamon and nutmeg. Cook for 1 minute, stirring frequently; mixture will be juicy. Spoon into a 9x13-inch baking pan. Combine the flour, ¾ cup sugar and salt in a bowl and mix well. Cut in the butter until crumbly. Sprinkle over the zucchini. Bake at 350 degrees for 40 minutes. Serve warm with whipped topping, whipped cream or ice cream. **Yield:** 12 to 15 servings.

Blanche E. Kuhlman, *Kuna Grange, Idaho*

Blueberry Buckle

¾ cup sugar
¼ cup shortening
1 egg
½ cup milk
2 cups flour
2 teaspoons baking powder
½ teaspoon salt
2 cups fresh or frozen blueberries
½ cup sugar
⅓ cup flour
½ teaspoon cinnamon
¼ cup (½ stick) butter or margarine, softened

Beat ¾ cup sugar, shortening and egg in a mixer bowl until blended. Add the milk and mix well. Stir in a mixture of 2 cups flour, baking powder and salt. Fold in the blueberries. Spoon into a greased and floured 9x9-inch baking pan. Combine ½ cup sugar, ⅓ cup flour and cinnamon in a bowl and mix well. Cut in the butter until crumbly. Sprinkle the crumb mixture over the prepared layer. Bake at 375 degrees for 45 to 50 minutes or until brown. **Yield:** 9 servings.

Eunice M. Gilbert, *Wallingford Grange, Connecticut*

Blackberry Cobbler

4 cups fresh or frozen blackberries
1 cup sugar
1¹/₂ cups flour
1 cup sugar
2 teaspoons baking powder
¹/₂ teaspoon salt
1 cup milk

Toss the blackberries and 1 cup sugar in a bowl. Spread evenly in a 9x13-inch baking dish. Combine the flour, 1 cup sugar, baking powder and salt in a bowl and mix well. Add the milk, stirring just until blended. Spoon over the blackberries. Bake at 375 degrees for 45 minutes. Serve warm or at room temperature. May substitute blueberries, loganberries, peaches or apricots for the blackberries. **Yield:** 6 to 8 servings.

Ella Vanderburg, *North Fork Grange, Oregon*

Cherry Delight

1¹/₄ cups flour
2 tablespoons (heaping) sugar
1 cup (2 sticks) butter or margarine
1 (21-ounce) can cherry pie filling
4 egg whites
1 cup sugar
¹/₄ teaspoon almond extract

Combine the flour and 2 tablespoons sugar in a bowl and mix well. Cut in the butter until crumbly. Pat the crumb mixture into a 9x13-inch baking pan. Bake at 350 degrees for 5 to 10 minutes or until brown. Let stand until cool. Spread the pie filling over the baked layer. Beat the egg whites in a mixer bowl until foamy. Add 1 cup sugar gradually, beating constantly until stiff peaks form. Beat in the flavoring. Spread over the pie filling. Bake at 250 degrees for 1 hour. **Yield:** 15 servings.

Lillian Kaltenbach, *Turtle Grange, Wisconsin*

The Interstate Commerce Act of 1887 was the first major legislation for which the Grange lobbied. The Act regulated railroads and commerce between states.

Cream Puff Dessert

1 cup water
1/2 cup (1 stick) butter
1 cup flour
4 eggs
3 (4-ounce) packages vanilla instant
   pudding mix
4 cups milk
8 ounces cream cheese, softened
8 ounces whipped topping
Chocolate syrup or grated chocolate
   candy bar

Bring the water and butter to a boil in a saucepan, stirring occasionally. Remove from heat. Add the flour and stir until blended and the mixture forms a ball. Let stand until cool. Add the eggs 1 at a time, mixing well after each addition. Spoon into a greased 9x13-inch baking pan. Bake at 350 degrees for 35 minutes. Let stand until cool. Whisk the pudding mix and milk in a bowl until blended. Beat the cream cheese in a mixer bowl until creamy. Stir into the pudding. Spread over the baked layer. Top with the whipped topping. Drizzle with chocolate syrup or sprinkle with the grated chocolate. Chill, covered, until serving time. **Yield:** 12 to 15 servings.

Debra Kieffer, *Marion Grange, Pennsylvania*
Nettie Martsolf, *Jefferson Grange, Ohio*

Old-Fashioned Apple Dumplings

2 cups flour
2 1/2 teaspoons baking powder
1/2 teaspoon salt
2/3 cup shortening
1/2 cup milk
6 medium baking apples, peeled,
   cored
Sugar and cinnamon to taste
2 cups packed brown sugar
2 cups water
1/4 teaspoon cinnamon
1/4 cup (1/2 stick) butter

Sift the flour, baking powder and salt into a bowl and mix well. Cut in the shortening until crumbly. Sprinkle the milk over the crumb mixture and mix just until the mixture adheres. Roll the pastry on a lightly floured surface. Cut into 6 squares large enough to enclose an apple. Place 1 apple in the center of each square. Fill the apple cavities with sugar and cinnamon to taste. Pat the pastry around each apple to enclose; twist the edges at the top to seal. Arrange the apples 1 inch apart in a greased baking pan. Combine the brown sugar, water and 1/4 teaspoon cinnamon in a saucepan. Cook for 5 minutes, stirring occasionally. Remove from heat. Stir in the butter. Pour over the apples. Bake at 375 degrees for 35 to 40 minutes, basting occasionally with the pan liquids. Serve hot with cream. **Yield:** 6 servings.

Elsie M. Fleming, *Stanton Grange, New Jersey*

Fruit Dessert

1 large can fruit cocktail, drained
1 (8-ounce) can pineapple chunks,
   drained
1 cup chopped pecans
1 cup miniature marshmallows
1 small can vanilla pudding
16 ounces whipped topping

Combine the fruit cocktail, pineapple, pecans and marshmallows in a bowl and mix gently. Spread in a 9x13-inch dish. Combine the pudding and whipped topping in a bowl and mix well. Add to the fruit mixture and mix well. Chill, covered, until serving time. **Yield:** 6 to 8 servings.

John Valentine, *High Priest of Demeter, National Grange*

Funnel Cakes

1¼ cups flour
2 tablespoons sugar
1 teaspoon baking soda
¾ teaspoon baking powder
¼ teaspoon salt
¾ cup milk
1 egg
4 cups corn oil
Confectioners' sugar to taste

Sift the flour, sugar, baking soda, baking powder and salt into a bowl and mix well. Whisk the milk and egg in a bowl until blended. Add to the flour mixture and mix well. Add additional milk if the batter is too stiff. Heat the oil in a skillet to 375 degrees. Cover the end of a funnel with 1 finger. Pour ¼ cup of the batter into the funnel. Hold the funnel over the hot oil, remove your finger and drizzle the batter in a spiral fashion. Fry for 2 minutes or until golden brown, turning once. Drain on paper towels. Sprinkle with confectioners' sugar. Repeat the process with the remaining batter. **Yield:** 6 funnel cakes.

Rada Krohn, *Rising Sun Grange, Wisconsin*

Gladness Dessert

1 envelope unflavored gelatin
½ cup cold water
1½ cups milk
1 cup sugar
1 tablespoon cornstarch
3 egg yolks, lightly beaten
3 egg whites, stiffly beaten
1 cup whipping cream
1 teaspoon vanilla extract
1 angel food cake, torn
1 cup packed brown sugar
¼ cup half-and-half
3 tablespoons butter
½ teaspoon vanilla extract

Soften the gelatin in the cold water. Combine the milk, sugar and cornstarch in a double boiler. Stir in the egg yolks. Cook until thickened, stirring frequently. Remove from heat. Stir in the gelatin mixture. Let stand until cool. Fold in the egg whites, whipping cream and 1 teaspoon vanilla. Arrange the angel food cake in a 9x13-inch dish. Spoon the gelatin mixture over the cake. Chill, covered, for 12 hours. Combine the brown sugar, half-and-half and butter in a saucepan. Cook for 1 minute or until the brown sugar dissolves, stirring constantly. Remove from heat. Stir in ½ teaspoon vanilla. Serve warm with the dessert. **Yield:** 12 to 14 servings.

Charlotte H. Holt, *Fairfield Grange, Wisconsin*

The Grange had an important role in the creation of Rural Free Delivery in 1902 and Parcel Post in 1912. Many petitions for RFD routes were signed at Grange meetings.

Heavenly Dream Dessert

1 cup chopped nuts
1 cup flour
1/2 cup (1 stick) margarine
8 ounces cream cheese, softened
1 cup confectioners' sugar
8 ounces whipped topping
1 (4-ounce) package vanilla instant
    pudding mix
1 cup milk
1 (4-ounce) package chocolate instant
    pudding mix
1 cup milk

Reserve 1/4 cup of the nuts. Combine the remaining nuts, flour and margarine in a bowl and mix until crumbly. Press the crumb mixture over the bottom of an 8x8-inch or 9x9-inch baking pan. Bake at 350 degrees for 10 to 12 minutes. Let stand until cool. Beat the cream cheese, confectioners' sugar and 1 1/2 cups of the whipped topping in a mixer bowl until blended. Spread over the baked layer. Whisk the vanilla pudding mix and 1 cup milk in a bowl until blended. Spoon over the prepared layers. Whisk the chocolate pudding mix and 1 cup milk in a bowl until blended. Spoon over the top. Spread with the remaining whipped topping. Sprinkle with the reserved nuts. Chill, covered, until serving time. May substitute any flavor pudding mix. **Yield:** 8 servings.

Barbara Dixon, *Brady Grange, Pennsylvania*

Mennonite Dessert

1 cup flour
1 cup chopped nuts
1/2 cup (1 stick) margarine, softened
8 ounces cream cheese, softened
1 cup confectioners' sugar
1 cup whipped topping
2 (4-ounce) packages any flavor instant
    pudding mix
3 cups milk
Whipped topping
Chopped nuts

Combine the flour, 1 cup nuts and margarine in a bowl and mix well. Press over the bottom of a 9x13-inch baking pan. Bake at 325 degrees for 25 minutes. Let stand until cool. Beat the cream cheese, confectioners' sugar and 1 cup whipped topping in a mixer bowl until blended. Spread over the baked layer. Beat the pudding mix and milk in a mixer bowl until thickened. Spoon over the prepared layers. Spread with additional whipped topping and sprinkle with additional chopped nuts. Chill, covered, until serving time. **Yield:** 8 to 10 servings.

Marion Rushia, *Connecticut River Grange, Vermont*

Pecan Cups

1 cup packed brown sugar
1/2 cup flour
1 cup chopped pecans
2/3 cup butter, melted
2 eggs, beaten

Combine the brown sugar and flour in a bowl and mix well. Stir in the pecans. Whisk the butter and eggs in a bowl until blended. Add to the brown sugar mixture and mix well. Fill greased miniature muffin cups 2/3 full. Bake at 350 degrees for 20 minutes. **Yield:** 2 dozen.

Jane M. Bonsall, *Brady Grange, Pennsylvania*

Cherry Pudding

1 (15-ounce) can cherries
1 cup sugar
1 cup flour
1 teaspoon baking powder
1/2 cup milk
3 tablespoons vegetable oil
1 egg, lightly beaten
1/2 teaspoon vanilla extract
1/2 cup chopped nuts (optional)
2 tablespoons butter
1/2 cup sugar
1 tablespoon flour

Drain the cherries, reserving 3/4 cup of the cherries and 1 cup of the juice. Double the recipe with the remaining cherries and juice if desired. Combine 1 cup sugar, 1 cup flour and baking powder in a bowl and mix well. Stir in the milk, oil, egg and vanilla. Add the reserved 3/4 cup cherries and nuts and mix well. Spoon into an 8x8-inch baking pan. Bake at 325 degrees for 40 to 45 minutes. Heat the butter in a saucepan until melted. Stir in 1 cup reserved juice, 1/2 cup sugar and 1 tablespoon flour. Cook until thickened, stirring frequently. Spread over the baked layer immediately or serve chilled. **Yield:** 8 to 10 servings.

Emily Felder, *First Lady, California State Grange*

Date and Walnut Pudding

2 cups water
3/4 cup packed dark brown sugar
3 tablespoons flour
1/4 teaspoon salt
2 cups milk
2 egg yolks, beaten
2 tablespoons butter
1 teaspoon vanilla extract
1 1/4 cups chopped dates
1/4 cup chopped walnuts

Add the water to the bottom half of a 3-quart double boiler. Combine the brown sugar, flour and salt in the top insert of the double boiler. Add just enough of the milk to form a smooth paste and mix well. Add the egg yolks and beat until blended. Stir in the remaining milk. Place over the water-filled saucepan. Cook over medium heat for 15 minutes or until thickened, stirring constantly. Stir in the butter and vanilla. Add the dates and walnuts and mix well. Let stand until cool. Serve with reduced-fat whipped topping or whipped cream if desired. **Yield:** 6 servings.

Vivian C. Shaw, *Granby Grange, Connecticut*

Grange-supported Rural Free Delivery led to rural America's fight for better roads. The good roads movement helped win support for the Federal Aid Road Act of 1916.

Hot Fudge Pudding Cake

3/4 cup milk
1/4 cup sugar
2 tablespoons baking cocoa
1/2 cup flour
1/3 cup sugar
3/4 teaspoon baking powder
2 tablespoons baking cocoa
1/8 teaspoon salt
1/4 cup milk
1/4 cup shortening, melted
1/2 teaspoon vanilla extract

Pour 3/4 cup milk into a bowl. Stir in a mixture of 1/4 cup sugar and 2 tablespoons baking cocoa. Set aside. Sift the flour, 1/3 cup sugar, baking powder, 2 tablespoons baking cocoa and salt into a bowl and mix well. Add 1/4 cup milk, shortening and vanilla and mix well. Spoon into a baking dish. Pour the cocoa mixture over the top. Bake at 350 degrees for 20 to 30 minutes or until the edges pull from the sides of the dish. Serve with whipped cream or ice cream. **Yield:** 6 servings.

George M. Standley, *Watatic Grange, New Hampshire*

Hot Fudge Cake

1 cup flour
3/4 cup sugar
1 teaspoon baking powder
6 tablespoons milk
1 1/2 tablespoons butter, melted
1 teaspoon vanilla extract
1/2 cup chopped walnuts
1 cup packed brown sugar
4 teaspoons baking cocoa
1 3/4 cups hot water

Combine the flour, sugar and baking powder in a bowl and mix well. Stir in the milk, butter and vanilla. Add the walnuts and mix well. Spoon into a 9x9-inch baking pan. Sprinkle with a mixture of the brown sugar and baking cocoa. Pour the hot water over the top; do not stir. Bake at 350 degrees for 45 minutes. Serve with vanilla ice cream. **Yield:** 16 servings.

Colleen P. Grunder, *Conquest Grange, New York*

Indian Pudding

1 cup milk
1/2 cup (scant) sugar
1/2 cup (scant) molasses
2 tablespoons cornmeal
2 tablespoons tapioca
1/4 to 1/3 cup butter
3 cups milk
1 egg, lightly beaten
1/2 teaspoon cinnamon
1/2 teaspoon ginger
1/4 teaspoon nutmeg
Salt to taste

Combine 1 cup milk, sugar, molasses, cornmeal, tapioca and butter in a saucepan. Bring to a boil, stirring constantly. Boil for 2 minutes or until thickened, stirring constantly. Stir in a mixture of the milk, egg, cinnamon, ginger, nutmeg and salt. Spoon into a 1 1/2-quart baking dish. Bake at 300 degrees for 1 hour or until a knife inserted in the center comes out clean, stirring occasionally. Serve warm or at room temperature with whipped cream. **Yield:** 6 to 8 servings.

Joan Hadlock, *Hammond Grange, New York*

Lemon Chiffon Pudding

1 (12-ounce) can evaporated milk
1 (3-ounce) package lemon gelatin
2 cups boiling water
2/3 cup sugar
3 tablespoons lemon juice
1/4 teaspoon salt
1 package sugar wafers, crushed

Chill the evaporated milk for 8 to 10 hours. Dissolve the gelatin in the boiling water in a bowl. Stir in the sugar, lemon juice and salt. Chill until partially set. Beat the evaporated milk in a mixer bowl until stiff peaks form. Add the gelatin mixture. Beat until blended. Spread half the sugar wafer crumbs in a 9x13-inch dish. Spread with the gelatin mixture. Top with the remaining sugar wafer crumbs. Chill, covered, for 3 hours. **Yield:** 12 to 15 servings.

Shirley Lawson, *Secretary, National Grange*

Molasses Suet Pudding

2 cups flour
1 teaspoon baking soda
1 teaspoon cinnamon
1/2 teaspoon salt
1/2 teaspoon nutmeg
1/4 teaspoon ground cloves
1 cup ground suet, or 1/3 cup
    vegetable oil
1 cup sour milk or buttermilk
1/3 cup molasses
1 cup raisins
1/2 cup chopped candied fruit
1/2 cup sugar
1 tablespoon cornstarch
1 tablespoon lemon zest
1/8 teaspoon salt
3/4 cup water
2 tablespoons rum
1 tablespoon butter

Combine the flour, baking soda, cinnamon, 1/2 teaspoon salt, nutmeg and cloves in a bowl and mix well. Stir in the suet, sour milk and molasses. Add the raisins and candied fruit and mix well. Spoon into a microwave-safe tube pan. Microwave, covered, on High for 7 to 8 minutes or until a knife inserted in the center comes out clean. Let stand for 5 minutes. Combine the sugar, cornstarch, zest and 1/8 teaspoon salt in a microwave-safe bowl and mix well. Stir in the water. Microwave for 3 1/2 minutes; stir. Stir in the rum and butter. Serve warm with the pudding. **Yield:** 12 to 15 servings.

Raymond G. Wilson, *Riverview Grange, Nebraska*

The Grange's work for support of agricultural and vocational education led to the Smith-Hughes Act of 1917. In 1954, the Grange also took sole credit for a $5 million appropriation increase for vocational education.

Old-Fashioned Rice Pudding

1 cup sugar
2 eggs
2 cups milk
1 tablespoon vanilla extract
2 teaspoons nutmeg
1 teaspoon cinnamon
1¹/₂ cups cooked long grain rice
³/₄ cup raisins
Flour
¹/₄ cup (¹/₂ stick) butter or margarine,
    melted

Beat the sugar and eggs in a mixer bowl until blended. Add the milk, vanilla, nutmeg and cinnamon and mix well. Rinse the rice in a colander under cold water for 10 minutes; drain. Stir into the milk mixture. Toss the raisins with a small amount of flour in a bowl. Stir the raisins and butter into the rice mixture. Spoon into a buttered 9x12-inch glass baking dish. Bake at 300 degrees for 1¹/₂ to 2 hours or until light brown. Serve at room temperature. **Yield:** 8 to 10 servings.

Beverly Mitchell, *Staff, National Grange*

Rhubarb Surprise Float

1 cup flour
1 tablespoon baking powder
¹/₄ teaspoon salt
¹/₄ cup (¹/₂ stick) butter, softened
¹/₂ cup sugar
1 egg
¹/₄ cup milk
3 cups chopped rhubarb
³/₄ cup sugar
¹/₂ cup boiling water
¹/₂ teaspoon nutmeg

Sift the flour, baking powder and salt together. Beat the butter in a mixer bowl until creamy. Add ¹/₂ cup sugar and beat until light and fluffy. Beat in the egg until blended. Add the dry ingredients alternately with the milk, mixing well after each addition. Spoon into a buttered 8x9-inch baking dish. Combine the rhubarb, ³/₄ cup sugar, boiling water and nutmeg in a bowl and mix well. Spoon over the prepared layer. Bake at 350 degrees for 45 to 55 minutes or until brown. Serve warm or chilled. Top with whipped cream if desired. **Yield:** 6 to 8 servings.

Joann Goodlaxson, *Rising Sun Grange, Wisconsin*

Pumpkin Crunch

1 cup sugar
3 eggs
1 (29-ounce) can pumpkin
1 (12-ounce) can evaporated milk
1 teaspoon cinnamon
¹/₄ teaspoon ginger
¹/₄ teaspoon ground cloves
¹/₄ teaspoon nutmeg
1 (2-layer) package yellow cake mix
1 cup chopped walnuts
1 cup (2 sticks) butter, melted
Whipped cream (optional)

Grease a 9x13-inch baking pan. Line the bottom and sides with waxed paper. Beat the sugar and eggs in a mixer bowl until blended. Add the pumpkin, evaporated milk, cinnamon, ginger, cloves and nutmeg and mix well. Spoon into the prepared pan. Sprinkle with the cake mix. Top with the walnuts and drizzle with the butter. Bake at 350 degrees for 1 hour or until set. Cool in the pan on a wire rack. Invert onto a serving platter. Top with whipped cream. **Yield:** 15 servings.

Ruby Howard, *Trinity Grange, North Carolina*

Pumpkin Roll

1 cup flour
2 teaspoons cinnamon
1 teaspoon baking powder
1 teaspoon ginger
1/2 teaspoon nutmeg
1/2 teaspoon salt
3 eggs
1 cup sugar
2/3 cup pumpkin
1 teaspoon lemon juice
1 cup chopped nuts (optional)
Confectioners' sugar to taste
6 to 8 ounces cream cheese, softened
3/4 cup confectioners' sugar
1/4 cup (1/2 stick) butter, softened
1 teaspoon vanilla extract

Grease and flour a jelly roll pan; line with waxed paper. Combine the flour, cinnamon, baking powder, ginger, nutmeg and salt in a bowl and mix well. Beat the eggs in a mixer bowl at high speed for 5 minutes. Add the sugar gradually, beating constantly until blended. Add the pumpkin and lemon juice and mix well. Stir in the flour mixture. Spread in the prepared pan. Sprinkle with nuts. Bake at 375 degrees for 15 minutes. Invert onto a towel dusted with confectioners' sugar to taste. Roll in the towel, starting with the short side. Let stand until cool. Beat the cream cheese, 3/4 cup confectioners' sugar, butter and vanilla in a mixer bowl until light and fluffy. Unroll the cake. Spread with the cream cheese mixture. Reroll to enclose the filling. Wrap in plastic wrap. Chill until serving time. **Yield:** 12 to 15 servings.

Maria Edelen, *First Lady, Iowa State Grange*

Anise Cookies

3 1/2 cups sifted flour
1 tablespoon baking powder
2 1/4 cups sugar
6 eggs
1 1/2 teaspoons anise oil

Sift the flour and baking powder together. Combine the sugar and eggs in a mixer bowl. Beat at medium speed for 30 minutes, scraping the bowl occasionally. Add the flour mixture. Beat for 3 minutes longer. Add the anise oil and beat until blended. Drop by teaspoonfuls 2 inches apart onto a greased and floured cookie sheet. Chill for 8 to 10 hours. Bake at 325 degrees for 10 to 12 minutes or until light brown. Remove to a wire rack immediately. Let stand until cool. **Yield:** 6 to 7 dozen cookies.

Doris M. Hunkele, *Mt. Nebo Grange, Pennsylvania*

The formation of the Rural Electrification Administration was due in large part to the Grange. REA gave low-cost loans to cooperatives, which were responsible for much of the electrification of rural America.

Apricot Coconut Cookies

1¼ cups flour
¼ cup sugar
1½ teaspoons baking powder
½ cup (1 stick) butter or margarine
3 ounces cream cheese
½ cup shredded coconut
½ cup apricot preserves
½ cup confectioners' sugar
2 tablespoons apricot preserves
1½ teaspoons butter, softened
1½ teaspoons milk

Combine the flour, sugar and baking powder in a bowl and mix well. Cut in the butter and cream cheese until crumbly. Stir in the coconut and ½ cup preserves. Drop by rounded teaspoonfuls 2 inches apart onto a greased cookie sheet. Bake at 350 degrees for 10 to 12 minutes or until golden brown. Cool on cookie sheet for 2 minutes. Remove to a wire rack to cool completely. Drizzle with a mixture of the confectioners' sugar, 2 tablespoons preserves, 1½ teaspoons butter and milk. **Yield:** 3 dozen cookies.

Marvin G. Fleming, *Stanton Grange, New Jersey*

Butter Cookies

½ cup (1 stick) butter, softened
6 tablespoons confectioners' sugar
1 teaspoon vanilla extract
⅛ teaspoon salt
1 cup flour
Chocolate sprinkles

Beat the butter, confectioners' sugar, vanilla and salt in a mixer bowl until creamy, scraping the bowl occasionally. Add the flour gradually, stirring until blended. Chill, covered, if needed to allow the dough to become firm enough to shape. Shape the dough into 1-inch balls. Arrange 1 inch apart on a lightly buttered cookie sheet. Press flat with a fork dipped in ice water. Top with chocolate sprinkles. Bake at 375 degrees for 8 to 10 minutes or until the edges are brown. Cool on cookie sheet for 2 minutes. Remove to a wire rack to cool completely. May double recipe. **Yield:** 30 cookies.

Florence Jones, *Medford Grange, New Jersey*

Cherry Delights

1 cup (2 sticks) margarine, softened
½ cup sugar
2½ cups flour
½ cup light corn syrup
2 egg yolks, lightly beaten
2 egg whites, lightly beaten
2 cups finely chopped nuts
Candied cherry halves

Beat the margarine and sugar in a mixer bowl until creamy. Stir in the flour, corn syrup and egg yolks. Chill, covered, until firm. Shape the dough into 1-inch balls. Dip the balls in the egg whites and coat with the nuts. Arrange on a greased cookie sheet. Press 1 cherry half in the center of each ball. Bake at 325 degrees for 15 to 20 minutes or until light brown. Cool on cookie sheet for 2 minutes. Remove to a wire rack to cool completely. **Yield:** 3 dozen cookies.

Anna Mae Weiss, *Fleetwood Grange, Pennsylvania*

Chocolate Peanut Butter Cookies

2 cups flour
1/2 cup baking cocoa
2 teaspoons baking powder
1/2 teaspoon salt
11/2 cups sugar
1/2 cup shortening
1/2 cup crunchy peanut butter
2 eggs
11/2 teaspoons vanilla extract
1/3 cup milk

Sift the flour, baking cocoa, baking powder and salt together. Beat the sugar, shortening and peanut butter in a mixer bowl until creamy. Add the eggs and vanilla and beat until blended. Add the flour mixture alternately with the milk, mixing well after each addition. Drop by teaspoonfuls onto an ungreased cookie sheet. Flatten in a lattice pattern with a fork. Sprinkle with additional sugar. Bake at 400 degrees for 8 to 9 minutes; cookies will be soft. Cool on cookie sheet for 2 minutes. Remove to a wire rack to cool completely. **Yield:** 2 dozen cookies.

Beulah L. Winter, *Home Grange, Michigan*

Chocolate Truffles

1 (2-layer) package chocolate cake mix
1/2 cup (1 stick) butter or margarine
1/2 cup baking cocoa
1/2 cup confectioners' sugar
1/2 cup apricot preserves
1 teaspoon vanilla extract
16 ounces semisweet chocolate
Chopped nuts or shredded coconut

Prepare and bake cake using package directions in a 9x13-inch cake pan. Let stand until cool. Heat the butter in a 3-quart saucepan over medium heat until melted. Stir in the baking cocoa and confectioners' sugar. Add the preserves and vanilla and mix until smooth and glossy. Remove from heat. Crumble the cake into the apricot mixture and mix well. Shape into 11/2-inch balls. Heat the chocolate in a saucepan over low heat until melted, stirring constantly. Remove from heat. Dip the balls individually into the chocolate and coat with nuts or coconut. Arrange on a sheet of waxed paper. Let stand for 1 hour or until set. **Yield:** 45 cookies.

Eleanor Burke, *Bethlehem Grange, Connecticut*

Famous Grange members in government include Franklin D. and Eleanor Roosevelt, Harry S. Truman, many Senate and House of Representatives members, and a few Secretaries of Agriculture.

Super-Duper Chocolate Cookies

2 cups flour
2 teaspoons baking powder
1/8 teaspoon salt
4 ounces unsweetened chocolate
1/2 cup shortening
2 cups sugar
2 teaspoons vanilla extract
4 eggs
1/2 cup chopped nuts
Confectioners' sugar to taste

Sift the flour, baking powder and salt together. Heat the chocolate and shortening in a double boiler until blended, stirring frequently. Remove from heat. Stir in the sugar and vanilla. Add the eggs 1 at a time, mixing well after each addition. Stir in the flour mixture. Add the nuts and mix well. Chill, covered, for several hours. Shape the dough into small balls; coat with confectioners' sugar. Arrange 2 inches apart on a cookie sheet. Bake at 350 degrees for 10 to 20 minutes or until crisp around the edges. Cool on cookie sheet for 2 minutes. Remove to a wire rack to cool completely. **Yield:** 6 dozen cookies.

Janet A. Eppley, *Valley Grange, Pennsylvania*

Chocolate Chip Cookies

3 cups flour
1 teaspoon baking soda
1 teaspoon salt
1 cup sugar
1 cup packed brown sugar
2/3 cup margarine, softened
2/3 cup shortening
2 eggs
2 teaspoons vanilla extract
2 cups chocolate chips

Sift the flour, baking soda and salt together. Beat the sugar, brown sugar, margarine and shortening in a mixer bowl until creamy, scraping the bowl occasionally. Add the eggs and vanilla and mix well. Stir in the dry ingredients. Add the chocolate chips and mix well. Shape the dough into 1-inch balls. Arrange 2 inches apart on an ungreased cookie sheet. Bake at 375 degrees for 9 to 10 minutes or until golden brown. Cool on cookie sheet for 2 minutes. Remove to a wire rack to cool completely. For a softer consistency, add an additional 1/2 cup flour. **Yield:** 7 to 8 dozen cookies.

Deborah L. Eckard, *Medford Grange, Maryland*

Slice-and-Bake Chocolate Chip Cookies

2 1/4 cups flour
1 teaspoon salt
1 teaspoon baking soda
1 cup shortening
3/4 cup packed brown sugar
3/4 cup sugar
2 eggs
1 teaspoon vanilla extract
1 1/2 cups miniature chocolate chips

Sift the flour, salt and baking soda together. Beat the shortening, brown sugar and sugar in a mixer bowl until creamy. Add the eggs and vanilla and mix well. Beat in the dry ingredients. Fold in the chocolate chips. Shape the dough into a log. Chill, wrapped in plastic wrap, for 2 hours or for up to 1 week. Cut into 1/2-inch slices. Arrange 2 inches apart on an ungreased cookie sheet. Bake at 350 degrees for 10 minutes. Cool on cookie sheet for 2 minutes. Remove to a wire rack to cool completely. May substitute any flavor chips or chopped nuts for the chocolate chips. **Yield:** 2 1/2 dozen cookies.

Sandra Saeler, *Jackson Grange, Pennsylvania*

Chocolate Chip Pumpkin Cookies

4 cups flour
2 teaspoons baking soda
1 teaspoon salt
1 teaspoon nutmeg
1 teaspoon cinnamon
1/2 teaspoon ginger
2 cups packed brown sugar
2 cups cooked pumpkin
1 cup (2 sticks) butter or shortening
2 teaspoons vanilla extract
2 cups chocolate chips
1 cup chopped nuts (optional)

Sift the flour, baking soda, salt, nutmeg, cinnamon and ginger together. Beat the brown sugar, pumpkin, butter and vanilla in a mixer bowl until creamy. Add the flour mixture and mix well. Stir in the chocolate chips and nuts. Drop by teaspoonfuls 2 inches apart onto a greased cookie sheet. Bake at 350 degrees for 12 to 15 minutes or until light brown. Cool on cookie sheet for 2 minutes. Remove to a wire rack to cool completely. Add an additional 1/2 to 1 cup flour for a stiffer dough.
Yield: 7 dozen cookies.

Linda Thruston, *Paradise Grange, California*

Coconut Macadamia Cookies

1 cup (2 sticks) butter or margarine,
    softened
1 cup packed brown sugar
1/2 cup sugar
1 egg
2 1/4 cups flour
1 teaspoon baking soda
1 cup flaked coconut
1 (3-ounce) jar macadamia nuts,
    coarsely chopped

Beat the butter, brown sugar, sugar and egg in a mixer bowl until creamy. Stir in a mixture of the flour and baking soda; dough will be stiff. Add the coconut and macadamia nuts and mix well. Drop by heaping teaspoonfuls 2 inches apart onto an ungreased cookie sheet. Bake at 375 degrees for 8 to 10 minutes or until light brown; centers will be soft. Cool on cookie sheet for 2 minutes. Remove to a wire rack to cool completely.
Yield: 4 1/2 dozen cookies.

Ann M. Knudsen, *Exeter Grange, Rhode Island*

With a push from the early Grange, Congress and President Lincoln established the Department of Agriculture in 1862.

Grandma's Cookies

4 cups flour
1 teaspoon baking soda or baking powder
1 teaspoon salt
1 teaspoon cream of tartar
2 cups packed brown sugar
1 cup (2 sticks) butter or shortening,
    softened
1 teaspoon vanilla extract
2 eggs
1 cup pecan pieces

Sift the flour, baking soda, salt and cream of tartar together. Beat the brown sugar, butter and vanilla in a mixer bowl until creamy. Add the eggs and beat until light and fluffy. Stir in the pecans. Add the flour mixture gradually, mixing well after each addition. Drop by teaspoonfuls 2 inches apart onto a cookie sheet. Flatten with a fork dipped in cold water. Bake at 400 degrees until light brown. Cool on cookie sheet for 2 minutes. Remove to a wire rack to cool completely. **Yield:** 8 dozen cookies.

Thelma Dollahite, *Blanco Valley Grange, Texas*

Grandma's Refrigerator Cookies

1 cup packed brown sugar
1 cup sugar
1/2 cup shortening
2 eggs, beaten
2 teaspoons vanilla extract
1/2 teaspoon salt
2 tablespoons boiling water
1 teaspoon baking soda
3 cups flour
1 teaspoon cream of tartar
1/2 cup raisins (optional)
1/2 cup chopped nuts (optional)

Beat the brown sugar, sugar and shortening in a mixer bowl until creamy. Add the eggs, vanilla and salt and beat until blended. Combine the boiling water and baking soda in a cup and mix well. Add the baking soda mixture, half the flour and cream of tartar to the creamed mixture and mix well. Beat in the remaining flour until blended. Stir in the raisins and nuts. Shape the dough into a log. Chill, wrapped in plastic wrap, for 8 to 10 hours; slice. Arrange 2 inches apart on a greased cookie sheet. Flatten with a fork. Sprinkle with additional sugar. Bake at 350 degrees for 10 minutes. Cool on cookie sheet for 2 minutes. Remove to a wire rack to cool completely. **Yield:** 3 dozen cookies.

Mardell McConnaha, *Bloomington Grange, Iowa*

Krum Kake

11/2 cups flour
2 tablespoons cornstarch
4 eggs
1 cup sugar
1/2 cup (1 stick) margarine, melted,
    cooled
1/2 teaspoon vanilla extract or
    cardamom seeds

Sift the flour and cornstarch together. Beat the eggs lightly in a mixer bowl. Add the sugar and beat lightly; do not overbeat. Add the margarine and vanilla. Stir in the flour mixture; dough will be sticky. Bake in a pizzelle iron using manufacturer's directions. Shape into a cone. Serve plain or fill with whipped cream. **Yield:** 11/2 dozen cookies.

Norman Brandt, *Wingold Grange, New Hampshire*

Lemon Cookies

2 cups sifted flour
3/4 teaspoon baking soda
1/4 teaspoon salt
3/4 cup shortening
2 (4-ounce) packages lemon instant
    pudding mix
1 cup sugar
3 eggs, lightly beaten

Sift the flour, baking soda and salt together. Beat the shortening in a mixer bowl until creamy. Add the pudding mix and sugar. Beat until light and fluffy. Add the eggs and mix well. Add the dry ingredients. Beat until blended. Drop by teaspoonfuls 2 inches apart onto a cookie sheet. Bake at 375 degrees for 8 to 10 minutes or until light brown. Cool on cookie sheet for 2 minutes. Remove to a wire rack to cool completely. **Yield:** 2 to 3 dozen cookies.

Claire Field, *First Lady, Minnesota State Grange*

Molasses Cookies

3 cups whole wheat flour
1 cup all-purpose flour
1 tablespoon baking powder
1 teaspoon baking soda
1 teaspoon salt
1 teaspoon ginger
1 teaspoon cinnamon
1 cup lard
1 cup sugar
2 eggs
1 cup sour milk
1 cup molasses

Combine the whole wheat flour, all-purpose flour, baking powder, baking soda, salt, ginger and cinnamon in a bowl and mix well. Beat the lard and sugar in a mixer bowl until creamy. Add the eggs and beat until light and fluffy. Beat in the sour milk and molasses. Add the flour mixture and mix until blended. Drop by spoonfuls onto a cookie sheet. Bake at 350 degrees for 8 to 10 minutes or until light brown. Cool on cookie sheet for 2 minutes. Remove to a wire rack to cool completely. **Yield:** 4 dozen cookies.

David L. Johnston, Sr., *Burns Grange, Michigan*

The National Grange's Legislative Affairs Department has had an office in Washington, D.C., since 1919.

Molasses Crinkles

2¹/₄ cups flour
2 teaspoons baking soda
1 teaspoon cinnamon
1 teaspoon ginger
¹/₂ teaspoon ground cloves
¹/₄ teaspoon salt
1 cup packed brown sugar
³/₄ cup butter, softened
¹/₄ cup molasses
1 egg

Sift the flour, baking soda, cinnamon, ginger, cloves and salt into a bowl and mix well. Beat the brown sugar, butter, molasses and egg in a mixer bowl until creamy. Add the flour mixture and mix well. Chill, covered, for 2 to 10 hours. Shape the dough into 1-inch balls. Dip the top of each ball in additional sugar. Arrange sugar side up 3 inches apart on a lightly greased cookie sheet. Bake at 375 degrees for 10 to 12 minutes or just until set. Cool on cookie sheet for 2 minutes. Remove to a wire rack to cool completely. **Yield:** 4 dozen cookies.

Barbara C. Barnette, *Glade Valley Grange, Maryland*

Oatmeal Crunchies

3 cups flour
2 teaspoons baking powder
2 teaspoons baking soda
1 teaspoon salt
4 cups packed brown sugar
2 cups shortening
4 eggs
2 teaspoons vanilla extract
6 cups quick-cooking oats
1¹/₂ cups raisins
1 cup chopped nuts
Confectioners' sugar

Sift the flour, baking powder, baking soda and salt together. Beat the brown sugar and shortening in a mixer bowl until creamy. Add the eggs and vanilla and beat until blended. Stir in the dry ingredients, oats, raisins and nuts. Chill, covered, until firm. Shape the dough into 1-inch balls. Spoon confectioners' sugar into a sealable plastic bag. Add the balls a few at a time and toss until heavily coated. Arrange 2 inches apart on a lightly greased cookie sheet. Bake at 375 degrees for 8 to 10 minutes or until light brown. Cool on cookie sheet for 2 minutes. Remove to a wire rack to cool completely. **Yield:** 8 dozen cookies.

Diana Nordquest, *Ohio Director of Women's Activities*

Vanishing Oatmeal Cookies

1¹/₂ cups flour
1 teaspoon baking soda
1 teaspoon cinnamon
¹/₂ teaspoon salt
1 cup (2 sticks) margarine, softened
1 cup packed brown sugar
¹/₂ cup sugar
2 eggs
1 teaspoon vanilla extract
3 cups rolled oats
1 cup raisins or chocolate chips

Combine the flour, baking soda, cinnamon and salt in a bowl and mix well. Beat the margarine, brown sugar and sugar in a mixer bowl until creamy. Add the eggs and vanilla and beat until blended. Beat in the flour mixture. Stir in the oats and raisins. Drop by teaspoonfuls 2 inches apart onto a cookie sheet. Bake at 350 degrees for 10 to 12 minutes or until light brown. Cool on cookie sheet for 1 minute. Remove to a wire rack to cool completely. **Yield:** 4 dozen cookies.

Becca D. Watts, *Mountville Grange, South Carolina*

Applesauce Oatmeal Cookies

2 cups sugar
1 cup shortening
2 eggs
3¹/₂ cups flour
1 teaspoon baking powder
2 teaspoons baking soda
1 teaspoon salt
2 teaspoons cinnamon
1 teaspoon ground cloves
1 teaspoon nutmeg
1 cup raisins
2 cups quick-cooking oats
2 cups applesauce

Beat the sugar and shortening in a mixer bowl until creamy. Add the eggs, flour, baking powder, baking soda, salt, cinnamon, cloves, nutmeg, raisins, oats and applesauce in the order listed, mixing well after each addition. Chill, covered, for 1 hour. Drop by teaspoonfuls onto a greased cookie sheet. Bake at 375 degrees for 12 to 15 minutes or until light brown. Cool on cookie sheet for 2 minutes. Remove to a wire rack to cool completely. **Yield:** 5 to 6 dozen cookies.

Alfred Myers, *Mossyrock Grange, Washington*

Orange Cookies

4¹/₂ cups flour
2 teaspoons baking powder
1 teaspoon baking soda
1 teaspoon salt
1 cup shortening
2 cups sugar
3 eggs, beaten
1 cup buttermilk
Juice and zest of 1 orange
Juice of 1 orange
2 tablespoons butter, softened
Confectioners' sugar

Sift the flour, baking powder, baking soda and salt together. Beat the shortening in a mixer bowl until creamy. Add the sugar and beat until light and fluffy. Beat in the eggs until blended. Add the flour mixture, buttermilk and juice and zest of 1 orange and mix well. Drop by teaspoonfuls 2 inches apart onto a cookie sheet. Bake at 375 degrees for 10 to 12 minutes or until light brown. Cool on cookie sheet for 2 minutes. Remove to a wire rack to cool completely. Beat orange juice and butter with enough confectioners' sugar to make of spreading consistency in a mixer bowl. Spread over the tops of the cookies. **Yield:** 4 dozen cookies.

Lura Carnes, *West Point Grange, Ohio*

As of 1999, the states of Pennsylvania, Ohio, Washington, and New York have the most local (Subordinate) Granges.

Peanut Butter Cookies

2³/4 cups sifted flour
2 teaspoons baking soda
1 cup butter, softened
1 cup sugar
1 cup packed brown sugar
1 cup peanut butter
2 eggs, beaten
1 teaspoon vanilla extract

Combine the flour and baking soda in a bowl and mix well. Beat the butter in a mixer bowl until creamy. Add the sugar and brown sugar. Beat until light and fluffy. Add the peanut butter. Beat until blended. Add the eggs and mix well. Add the flour mixture and mix well. Beat in the vanilla. Shape by heaping teaspoonfuls into balls. Arrange on a greased cookie sheet. Flatten in a crisscross pattern with a fork dipped in additional sugar. Bake at 350 degrees until light brown and crisp. Cool on cookie sheet for 2 minutes. Remove to a wire rack to cool completely. **Yield:** 5 to 6 dozen cookies.

Sue Gray, *First Lady, Connecticut State Grange*

Giant Peanut Butter Cookies

2¹/2 cups sifted flour
1 cup nonfat dry milk powder
1¹/2 teaspoons baking soda
1 teaspoon baking powder
¹/2 teaspoon salt
1 cup (2 sticks) margarine, softened
1 cup creamy peanut butter
1 cup sugar
1 cup packed light brown sugar
2 eggs

Sift the flour, milk powder, baking soda, baking powder and salt together. Beat the margarine and peanut butter in a mixer bowl until creamy. Add the sugar, brown sugar and eggs gradually, mixing well after each addition. Stir in the flour mixture. Let stand for 15 minutes. Shape the dough into 1-inch balls. Arrange 3 inches apart on a lightly greased cookie sheet. Flatten the balls in a crisscross pattern with a fork dipped in additional flour. Bake at 375 degrees for 10 to 12 minutes or until light brown. Cool on cookie sheet for 2 minutes. Remove to a wire rack to cool completely. **Yield:** 4 dozen cookies.

Cathy Howe Pollard, *Hawk's Mt. Grange, Vermont*

Pecan Cookies

2¹/2 cups flour
¹/2 teaspoon baking soda
¹/4 teaspoon salt
2¹/2 cups packed brown sugar
¹/2 cup shortening
¹/2 cup (1 stick) butter, softened
2 eggs, beaten
1¹/2 cups chopped pecans

Sift the flour, baking soda and salt together. Beat the brown sugar, shortening and butter in a mixer bowl until creamy. Add the eggs and beat until blended. Add the dry ingredients and mix well. Stir in the pecans. Drop by teaspoonfuls 2 inches apart onto a greased cookie sheet. Bake at 350 degrees for 12 to 15 minutes or until light brown. Cool on cookie sheet for 2 minutes. Remove to a wire rack to cool completely. **Yield:** 4 dozen cookies.

Earlene Foster, *First Lady, West Virginia State Grange*

Pecan Ice Box Cookies

3 cups flour
1/2 teaspoon baking soda
1/2 teaspoon baking powder
1 cup packed brown sugar
1 cup sugar
1 cup (2 sticks) butter, softened
1 egg
1 cup finely chopped pecans

Combine the flour, baking soda and baking powder in a bowl and mix well. Beat the brown sugar, sugar and butter in a mixer bowl until creamy. Add the egg and mix well. Add the dry ingredients gradually, beating well after each addition. Stir in the pecans. Shape the dough into several logs 2 inches in diameter. Chill, wrapped in waxed paper, for 8 to 10 hours. Cut each log into thin slices. Arrange the slices 2 inches apart on a cookie sheet. Bake at 375 degrees until light brown. Cool on cookie sheet for 2 minutes. Remove to a wire rack to cool completely. **Yield:** 3 dozen cookies.

Frank Knight, *Blue Bonnet Grange, Texas*

Peppermint Pinwheels

1 1/2 cups flour
2 teaspoons baking powder
1/2 teaspoon salt
1 cup sugar
1/2 cup (1 stick) butter, softened
1 egg
1 teaspoon peppermint extract
2 ounces unsweetened chocolate, melted

Sift the flour, baking powder and salt together. Beat the sugar and butter in a mixer bowl until creamy. Add the egg and flavoring and beat until blended. Fold in the dry ingredients. Divide the dough into 2 equal portions. Combine 1 portion of the dough and the chocolate in a bowl and mix well. Chill both portions in the refrigerator. Roll each portion into a 1/8-inch-thick rectangle on a lightly floured surface. Stack the chocolate rectangle on the plain rectangle. Roll as for a jelly roll. Chill, wrapped in waxed paper, in the refrigerator. Cut the roll into thin slices. Arrange the slices 2 inches apart on a greased cookie sheet. Bake at 400 degrees for 10 to 12 minutes or until light brown. Cool on cookie sheet for 2 minutes. Remove to a wire rack to cool completely. **Yield:** 1 1/2 to 2 dozen cookies.

Alice H. Eckard, *Medford Grange, Maryland*

Grange membership, nationally, peaked in 1952 with 858,105 members.

Peppernuts

1/2 cup sugar
6 tablespoons butter, softened
6 tablespoons lard or shortening
1/2 cup dark corn syrup
1/2 cup honey
1/4 cup sour cream
Oil of peppermint to taste
3 cups flour
1/4 teaspoon baking soda
1/8 teaspoon ground cloves
1/8 teaspoon nutmeg
1/8 teaspoon cinnamon
Dash of ginger, allspice and pepper

Beat the sugar, butter and lard in a mixer bowl until creamy. Add the corn syrup, honey and sour cream and mix well. Beat in the oil of peppermint. Add a mixture of the flour, baking soda, cloves, nutmeg, cinnamon, ginger, allspice and pepper and mix well. Shape the dough into logs 1 inch in diameter. Chill, wrapped in waxed paper, in the refrigerator until just before baking. Cut each log into 1/8-inch slices. Arrange the slices 2 inches apart on a cookie sheet. Bake at 350 degrees for 10 minutes or until the edges are light brown. Cool on cookie sheet for 2 minutes. Remove to a wire rack to cool completely. For variety, just add the oil of peppermint to a portion of the dough. May substitute oil of anise for the peppermint. **Yield:** 3 to 4 dozen cookies.

Ruth Esther Shorthill, *Indian Creek Grange, Kansas*

Pineapple Cookies

3 1/2 cups flour
1 teaspoon baking soda
1 teaspoon salt
1 1/2 cups sugar
1/2 cup shortening
2 eggs
1 teaspoon vanilla extract
1 cup crushed pineapple

Sift the flour, baking soda and salt together. Beat the sugar and shortening in a mixer bowl until creamy. Add the eggs and vanilla and beat until blended. Fold in the pineapple. Stir in the dry ingredients. Drop by spoonfuls 2 inches apart onto a greased cookie sheet. Bake at 400 degrees until light brown. Cool on cookie sheet for 2 minutes. Remove to a wire rack to cool completely. **Yield:** 3 to 4 dozen cookies.

Alanna Barrett, *Golden Rod Grange, New Hampshire*

Pineapple Raisin Cookies

2 cups sifted flour
1 teaspoon baking powder
1/2 teaspoon salt
1/2 teaspoon baking soda
1 cup packed light brown sugar
1/2 cup (1 stick) butter, softened
1 egg
1 teaspoon vanilla extract
3/4 cup crushed pineapple
1/2 cup raisins and/or chopped nuts

Combine the flour, baking powder, salt and baking soda in a bowl and mix well. Beat the brown sugar and butter in a mixer bowl until creamy. Add the egg and vanilla and beat until blended. Stir in the pineapple. Add the flour mixture and mix well. Stir in the raisins and/or nuts. Drop by teaspoonfuls onto a greased cookie sheet. Bake at 375 degrees for 12 to 15 minutes or until light brown. Cool on cookie sheet for 2 minutes. Remove to a wire rack to cool completely. **Yield:** 3 dozen cookies.

Grace Gray, *Hurricane Creek Grange, Oregon*

Potato Chip Cookies

1 cup (2 sticks) butter, softened
1/2 cup sugar
1 egg yolk
1 teaspoon vanilla extract
2 1/2 cups flour
1/2 cup crushed potato chips
1/2 cup chopped nuts
1/2 cup chocolate chips

Beat the butter, sugar, egg yolk and vanilla in a mixer bowl until light and fluffy. Add the flour 1/2 cup at a time, beating well after each addition. Stir in the potato chips and nuts. Shape the dough into small balls. Arrange 2 inches apart on a greased cookie sheet. Make an indentation in each cookie with the back of a spoon or your thumb. Fill the indentations with chocolate pieces. Bake at 325 degrees for 25 minutes. Cool on cookie sheet for 2 minutes. Remove to a wire rack to cool completely. **Yield:** 2 to 3 dozen cookies.

Beatrice DeFino, *Kendrew Grange, New York*

Raisin-Filled Cookies

2 1/2 cups raisins
2 cups packed brown sugar
6 tablespoons (heaping) flour
2 cups water
4 cups flour
1 teaspoon baking soda
1 cup shortening
2 cups packed brown sugar
3 eggs, beaten
1 teaspoon vanilla extract

Combine the raisins, 2 cups brown sugar, 6 tablespoons flour and water in a saucepan. Cook until thickened, stirring constantly. Let stand until cool. Sift 4 cups flour and baking soda together. Beat the shortening in a mixer bowl until creamy. Add 2 cups brown sugar, eggs and vanilla and beat until blended. Add the dry ingredients and mix well. Roll the dough thin on a lightly floured surface; cut with a round cutter. Spoon the raisin mixture over half the rounds. Top with the remaining rounds. Arrange 2 inches apart on a cookie sheet. Bake at 350 degrees for 15 minutes. Cool on cookie sheet for 2 minutes. Remove to a wire rack to cool completely. **Yield:** 2 dozen cookies.

Ruth Ann Kensinger, *Lincoln Grange, Pennsylvania*

As of 1999, the states with the largest fraternal Grange membership are Washington, Oregon, Pennsylvania, and California.

Sugar Cookies

3 cups flour
1 cup (2 sticks) butter or margarine,
   softened
1 teaspoon baking soda
1/2 teaspoon cream of tartar
1 cup sugar
2 eggs
1 teaspoon vanilla extract

Beat the flour, butter, baking soda and cream of tartar in a mixer bowl until blended. Whisk the sugar, eggs and vanilla in a bowl until smooth. Add to the flour mixture and mix well. Chill, covered, for 8 to 10 hours. Roll the dough on a lightly floured surface. Cut into desired shapes. Arrange 2 inches apart on a cookie sheet. Bake at 425 degrees for 4 minutes or until the edges are light brown. Cool on the cookie sheet for 2 minutes. Remove to a wire rack to cool completely. **Yield:** 3 dozen cookies.

Jeanne Amsden, *Woodland Grange, Iowa*

Soft Sugar Cookies

6 cups flour
2 teaspoons baking soda
2 teaspoons baking powder
1 teaspoon cream of tartar
1/2 teaspoon salt
1 cup buttermilk
1 tablespoon lemon juice
1 tablespoon vanilla extract
3 eggs
2 cups sugar
1 cup shortening

Mix the first 5 ingredients in a bowl. Mix the buttermilk, lemon juice and vanilla in a bowl. Beat the eggs in a mixer bowl at high speed for 1 minute. Add the sugar and shortening and beat until creamy. Add the flour mixture alternately with the buttermilk mixture, mixing well after each addition. Roll 1/4 inch thick on a lightly floured surface. Cut into desired shapes. Arrange on a cookie sheet. Sprinkle with additional sugar. Bake at 375 degrees for 8 to 10 minutes or until light brown. Cool on cookie sheet for 2 minutes. Remove to a wire rack to cool completely. **Yield:** 5 dozen cookies.

Jean R. Rishel, *Penns Valley Grange, Pennsylvania*

Sugarless Gelatin Pastel Cookies

2 cups flour
1/4 teaspoon baking powder
1/4 teaspoon salt (optional)
1/2 cup (1 stick) butter or margarine,
   softened
1/4 cup shortening
1 egg
2 teaspoons vanilla extract
1 small package any flavor sugar-free
   gelatin
1 packet sugar substitute

Mix the first 3 ingredients in a bowl. Beat the butter and shortening in a mixer bowl until creamy. Beat in the egg and vanilla. Add the flour mixture gradually, mixing well after each addition. Beat in the gelatin and sugar substitute just until mixed; do not overbeat. Roll 1/4 to 1/3 inch thick on a lightly floured surface. Cut into the desired shapes. Arrange on an ungreased cookie sheet. Sprinkle with additional sugar-free gelatin, shredded coconut and/or other sugar-free decorations as desired. Bake at 375 degrees for 10 to 12 minutes or until light brown. Cool on cookie sheet for 2 minutes. Remove to a wire rack to cool completely. **Yield:** 6 to 7 dozen cookies.

Charity Rinker, *Ringoes Grange, New Jersey*

Sugarless Cookies

1 cup flour
1 cup quick-cooking oats
1 1/2 teaspoons cinnamon
1 teaspoon baking soda
1 teaspoon ground cloves
1 teaspoon allspice
1/2 teaspoon salt (optional)
1/4 teaspoon nutmeg
1 cup unsweetened applesauce
1/2 cup vegetable oil
2 eggs, lightly beaten
1 teaspoon vanilla extract
1 1/2 cups raisins
1/2 cup chopped nuts

Combine the flour, oats, cinnamon, baking soda, cloves, allspice, salt and nutmeg in a bowl and mix well. Add the applesauce, oil, eggs and vanilla and mix well. Stir in the raisins and nuts. Drop by teaspoonfuls onto a greased cookie sheet. Bake at 375 degrees for 12 minutes. Cool on cookie sheet for 2 minutes. Remove to a wire rack to cool completely. **Yield:** 4 dozen cookies.

Margaret M. Storm, *Pleasant Hill Grange, Pennsylvania*

Ten-Cup Cookies

1 cup flour
1 tablespoon baking soda
1 teaspoon baking powder
1 cup peanut butter
1 cup (2 sticks) butter or margarine,
    softened
1 cup sugar
1 cup packed brown sugar
2 eggs
1 cup quick-cooking oats
1 cup chopped pecans
1 cup chocolate chips
1 cup raisins
1 cup shredded coconut

Combine the flour, baking soda and baking powder in a bowl and mix well. Beat the peanut butter and butter in a mixer bowl until creamy. Add the sugar, brown sugar and eggs and beat until light and fluffy. Add the dry ingredients and mix well. Stir in the oats, pecans, chocolate chips, raisins and coconut. Drop by teaspoonfuls 2 inches apart onto a greased cookie sheet. Bake at 350 degrees for 12 to 15 minutes or until light brown. Cool on cookie sheet for 2 minutes. Remove to a wire rack to cool completely. **Yield:** 5 to 6 dozen cookies.

Betty Rhine, *Harbor Springs Grange, Michigan*

Each year, the National Grange selects a State Grange Youth Director of the Nation for states with fewer than 100 Subordinate Granges and one for the states that have more than 100 Subordinate Granges.

World's Best Cookies

3¹/₂ cups flour
1 teaspoon baking soda
1 teaspoon salt
1 cup crushed cornflakes
1 cup rolled oats
¹/₂ cup chopped nuts
¹/₂ cup shredded coconut
1 cup (2 sticks) margarine, softened
1 cup packed brown sugar
¹/₂ cup vegetable oil
1 egg or 2 egg whites, lightly beaten
1 teaspoon vanilla extract

Combine the flour, baking soda and salt in a bowl and mix well. Stir in the cornflakes, oats, nuts and coconut. Beat the margarine, brown sugar, oil, egg and vanilla in a mixer bowl until creamy. Add the flour mixture and mix well. Shape into 1-inch balls. Arrange 2 inches apart on an ungreased cookie sheet. Flatten with a glass dipped in cold water. Bake at 325 degrees for 12 to 15 minutes or until light brown. **Yield:** 6 dozen cookies.

Linda Pugh, *Ada Grange, Oregon*

Apricot Bars

2 cups flour
¹/₄ teaspoon baking powder
³/₄ cup (1¹/₂ sticks) margarine, softened
1 cup sugar
1 egg
1¹/₃ cups shredded coconut
¹/₂ cup chopped walnuts
¹/₂ teaspoon vanilla extract
1 (12-ounce) jar apricot preserves

Mix the flour and baking powder in a bowl. Beat the margarine and sugar in a mixer bowl until creamy. Beat in the egg. Add the flour mixture gradually, mixing well after each addition. Stir in the coconut, walnuts and vanilla. Pat ²/₃ of the dough over the bottom of a greased 9x13-inch baking pan. Spread with the preserves. Crumble the remaining dough over the top. Bake at 350 degrees for 30 to 35 minutes or until golden brown. Cool in pan on a wire rack. Cut into bars. **Yield:** 3 dozen bars.

Anna Van Hulle, *Waller Road Grange, Washington*

Apple Pie Bars

2¹/₂ cups flour
1 tablespoon sugar
1 teaspoon salt
1 cup shortening
²/₃ cup milk
1 egg yolk, lightly beaten
¹/₂ cup crushed cornflakes
8 to 10 apples, sliced
1¹/₄ cups sugar
1 teaspoon cinnamon
1 egg white
1 cup confectioners' sugar
Half-and-half

Combine the flour, 1 tablespoon sugar and salt in a bowl and mix well. Cut in the shortening until crumbly. Stir in a mixture of the milk and egg yolk. Divide the pastry into 2 portions. Roll 1 portion to fit a 10x15-inch baking pan on a lightly floured surface. Fit the pastry into the pan. Sprinkle with the cornflakes. Arrange the apples over the cornflakes. Sprinkle with 1¹/₄ cups sugar and cinnamon. Roll the remaining pastry on a lightly floured surface. Place over the top. Pinch the edges to seal. Whisk the egg white in a mixer bowl until foamy. Brush over the pastry. Bake at 375 degrees for 1 hour or until brown. Combine the confectioners' sugar and half-and-half in a bowl, stirring until of a glaze consistency. Drizzle over the warm pastry. Cut into bars. **Yield:** 2 dozen bars.

Burton E. Meyers, *Winthrop Grange, New Hampshire*

Applesauce Bars

1 cup sugar
3/4 cup shortening or vegetable oil
2 eggs
1 teaspoon vanilla extract
2 cups flour
1 teaspoon cinnamon
1/2 teaspoon salt
1 teaspoon baking powder
2 teaspoons baking soda
1/2 cup chopped walnuts or pecans
1/2 cup chopped dates (optional)
2 cups applesauce
1 cup sifted confectioners' sugar
11/2 tablespoons (about) milk
1/4 teaspoon vanilla extract

Beat the sugar and shortening in a mixer bowl until creamy. Add the eggs and 1 teaspoon vanilla and beat until blended. Add the flour, cinnamon, salt, baking powder, baking soda, nuts, dates and applesauce in the order listed, mixing well after each addition. Spread in a greased and floured 10x15-inch baking pan. Bake at 350 degrees for 30 minutes. Combine the confectioners' sugar, milk and 1/4 teaspoon vanilla in a bowl, stirring until of a spreadable consistency. Spread over the top while warm. Let stand until cool. Cut into bars. May bake in a bundt pan for 45 minutes. **Yield:** 3 dozen bars.

Myra Beck, *Minnesota Director of Women's Activities*

Two-Tone Banana Bars

11/2 cups flour
1 teaspoon baking soda
1 teaspoon baking powder
1/2 teaspoon salt
1 cup sugar
1/2 cup (1 stick) margarine, softened
1 egg
11/2 cups mashed bananas
1/4 cup baking cocoa

Combine the flour, baking soda, baking powder and salt in a bowl and mix well. Beat the sugar, margarine and egg in a mixer bowl until creamy. Add the bananas and beat until blended. Add the dry ingredients and mix well. Divide the batter into 2 equal portions. Stir the baking cocoa into 1 portion in a bowl. Spread in a greased 9x13-inch baking pan. Top with the remaining batter. Swirl with a knife. Bake at 350 degrees for 25 minutes. Cool in pan on a wire rack. Cut into bars. **Yield:** 2 dozen bars.

Edna I. Wilson, *Ludlow Grange, Massachusetts*

At the National Convention, State Granges are assigned officers that are to be filled by youth/ young adults from their respective states. The officers open the Friday session of the National Grange Convention each year.

Blueberry Squares

1 cup (2 sticks) butter or margarine,
  softened
2 cups sugar
4 eggs
1 teaspoon vanilla extract
3 cups flour
1 (21-ounce) can blueberry pie filling

Beat the butter and sugar in a mixer bowl until creamy. Add the eggs and vanilla and beat until blended. Add the flour gradually, mixing well after each addition. Spread half the batter in a greased 9x13-inch baking pan. Top with the pie filling. Drop the remaining batter by spoonfuls over the pie filling. Bake at 350 degrees for 45 minutes. Cool in pan on a wire rack. Cut into squares. **Yield:** 20 squares.

Carol Reynolds, *Dunstable Grange, Massachusetts*

Yummy Cherry Bars

2 cups flour
2 cups quick-cooking oats
1 3/4 cups (3 1/2 sticks) butter, melted
1 1/4 cups sugar
1/2 cup chopped pecans
1/2 teaspoon baking soda
1 (21-ounce) can cherry pie filling
1 cup miniature marshmallows

Combine the flour, oats, butter, sugar, pecans and baking soda in a mixer bowl. Beat at low speed for 2 to 3 minutes or until crumbly, scraping the bowl frequently. Reserve 1 1/2 cups of the crumb mixture. Pat the remaining crumb mixture over the bottom of a buttered 9x13-inch baking pan. Bake at 350 degrees for 12 to 15 minutes or until the edges are brown. Spread with the pie filling. Sprinkle with the marshmallows. Top with the remaining crumb mixture. Bake for 25 minutes longer or until light brown. Cool in pan on a wire rack. Cut into bars. **Yield:** 3 dozen bars.

Gene Edelen, *Treasurer, National Grange*

Cherry Squares

3 cups sifted flour
1 tablespoon baking powder
1 1/2 cups sugar
3/4 cup vegetable oil
Juice of 1 medium orange
1 teaspoon vanilla extract
3 eggs
1 (21-ounce) can cherry pie filling
1 teaspoon almond extract
1/4 cup sugar
1 teaspoon cinnamon

Combine the flour and baking powder in a bowl and mix well. Beat 1 1/2 cups sugar and oil in a mixer bowl until blended. Add the orange juice and vanilla and mix well. Add the eggs 1 at a time, mixing well after each addition. Fold in the flour mixture. Spread half the batter in a greased 9x12-inch baking pan. Spread with a mixture of the pie filling and almond extract. Top with the remaining batter. Sprinkle with a mixture of 1/4 cup sugar and cinnamon. Bake at 350 degrees for 15 minutes. Reduce the oven temperature to 325 degrees. Bake for 30 minutes longer. Cool in pan on a wire rack. Cut into squares. Serve with ice cream or whipped topping if desired. **Yield:** 18 squares.

Charlotte Dykeman, *Fletcher Grange, Vermont*

Blondies

1/2 cup (1 stick) butter or margarine
1/2 cup packed brown sugar
1 cup flour
1/2 teaspoon baking powder
1/2 teaspoon salt
1/8 teaspoon baking soda
1 egg, lightly beaten
1 teaspoon vanilla extract
1/2 cup chopped nuts

Combine the butter and brown sugar in a saucepan. Cook until blended, stirring frequently. Let stand until cool. Sift the flour, baking powder, salt and baking soda together. Stir the egg and vanilla into the brown sugar mixture. Add the flour mixture and nuts and stir just until mixed. Spoon into a greased and floured 8x8-inch baking pan. Bake at 350 degrees for 20 to 25 minutes or until the edges pull from the sides of the pan. Cool in pan on a wire rack. Cut into bars. May double the recipe and bake in a 9x13-inch baking pan. **Yield:** 16 bars.

Peggy York, *Alamo Grange, Texas*

White Chocolate Blondies

3 cups flour
1 teaspoon baking powder
1/2 teaspoon salt
6 ounces white baking chocolate
1 cup (2 sticks) butter or margarine
3 cups sugar
6 eggs
2 teaspoons vanilla extract
2 cups vanilla chips or white
    chocolate chips
1 cup chopped pecans

Combine the flour, baking powder and salt in a bowl and mix well. Combine the white chocolate and butter in a double boiler. Heat over hot water until blended, stirring frequently. Cool for 20 minutes. Beat the sugar and eggs in a mixer bowl for 4 minutes or until thick and pale yellow. Beat in the melted chocolate and vanilla. Add the flour mixture and mix well. Stir in the vanilla chips and pecans. Spoon into a greased 10x15-inch baking pan. Bake at 350 degrees for 40 to 45 minutes or until golden brown. Cool in pan on a wire rack. Cut into bars. **Yield:** 4 dozen bars.

Lois Barber, *Gardner Grange, Kansas*

The National Grange Youth Department has been in existence for more than fifty years.

Brownies From Scratch

1 cup sugar
1/2 cup vegetable oil
1 teaspoon vanilla extract
1/2 cup flour
1/3 cup baking cocoa
2 eggs, beaten

Combine the sugar, oil and vanilla in a bowl and mix well. Stir in the flour, baking cocoa and eggs. Spoon into a greased 9x9-inch baking pan. Bake at 350 degrees for 20 to 25 minutes or until the edges pull from the sides of the pan. Cool in pan on a wire rack. Cut into bars. Double the recipe and bake in a 9x13-inch baking pan. **Yield:** 1 dozen brownies.

Carolyn Hammett, *South Carolina Director of Women's Activities*

Aunt Grace's Brownies

4 egg yolks
2 cups sugar
1 1/2 cups flour
1 cup shortening, melted or
    vegetable oil
1/4 cup milk
1/4 cup baking cocoa
2 teaspoons vanilla extract
1/2 teaspoon salt
Chopped nuts (optional)
Shredded coconut (optional)
4 egg whites, stiffly beaten

Beat the egg yolks in a mixer bowl until fluffy. Add the sugar, flour, shortening, milk, baking cocoa, vanilla and salt and mix well. Stir in the nuts and coconut. Fold in the egg whites. Spoon the batter into a 9x13-inch baking pan. Bake at 350 degrees for 25 to 30 minutes or until the edges pull from the sides of the pan. Cool in pan on a wire rack. Cut into bars.
Yield: 15 to 18 brownies.

Jeff Proof, *Lawsville Grange, Pennsylvania*

Congo Bars

2 2/3 cups flour
2 1/2 teaspoons baking powder
1/2 teaspoon salt
2 cups packed brown sugar
3/4 to 1 cup vegetable oil
3 eggs
2 cups chocolate chips
1/2 cup chopped walnuts (optional)

Combine the flour, baking powder and salt in a bowl and mix well. Beat the brown sugar, oil and eggs in a mixer bowl for 2 minutes or until smooth. Beat in the dry ingredients until blended. Stir in the chocolate chips and walnuts; batter will be very thick. Spoon into a greased 9x13-inch baking pan. Bake at 350 degrees for 30 minutes or until the edges pull from the sides of the pan. Cool in pan on a wire rack. Cut into bars.
Yield: 4 dozen bars.

Kathy Evans, *New Plymouth Grange, Idaho*

Deluxe Chocolate Marshmallow Bars

1¹/₃ cups flour
3 tablespoons baking cocoa
¹/₂ teaspoon baking powder
¹/₂ teaspoon salt
1¹/₂ cups sugar
³/₄ cup (1¹/₂ sticks) butter or margarine,
    softened
3 eggs
1 teaspoon vanilla extract
¹/₂ cup chopped nuts (optional)
4 cups miniature marshmallows
1¹/₃ cups chocolate chips
1 cup peanut butter
3 tablespoons butter
2 cups crisp rice cereal

Combine the flour, baking cocoa, baking powder and salt in a bowl and mix well. Beat the sugar and ³/₄ cup butter in a mixer bowl until creamy. Add the eggs and vanilla and beat until light and fluffy. Add the flour mixture and mix well. Stir in the nuts. Spread in a greased 10x15-inch baking pan. Bake at 350 degrees for 15 to 18 minutes or until the edges pull from the sides of the pan. Sprinkle with the marshmallows. Bake for 2 to 3 minutes or until the marshmallows melt. Spread the marshmallows evenly over the surface with a knife dipped in water. Let stand until cool. Combine the chocolate chips, peanut butter and 3 tablespoons butter in a saucepan. Cook over low heat until blended, stirring constantly. Remove from heat. Stir in the cereal. Spread over the baked layer. Chill, covered, until set. Cut into bars. **Yield:** 3 dozen bars.

Deb Beatty, *Bloomington Grange, Iowa*
Mary Briggs, *Penola Grange, Indiana*

Chocolate Raspberry Bars

1 cup flour
¹/₄ cup confectioners' sugar
¹/₂ cup (1 stick) butter or margarine
¹/₂ cup seedless raspberry jam
4 ounces cream cheese, softened
2 tablespoons milk
1 cup vanilla chips, melted
³/₄ cup semisweet chocolate chips
2 tablespoons shortening

Combine the flour and confectioners' sugar in a bowl and mix well. Cut in the butter until crumbly. Press over the bottom of an ungreased 9x9-inch baking pan. Bake at 375 degrees for 15 to 18 minutes or until brown. Spread the jam over the warm baked layer. Beat the cream cheese and milk in a mixer bowl until smooth. Add the vanilla chips and beat until blended. Spread over the jam. Let stand until cool. Chill, covered, for 1 hour or until set. Combine the semisweet chocolate chips and shortening in a saucepan. Cook over low heat until blended, stirring constantly. Spread over the prepared layers. Chill for 10 minutes. Cut into bars. **Yield:** 3 dozen bars.

E. Joy Brown, *York Grange, Idaho*

Each State Grange selects a Grange member to be a State Grange Youth Director.

Diabetic Fruit Bars

1 cup chopped dates
1 cup chopped dried prunes
1 cup raisins
2 cups water
1/4 cup (1/2 stick) margarine, softened
4 eggs
2 teaspoons vanilla extract
1/2 cup unsweetened applesauce
2 cups flour
2 teaspoons baking soda
1 teaspoon cinnamon
1/2 teaspoon salt

Combine the dates, prunes, raisins and water in a saucepan. Cook until tender, stirring occasionally. Cool slightly. Add the margarine, stirring until melted. Let stand until completely cool. Whisk the eggs and vanilla in a bowl until blended. Stir in the applesauce. Add a mixture of the flour, baking soda, cinnamon and salt and mix well. Stir in the date mixture. Spoon into a greased 9x13-inch baking pan. Bake at 350 degrees for 30 to 35 minutes or until the edges pull from the sides of the pan. Cut into bars. **Yield:** 24 to 30 bars.

Lena Warden, *Charity Grange, Oregon*

Fruit-Filled Squares

2 cups sugar
1 cup (2 sticks) margarine, softened
4 eggs, beaten
3 cups flour
1 teaspoon vanilla extract
1 teaspoon almond extract
1 (21-ounce) can any flavor pie filling

Beat the sugar and margarine in a mixer bowl until creamy. Add the eggs and beat until blended. Beat in the flour. Add the flavorings and mix well. Spread 3/4 of the batter in a 9x13-inch baking pan. Spread with the pie filling. Drop the remaining batter by spoonfuls over the top; do not spread. Bake at 350 degrees for 40 to 45 minutes or until brown. Cool in pan on a wire rack. Cut into squares. **Yield:** 15 squares.

Goldie French, *Golden Rod Grange, New Hampshire*

Fruit and Nut Squares

1 cup sifted flour
1 teaspoon baking soda
1/2 teaspoon cinnamon
1 cup water
1/2 cup chopped prunes
1/2 cup chopped dates
1/2 cup raisins
1/2 cup (1 stick) butter or margarine
2 eggs, beaten
1 teaspoon vanilla extract
1/2 cup chopped walnuts

Sift the flour, baking soda and cinnamon together. Combine the water, prunes, dates and raisins in a saucepan. Bring to a boil over medium-high heat; reduce heat to medium-low. Cook for 4 minutes, stirring occasionally. Remove from heat. Add the butter, stirring until melted. Let stand until cool. Stir in the eggs, vanilla and walnuts. Add the flour mixture and mix well. Spoon into a greased 9x9-inch baking pan. Bake at 350 degrees for 30 minutes or until a wooden pick inserted in the center comes out clean. Cool in pan on a wire rack. Cut into 2 1/4-inch squares. **Yield:** 16 squares.

Marian Grutsch, *Peninsula Grange, Michigan*

Lemon Squares

2 cups flour
1 cup confectioners' sugar
1 cup (2 sticks) margarine, melted
4 eggs
2 cups sugar
6 tablespoons lemon juice
1/4 cup flour
1 teaspoon baking powder

Combine 2 cups flour, confectioners' sugar and margarine in a bowl and mix well. Pat over the bottom of a greased 9x13-inch baking pan. Bake at 350 degrees for 20 minutes. Whisk the eggs in a bowl. Add the sugar and lemon juice and whisk until blended. Add a mixture of 1/4 cup flour and baking powder and mix well. Spoon over the baked layer. Bake at 350 to 375 degrees for 20 to 25 minutes or until set and light brown. Cool in pan on a wire rack. Cut into squares. **Yield:** 2 to 3 dozen squares.

Joyce Ann Blosser, *Clear Creek Valley Grange, Ohio*

Maple Nut Bars

1 1/2 cups flour
2 tablespoons brown sugar
1/2 cup (1 stick) butter
2 eggs
1/2 cup packed brown sugar
1/2 cup maple syrup
2 tablespoons butter, melted
1 teaspoon vanilla extract
1/2 cup chopped walnuts

Combine the flour and 2 tablespoons brown sugar in a bowl. Cut in 1/2 cup butter until crumbly. Pat the crumb mixture over the bottom of an ungreased 8x12-inch baking pan. Bake at 350 degrees for 15 minutes. Whisk the eggs lightly in a bowl. Stir in 1/2 cup brown sugar, maple syrup, 2 tablespoons butter and vanilla. Add the walnuts and mix well. Spoon over the baked layer. Bake for 25 minutes longer or until set. Cool slightly in pan on a wire rack. Cut into bars. Store, covered, in the refrigerator. **Yield:** 32 bars.

Pauline Hunt, *Glastonbury Grange, Connecticut*

The Grange Youth Program has offered many great programs over the years. They include the Grange Interstate Youth Exchange, Youth Representative Awards, Spirit of Grange Award, GISYE II Program, National Public Speaking Contests, and Sign-A-Song Contests.

Scotcheroos

1 cup sugar
1 cup corn syrup
1 cup peanut butter
6 cups crisp rice cereal
1 cup semisweet chocolate chips
1 cup butterscotch chips

Bring the sugar and corn syrup to a boil in a large saucepan, stirring frequently. Remove from heat. Fold in the peanut butter and cereal. Press the cereal mixture into a buttered 9x13-inch dish. Let stand until firm. Heat the chocolate chips and butterscotch chips in a double boiler until blended, stirring frequently. Spread over the prepared layer. Let stand until set. Cut into bars. **Yield:** 3 to 4 dozen bars.

Bernard Shoemaker, *Steward, National Grange*

Seven-Layer Bars

1/4 cup (1/2 stick) plus 1 tablespoon
    butter or margarine
1 1/2 cups graham cracker crumbs
1 cup flaked coconut
1 cup semisweet chocolate chips
1 cup butterscotch chips
1 cup chopped pecans or walnuts
1 (14-ounce) can sweetened
    condensed milk

Heat the butter in a 9x9-inch baking pan in a 350-degree oven until melted. Layer the graham cracker crumbs, coconut, chocolate chips, butterscotch chips and pecans in the order listed over the butter. Drizzle the condensed milk over the top. Bake at 325 degrees for 30 minutes. Cool in pan for several minutes. Cut into 1 1/2-inch bars. Remove to a wire rack to cool completely. May freeze for future use. **Yield:** 3 dozen bars.

Ellen Parady, *Sabbathday Lake Grange, Maine*

Chocolate Cream Cheese Frosting

1/4 cup (1/2 stick) butter or margarine
1/4 cup milk
2 ounces cream cheese
1 ounce unsweetened chocolate
1 (1-pound) package confectioners' sugar
1 teaspoon vanilla extract

Combine the butter, milk, cream cheese and chocolate in a saucepan. Cook over low heat until blended, stirring constantly. Remove from heat. Add the confectioners' sugar and vanilla and stir until smooth. **Yield:** 3 cups.

Ila Strange, *Blanchard Grange, Washington*

Rocky Road Bars

1/2 cup (1 stick) butter or margarine
1 ounce unsweetened chocolate
1 cup sugar
1 cup flour
2 eggs, lightly beaten
1 1/2 teaspoons baking powder
1 teaspoon vanilla extract
1/2 cup chopped nuts
6 ounces cream cheese, softened
1/2 cup sugar
1/4 cup butter, softened
2 tablespoons flour
1 egg
1/2 teaspoon vanilla extract
2 cups marshmallows
Chocolate Cream Cheese Frosting
    (page 214)

Heat 1/2 cup butter and chocolate in a saucepan over low heat until blended, stirring frequently. Remove from heat. Stir in 1 cup sugar, 1 cup flour, 2 eggs, baking powder and 1 teaspoon vanilla. Add the nuts and mix well. Spoon into a greased and floured 9x13-inch baking pan. Beat the cream cheese, 1/2 cup sugar, 1/4 cup butter, 2 tablespoons flour, 1 egg and 1/2 teaspoon vanilla in a mixer bowl until smooth. Spread over the prepared layer. Bake at 350 degrees for 25 to 35 minutes or until the edges pull from the sides of the pan. Sprinkle with the marshmallows. Bake for 2 minutes longer. Spread with the Chocolate Cream Cheese Frosting immediately and swirl. Let stand until cool. Cut into bars. **Yield:** 2 dozen bars.

Ila Strange, *Blanchard Grange, Washington*

Scandinavian Almond Bars

1/2 cup (1 stick) butter, softened
1 cup sugar
1 egg
1/2 teaspoon almond extract
1 3/4 cups flour
2 teaspoons baking powder
1/4 teaspoon salt
1/4 cup (about) milk
1/2 cup sliced almonds, chopped
1 cup confectioners' sugar
3 to 4 teaspoons milk
1/4 teaspoon almond extract

Beat the butter in a mixer bowl until creamy. Add the sugar and beat until light and fluffy. Beat in the egg and 1/2 teaspoon almond extract. Stir in a mixture of the flour, baking powder and salt. Divide the dough into 4 equal portions. Shape each portion into a 12-inch rope. Arrange 2 of the ropes 4 to 5 inches apart on an ungreased baking sheet. Flatten each rope to a width of 3 inches. Repeat the process with the remaining 2 dough portions. Brush with 1/4 cup milk and sprinkle with the almonds. Bake at 325 degrees for 12 to 14 minutes or until the edges are light brown. Cut the warm logs diagonally into 1-inch bars. Remove to a wire rack to cool. Drizzle with a mixture of the confectioners' sugar, 3 to 4 teaspoons milk and 1/4 teaspoon almond extract. **Yield:** 3 dozen bars.

Jane Miller, *Connecticut Director of Women's Activities*

Each year the National Grange offers six regional youth/young adult conferences.

Sour Cream Raisin Bars

2 cups raisins
1 cup water
1 cup packed brown sugar
1 cup (2 sticks) butter, softened
1³/4 cups each rolled oats and flour
1 teaspoon baking soda
1¹/2 cups sour cream
1 cup sugar
2¹/2 tablespoons cornstarch
3 egg yolks, lightly beaten
1 teaspoon vanilla extract
¹/2 teaspoon cinnamon

Bring the raisins and water to a boil in a saucepan. Simmer for 10 minutes; drain. Let stand until cool. Beat the brown sugar and butter in a mixer bowl until creamy. Mix in the oats, flour and baking soda. Pat half the oat mixture over the bottom of a 9x13-inch baking pan. Bake at 350 degrees for 10 minutes. Mix the next 4 ingredients in a saucepan. Bring to a boil. Cook until thickened, stirring constantly. Stir in the raisins, vanilla and cinnamon. Spoon over the baked layer. Crumble the remaining oat mixture over the top. Bake for 30 minutes. Cut into 1¹/2x2-inch bars when cool. **Yield:** 4 dozen bars.

Mary Johnson, *Chaplain, National Grange*

Three-Layer Squares

1 cup flour
¹/2 cup (1 stick) butter, softened
2 tablespoons flour
¹/2 teaspoon salt
¹/4 teaspoon baking powder
1 cup chopped nuts
¹/2 cup shredded coconut
1¹/2 cups packed brown sugar
2 eggs, beaten
1 teaspoon vanilla extract
1¹/2 cups confectioners' sugar
2 tablespoons butter, softened
2 tablespoons orange juice
1 tablespoon lemon juice

Beat 1 cup flour and ¹/2 cup butter in a mixer bowl until blended. Pat over the bottom of a 9x12-inch baking pan. Bake at 375 degrees for 12 to 15 minutes or until light brown. Sift 2 tablespoons flour, salt and baking powder into a bowl and mix well. Stir in the nuts and coconut. Combine the brown sugar, eggs and vanilla in a bowl and mix well. Add the flour mixture and mix well. Spoon over the baked layer. Bake at 375 degrees for 20 minutes. Cool in pan on a wire rack. Combine the confectioners' sugar, 2 tablespoons butter, orange juice and lemon juice in a mixer bowl. Beat until of a spreading consistency. Spread over the baked layer. Cut into 2x2-inch squares. **Yield:** 2 dozen squares.

Helen Barber, *Dansville Grange, New York*

Toffee Nut Bars

¹/2 cup packed brown sugar
¹/2 cup shortening
1 cup sifted flour
2 eggs
1 cup packed brown sugar
1 teaspoon vanilla
2 tablespoons sifted flour
1 teaspoon baking powder
¹/2 teaspoon salt
1 cup shredded coconut
1 cup chopped nuts

Combine ¹/2 cup brown sugar and shortening in a bowl and mix well. Stir in 1 cup flour. Press over the bottom of an ungreased 7x11-inch baking pan. Bake at 350 degrees for 10 minutes. Whisk the eggs in a bowl until blended. Stir in 1 cup brown sugar and vanilla. Add a mixture of 2 tablespoons flour, baking powder and salt and mix well. Stir in the coconut and nuts. Spoon over the baked layer. Bake for 25 minutes longer. Cool in pan on a wire rack. Cut into 2x2-inch bars. **Yield:** 20 bars.

Marion Boston, *Locust Grove Grange, Idaho*

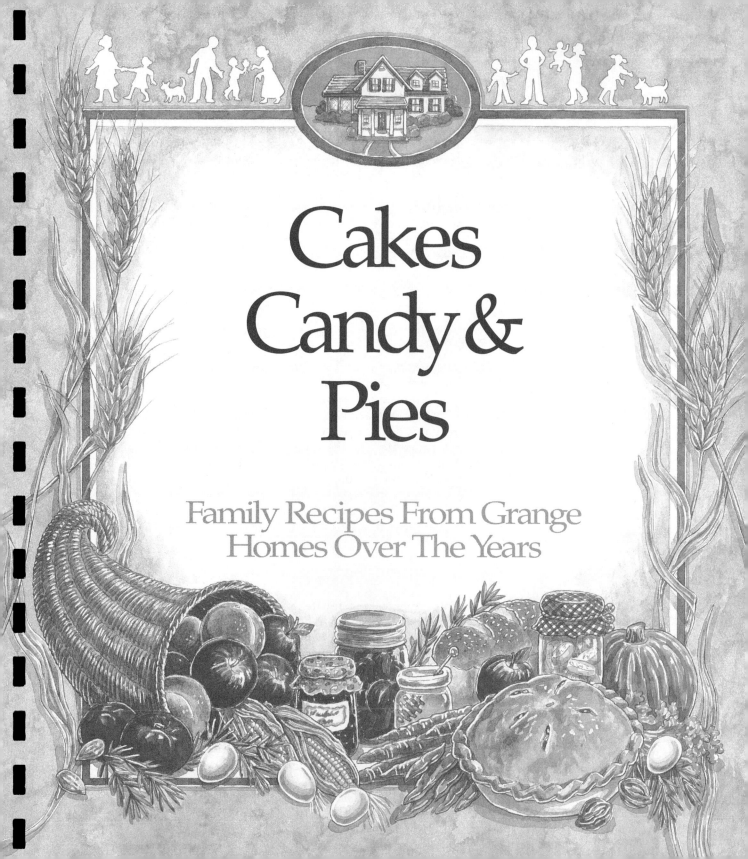

Cakes
Candy &
Pies

Family Recipes From Grange
Homes Over The Years

Anytime Cake

1/4 cup ground nuts
1/4 cup sugar
1 teaspoon cinnamon
2 1/2 cups flour
1 teaspoon baking soda
1/2 teaspoon baking powder
1/4 teaspoon salt
1 cup sugar
1 cup shortening
3 eggs
1 1/2 teaspoons vanilla extract
1 cup sour cream

Combine the nuts, 1/4 cup sugar and cinnamon in a bowl and mix well. Sift the flour, baking soda, baking powder and salt together. Beat 1 cup sugar and shortening in a mixer bowl until light and fluffy. Add the eggs and vanilla and beat until blended. Add the dry ingredients alternately with the sour cream, mixing well after each addition. Layer the batter and nut mixture 1/3 at a time in a greased and floured tube pan, swirling with a knife before sprinkling with the remaining portion of nut mixture. Bake at 350 degrees for 45 to 50 minutes or until the cake tests done. Cool in pan for several minutes. Invert onto a serving plate. **Yield:** 16 servings.

Shirley Davy, *Westbrook Grange, Connecticut*

Apple Cake

2 cups flour
2 cups packed brown sugar
1/2 cup (1 stick) butter
1 cup chopped pecans
1 cup sour cream
1 egg, beaten
1 1/2 teaspoons cinnamon
1 teaspoon baking soda
1 teaspoon vanilla extract
1/2 teaspoon salt
2 cups finely chopped apples

Combine the flour and brown sugar in a bowl and mix well. Cut in the butter until crumbly. Stir in the pecans. Pat 1 to 1 1/3 cups of the crumb mixture over the bottom of each of 2 ungreased 8x8-inch or 9x9-inch baking pans. Stir the sour cream, egg, cinnamon, baking soda, vanilla and salt into the remaining crumb mixture. Add the apples and mix well. Spoon half of the apple mixture into each prepared pan. Bake at 350 degrees for 25 to 30 minutes or until brown. Serve plain or with your favorite topping. **Yield:** 6 to 8 servings.

Marvin Schweppe, *Leon Valley Grange, Texas*

Apple Swirl Cake

3 cups sifted flour
2 tablespoons baking powder
1/2 teaspoon salt
2 cups chopped peeled apples
3 tablespoons sugar
1 teaspoon cinnamon
2 cups sugar
1 cup vegetable oil
1/4 cup orange juice
4 eggs
2 teaspoons vanilla extract
Confectioners' sugar to taste

Sift the flour, baking powder and salt together. Toss the apples with 3 tablespoons sugar and cinnamon in a bowl. Beat 2 cups sugar and oil in a mixer bowl until blended. Add the orange juice, eggs and vanilla and mix well. Add the dry ingredients and beat until smooth. Layer 1/3 of the batter and 1/2 of the apple mixture in a greased and floured bundt pan. Spread with 1/2 of the remaining batter and sprinkle with the remaining apple mixture. Top with the remaining batter. Bake at 325 degrees for 1 hour or until the cake tests done. Cool in pan on a wire rack for 10 to 15 minutes. Invert onto a serving platter to cool completely. Dust with confectioners' sugar. **Yield:** 16 servings.

Helen E. Rinker, *Klondike-Piney Grange, Wyoming*

Spanish Bar Cake

1 (21-ounce) can apple pie filling
4 eggs
1 tablespoon apple pie spice
1/4 teaspoon ground cloves
1 (2-layer) package yellow cake mix
1 cup raisins
1 cup chopped walnuts
Spicy Cream Cheese Frosting (below)

Process the pie filling, eggs, apple pie spice and cloves in a blender or food processor until smooth. Combine the pie filling mixture with the cake mix in a mixer bowl. Beat for 4 to 5 minutes. Stir in the raisins and walnuts. Spoon the batter into a greased 9x13-inch cake pan. Bake at 325 degrees until the cake tests done. Cool in pan on a wire rack for 15 minutes. Invert onto a serving platter to cool completely. Spread with the Spicy Cream Cheese Frosting when cool. **Yield:** 15 servings.

Beatrice Benedik, *Stanton Grange, New Jersey*

Spicy Cream Cheese Frosting

3 1/2 cups confectioners' sugar
8 ounces cream cheese, softened
1/2 cup (1 stick) butter, softened
1/3 cup dark corn syrup
1 tablespoon grated dried orange zest
1/4 teaspoon ground cloves

Combine the confectioners' sugar, cream cheese, butter, corn syrup, orange zest and cloves in a mixer bowl. Beat until of spreading consistency. **Yield:** 15 servings.

Beatrice Benedik, *Stanton Grange, New Jersey*

The Grange was organized in Washington, D.C., on December 4, 1867, by seven founders.

Apricot Slip Cake

1/2 cup dried apricots
1/4 cup sugar
1 1/2 cups cake flour
2 teaspoons baking powder
1/2 teaspoon baking soda
1/3 teaspoon salt
1 cup packed brown sugar
1/2 cup sour cream
1/2 cup milk
2 egg yolks
1 teaspoon vanilla extract
2 egg whites, stiffly beaten
1 cup packed brown sugar
3 tablespoons butter
1/2 cup chopped nuts
1/3 cup shredded coconut

Combine the apricots with enough water to cover in a saucepan. Bring to a boil. Boil for 15 minutes. Stir in the sugar. Cook for 5 minutes longer; drain. Sift the cake flour, baking powder, baking soda and salt together. Combine 1 cup brown sugar, sour cream, milk, egg yolks and vanilla in a bowl and mix well. Stir in the dry ingredients. Fold in the egg whites. Spoon into a 9x13-inch cake pan. Arrange the apricots over the top. Combine 1 cup brown sugar and butter in a saucepan. Cook until blended, stirring frequently. Stir in the nuts and coconut. Spoon over the top. Bake at 325 degrees for 40 minutes. **Yield:** 15 servings.

Donna Simmons, *Pleasant Valley Grange, Oregon*

Banana Cake

2 cups flour
3/4 teaspoon baking soda
1/2 teaspoon baking powder
1 1/4 cups sugar
1/2 cup shortening
2 eggs
1 cup mashed banana
1/4 cup sour milk
1/2 teaspoon salt
1 teaspoon vanilla extract

Sift the flour, baking soda and baking powder together twice. Beat the sugar and shortening in a mixer bowl until creamy. Add the eggs and beat until blended. Add the dry ingredients and mix well. Mix in the banana, sour milk and salt. Stir in the vanilla. Spoon the batter into a greased 9x13-inch cake pan. Bake at 375 degrees for 30 minutes. **Yield:** 12 servings.

Hazel Downey, *Missouri Director of Women's Activities*

Chocolate Pumpkin Cake

2 cups flour
2 teaspoons baking powder
1 1/2 teaspoons cinnamon
1 teaspoon baking soda
1/2 teaspoon salt
1/2 teaspoon ground cloves
1/4 teaspoon allspice
4 eggs
2 cups sugar
3/4 cup vegetable oil
2 cups cooked pumpkin
1 cup All-Bran
1 cup chocolate chips

Sift the flour, baking powder, cinnamon, baking soda, salt, cloves and allspice into a bowl and mix well. Beat the eggs in a mixer bowl until blended. Add the sugar and oil and beat until smooth. Stir in the pumpkin. Add the dry ingredients alternately with the cereal, mixing well after each addition. Stir in the chocolate chips. Spoon into an ungreased tube pan. Bake at 350 degrees for 45 minutes. Invert onto a serving plate. **Yield:** 16 servings.

Norris Woolley, *Villenova Grange, New York*

Chocolate Raspberry Torte

1 (2-layer) package German chocolate
  cake mix
3 ounces cream cheese, softened
1 (4-ounce) package vanilla instant
  pudding mix
3/4 cup milk
8 ounces whipped topping
2 cups fresh raspberries
Confectioners' sugar to taste

Prepare the cake using package directions for 3 greased and floured 9-inch-round cake pans. Bake at 350 degrees for 25 to 30 minutes or until the layers test done. Cool in pans for 10 minutes. Invert onto wire racks to cool completely. Beat the cream cheese in a mixer bowl until light and fluffy. Add a mixture of the pudding mix and milk and beat until blended. Fold in the whipped topping and raspberries. Place 1 cake layer on a serving platter. Spread with half the raspberry mixture. Layer with another cake layer. Spread with the remaining raspberry mixture. Top with the remaining cake layer. Dust with confectioners' sugar. Garnish with sprigs of fresh mint and additional raspberries. Store, covered, in the refrigerator. May substitute frozen drained raspberries for the fresh raspberries. **Yield:** 12 servings.

Barbara Yochum, *Steuben Grange, Pennsylvania*

Chocolate Zucchini Cake

2 1/2 cups flour
1/4 cup baking cocoa
1 teaspoon baking soda
1/2 teaspoon cinnamon
1/2 teaspoon nutmeg
1 3/4 cups sugar
1/2 cup (1 stick) margarine, softened
1/2 cup vegetable oil
2 eggs
1/2 cup sour milk
2 cups grated zucchini
1 teaspoon vanilla extract
1 cup chocolate chips

Combine the flour, baking cocoa, baking soda, cinnamon and nutmeg in a bowl and mix well. Beat the sugar, margarine and oil in a mixer bowl until creamy. Add the eggs and beat until blended. Add the flour mixture alternately with the sour milk, mixing well after each addition. Stir in the zucchini and vanilla. Spoon the batter into a greased bundt pan or 9x13-inch cake pan. Sprinkle with the chocolate chips. Bake at 350 degrees for 40 to 45 minutes or until the cake tests done. Invert onto a serving plate. **Yield:** 18 servings.

Donna Bulger, *Vermont Director of Women's Activities*

The Grange works to make the family a stronger unit.

Mississippi Mud Cake

1 cup (2 sticks) margarine, softened
2 cups sugar
4 eggs
1 1/2 cups flour
1/2 cup baking cocoa
1 teaspoon vanilla extract
1/2 teaspoon salt
1 cup chopped walnuts
1 (10-ounce) package miniature
    marshmallows
Chocolate Frosting (below)

Beat the margarine in a mixer bowl until creamy. Add the sugar and eggs and beat until blended. Add the flour, baking cocoa, vanilla and salt and mix well. Stir in the walnuts. Spoon the batter into a greased and floured 9x13-inch cake pan. Bake at 350 degrees for 35 minutes. Sprinkle with the marshmallows and press gently. Cool in pan on a wire rack. Spread with the Chocolate Frosting. The flavor is enhanced if baked 1 day in advance. **Yield:** 15 to 20 servings.

Maxine E. Robinson, *Pine Run Grange, Pennsylvania*

Chocolate Frosting

1/4 cup (1/2 stick) margarine, softened
1 (1-pound) package confectioners' sugar
1/3 cup baking cocoa
1/4 cup (or more) milk
1/2 teaspoon vanilla extract

Beat the margarine in a mixer bowl until creamy. Add the confectioners' sugar, baking cocoa, milk and vanilla and beat until of a spreading consistency, scraping the bowl occasionally. **Yield:** 15 to 20 servings.

Maxine E. Robinson, *Pine Run Grange, Pennsylvania*

Coconut Devil's Food Cake

2 cups sifted cake flour
1 teaspoon baking soda
1/2 teaspoon salt
1/2 cup (1 stick) butter, softened
1 3/4 cups sugar
1 egg
2 egg yolks
2 1/2 to 3 ounces unsweetened
    chocolate, melted
1 cup milk
1 teaspoon vanilla extract
1 cup shredded coconut, chopped

Line 2 deep 9-inch round cake pans with baking parchment. Sift the flour, baking soda and salt together 3 times. Beat the butter in a mixer bowl until creamy. Add the sugar gradually, beating constantly until light and fluffy. Add the egg and egg yolks 1 at a time and mix well after each addition. Add the chocolate and beat until blended. Add the dry ingredients alternately with the milk, beating well after each addition. Stir in the vanilla. Fold in the coconut. Spoon the batter into the prepared cake pans. Bake at 350 degrees for 30 to 35 minutes or until the layers test done. Cool in pans for 10 minutes. Invert onto wire racks to cool completely. Spread your favorite chocolate seven-minute frosting between the layers and over the top and side of the cake. Sprinkle with additional coconut. **Yield:** 20 servings.

Agnes E. Homan, *Progress Grange, Pennsylvania*

Amazing Corn Cake

2¹/4 cups flour
1 tablespoon baking powder
1 teaspoon baking soda
1 teaspoon salt
1 teaspoon cinnamon
1 (17-ounce) can cream-style corn
³/4 cup sugar
¹/2 cup packed brown sugar
1 cup vegetable oil
3 eggs
¹/2 cup raisins
¹/2 cup chopped nuts
Brown Sugar Frosting (below)

Combine the flour, baking powder, baking soda, salt and cinnamon in a bowl and mix well. Beat the corn, sugar and brown sugar in a mixer bowl. Add the oil and eggs and beat until blended. Add the flour mixture and mix well. Fold in the raisins and nuts. Spoon the batter into a greased 9x13-inch cake pan. Bake at 350 degrees for 30 to 35 minutes or until the cake tests done. Cool in pan on a wire rack. Spread with the Brown Sugar Frosting. **Yield:** 12 servings.

Lucille Cullen, *Outlook Grange, Washington*

Brown Sugar Frosting

¹/2 cup packed brown sugar
¹/4 cup (¹/2 stick) butter
¹/4 cup milk
2 to 3 cups confectioners' sugar

Combine the brown sugar, butter and milk in a saucepan. Bring to a boil, stirring frequently. Remove from heat. Add the confectioners' sugar gradually, mixing constantly until of a spreading consistency. **Yield:** 12 servings.

Lucille Cullen, *Outlook Grange, Washington*

Art and photography contests are held annually with winners from the local Granges competing for top honors at the National Convention.

Mexican Fruitcake

1 (20-ounce) can crushed pineapple
2 teaspoons baking soda
2 cups flour
2 cups sugar
1 teaspoon salt
1 cup chopped walnuts
2 eggs, lightly beaten
Cream Cheese Frosting (below)
1/2 cup finely chopped walnuts

Combine the undrained pineapple and baking soda in a bowl and mix well. Sift the flour, sugar and salt into a bowl and mix well. Fold in the pineapple mixture. Add 1 cup walnuts and eggs and mix well. Spoon into a greased and floured 9x13-inch cake pan. Bake at 325 degrees for 30 minutes or until a wooden pick inserted in the center comes out clean. Cool in pan on a wire rack for 30 minutes. Spread with the Cream Cheese Frosting. Sprinkle with 1/2 cup walnuts. **Yield:** 15 to 20 servings.

Lisa Abernethy, *Gate City Grange, North Carolina*

Cream Cheese Frosting

8 ounces cream cheese, softened
1/2 cup (1 stick) margarine, softened
1 (1-pound) package confectioners' sugar
1 teaspoon vanilla extract

Beat the cream cheese and margarine in a mixer bowl until creamy. Add the confectioners' sugar gradually, beating constantly until of a spreading consistency. Beat in the vanilla. **Yield:** 15 to 20 servings.

Lisa Abernethy, *Gate City Grange, North Carolina*

Sausage Fruitcakes

1 (16-ounce) package raisins
2 cups boiling water
1 pound sausage, crumbled
2 teaspoons baking soda
1/4 cup vinegar
4 1/2 cups flour
2 cups sugar
1 tablespoon salt
2 teaspoons vanilla extract
1 teaspoon nutmeg
1 teaspoon cinnamon
1/2 teaspoon ground cloves
2 cups chopped walnuts

Soak the raisins in the boiling water in a bowl for 20 minutes. Drain, reserving the liquid. Combine the reserved liquid and sausage in a bowl and mix well. Dissolve the baking soda in the vinegar. Stir into the sausage mixture. Add the flour, sugar, salt, vanilla, nutmeg, cinnamon and cloves and mix well. Stir in the raisins and walnuts. Spoon the batter into two 5x9-inch loaf pans sprayed with nonstick cooking spray. Bake at 350 degrees for 1 hour or until a wooden pick inserted in the center comes out clean. Remove to wire racks to cool. May bake in a bundt pan. **Yield:** 16 servings.

Edna S. Jones, *Shermanata Grange, Pennsylvania*

Grange Christmas Cake

3 cups flour
1 teaspoon cinnamon
1 teaspoon ground cloves
1 teaspoon salt
3 cups water
1 (16-ounce) package raisins
1 (9-ounce) package condensed
    mincemeat
2 teaspoons baking soda
1 1/3 cups sugar
1/2 cup (1 stick) butter, softened
2 eggs
1 cup chopped nuts

Sift the flour, cinnamon, cloves and salt together. Bring the water, raisins and mincemeat to a boil in a saucepan, stirring occasionally. Remove from heat. Let stand until cool. Stir in the baking soda. Beat the sugar and butter in a mixer bowl until creamy. Add the eggs and beat until blended. Stir in the raisin mixture. Add the flour mixture and mix well. Stir in the nuts. Spoon the batter into a greased 10-inch tube pan. Bake at 300 degrees for 1 1/2 to 2 hours or until the cake tests done. Invert on a funnel to cool completely. Loosen the cake from the side of the pan. Invert onto a serving plate. **Yield:** 16 to 20 servings.

Nancy D. Wolfe, *Brandywine Grange, Maryland*

Hawaiian Wedding Cake

1 (2-layer) package yellow cake mix
1 (6-ounce) package vanilla instant
    pudding mix
1 1/2 cups milk
8 ounces cream cheese, softened
1/4 cup milk
1 (20-ounce) can crushed pineapple,
    drained
Whipped topping or whipped cream
Shredded coconut

Prepare and bake the cake using package directions for a 12x18-inch cake pan. Cool in pan on a wire rack. Whisk the pudding mix and 1 1/2 cups milk in a bowl until thickened. Beat the cream cheese and 1/4 cup milk in a mixer bowl until blended. Add the pudding and beat until blended. Stir in the pineapple. Spoon over the top of the cake. Spread with whipped topping. Sprinkle with coconut. Chill, covered, until serving time.
Yield: 24 servings.

Ned W. Turner, *Elk Plain Grange, Washington*

There has been some kind of talent contest at National Grange for more than sixty years.

Love Cake

3 cups sifted flour
1 tablespoon baking soda
1 (1-pound) package confectioners' sugar
1 cup freshly shredded coconut
3/4 cup shortening
4 egg yolks
1 teaspoon vanilla extract
1 cup milk
4 egg whites, stiffly beaten
Love Cake Frosting (below)

Mix the flour and baking soda in a bowl. Beat the confectioners' sugar, coconut and shortening in a mixer bowl until creamy. Add the egg yolks and vanilla and beat until blended. Add the flour mixture alternately with the milk, mixing well after each addition. Fold in the egg whites. Spoon into a nonstick 9x13-inch cake pan. Bake at 350 degrees for 30 to 35 minutes or until the cake tests done. Cool in pan on a wire rack. Spread with the Love Cake Frosting. The flavor of the cake is enhanced if frozen for about 3 weeks before serving. **Yield:** 24 servings.

Dorothy Krouse, *Northumberland Grange, Pennsylvania*

Love Cake Frosting

1/2 cup milk
2 1/2 tablespoons flour
1/2 cup confectioners' sugar
1/2 cup shortening
1 teaspoon vanilla extract

Combine the milk and flour in a saucepan and mix well. Cook until the mixture is of the consistency of a paste, stirring constantly. Remove from heat. Let stand until cool. Beat the confectioners' sugar, shortening and vanilla in a mixer bowl until creamy. Add the pasty mixture. Beat until light and fluffy. **Yield:** 24 servings.

Dorothy Krouse, *Northumberland Grange, Pennsylvania*

Orange Chiffon Cake

8 egg whites
1/2 teaspoon cream of tartar
2 1/4 cups sifted flour
1 1/2 cups sugar
1 tablespoon baking powder
3/4 cup orange juice
1/2 cup vegetable oil
5 egg yolks
1 teaspoon grated orange zest
1 teaspoon vanilla extract

Beat the egg whites and cream of tartar in a mixer bowl until stiff peaks form. Combine the flour, sugar and baking powder in a mixer bowl and mix well. Add the orange juice, oil, egg yolks, zest and vanilla. Beat at low speed until smooth. Fold the orange juice mixture into the egg whites. Spoon the batter into a greased and floured tube or bundt pan. Bake at 325 degrees for 65 to 70 minutes or until the top springs back when lightly touched. Invert onto a serving platter immediately. Remove the cake from the pan when cool. Frost as desired. **Yield:** 16 to 18 servings.

Evelyn Ray, *San Dimas Grange, California*

Peanut Butter Sheet Cake

2 cups flour
2 cups sugar
1 teaspoon salt
1 teaspoon baking soda
1 cup water
1 cup (2 sticks) margarine
1/2 cup crunchy peanut butter
1/2 cup buttermilk
2 eggs, lightly beaten
Peanut Butter Frosting (below)

Combine the flour, sugar, salt and baking soda in a bowl and mix well. Bring the water, margarine and peanut butter to a boil in a saucepan, stirring frequently. Pour over the flour mixture and mix well. Stir in the buttermilk. Add the eggs and mix well. Spoon into a greased sheet cake pan. Bake at 350 degrees for 20 to 25 minutes or until the cake tests done. Cool in pan on a wire rack. Spread with the hot Peanut Butter Frosting. **Yield:** 24 servings.

Marie C. Thelen, *Olive Grange, Michigan*

Peanut Butter Frosting

1/2 cup (1 stick) margarine
1/2 cup crunchy peanut butter
6 tablespoons buttermilk
4 cups confectioners' sugar
1 teaspoon vanilla extract

Combine the margarine, peanut butter and buttermilk in a saucepan. Bring to a boil, stirring frequently. Remove from heat. Add the confectioners' sugar and vanilla and beat until of a spreading consistency. **Yield:** 24 servings.

Marie C. Thelen, *Olive Grange, Michigan*

As of 1999, Granges are found in thirty-seven states and in the District of Columbia.

Pear Cake

1 large can pears
2 cups flour
1 teaspoon baking soda
1 teaspoon baking powder
2 cups sugar
1/3 cup vegetable oil
2 eggs
1 teaspoon vanilla extract
1 cup chopped nuts

Drain the pears, reserving the juice. Chop the pears. Combine the flour, baking soda and baking powder in a bowl and mix well. Beat the sugar and oil in a mixer bowl until blended. Add the eggs and vanilla and beat until smooth. Beat in the flour mixture. Add the pears and reserved juice and mix well. Stir in the nuts. Spoon the batter into a greased 9x13-inch cake pan. Bake at 350 degrees for 45 to 60 minutes or until the cake tests done. **Yield:** 18 servings.

Claudine Anderson, *Paradise Grange, California*

Pecan Christmas Cake

4 cups chopped pecans
1 1/2 cups golden raisins
3 cups sifted flour
1 teaspoon baking powder
1/4 teaspoon salt
2 cups (4 sticks) butter, softened
2 cups sugar
6 eggs
1 tablespoon lemon juice
1 tablespoon vanilla extract
1 teaspoon grated lemon zest

Toss the pecans and raisins with 1/2 cup of the flour in a bowl. Sift the remaining 2 1/2 cups flour, baking powder and salt together. Beat the butter and sugar in a mixer bowl until light and fluffy. Add the eggs 1 at a time, mixing well after each addition. Stir in the lemon juice, vanilla and zest. Add the pecan mixture alternately with the dry ingredients, mixing well after each addition. Spoon the batter into a greased paper-lined 10-inch tube pan. Bake at 300 degrees for 1 hour and 50 minutes. Cool in pan on a wire rack. Invert onto a serving platter. The flavor of this cake is enhanced if frozen for 3 weeks before serving. Do not substitute margarine for the butter. **Yield:** 16 servings.

Marcella Troth, *Kansas Director of Women's Activities*

Pineapple Cake

1 (20-ounce) can crushed pineapple
2 cups sugar
2 cups flour
2 eggs
2 teaspoons baking soda
1 teaspoon vanilla extract
8 ounces cream cheese, softened
1/2 cup (1 stick) margarine, softened
2 cups confectioners' sugar
1 teaspoon vanilla extract

Combine the undrained pineapple, sugar, flour, eggs, baking soda and 1 teaspoon vanilla in a mixer bowl. Beat until blended. Spoon the batter into a 9x12-inch cake pan. Bake for 45 minutes. Cool in pan on a wire rack. Beat the cream cheese and margarine in a mixer bowl until creamy. Add the confectioners' sugar and 1 teaspoon vanilla and beat until of a spreading consistency. Spread over the top of the cake. **Yield:** 12 to 15 servings.

Reverend David C. Newkirk, *Mayfield Grange, New York*

Chocolate Pound Cake

3 cups flour
1/4 cup baking cocoa
1/2 teaspoon baking powder
1/2 teaspoon salt
3 cups sugar
1 cup shortening
6 eggs
2 teaspoons vanilla extract
1 cup milk
Creamy Chocolate Frosting (below)

Sift the flour, baking cocoa, baking powder and salt together. Beat the sugar and shortening in a mixer bowl until creamy. Add the eggs 1 at a time, mixing well after each addition. Beat in the vanilla. Add the flour mixture alternately with the milk, mixing well after each addition and beginning and ending with the flour mixture . Spoon the batter into a greased and floured or lined 10-inch tube pan. Bake at 325 degrees for 1 1/2 hours or until a wooden pick inserted in the center comes out clean. Cool in pan for several minutes. Invert onto a serving plate to cool completely. Spread the Creamy Chocolate Frosting over the top and side of the cake. **Yield:** 16 servings.

Mary Ann Clary, *Macedonia Grange, South Carolina*

Creamy Chocolate Frosting

1 (1-pound) package confectioners' sugar
1/4 cup baking cocoa
1/2 cup (1 stick) margarine, melted
1/4 cup (or more) evaporated milk

Sift the confectioners' sugar and baking cocoa into a mixer bowl. Add the margarine and evaporated milk. Beat until of a spreading consistency, adding additional evaporated milk as needed for the desired consistency. **Yield:** 16 servings.

Mary Ann Clary, *Macedonia Grange, South Carolina*

The Deaf Activities Department gives scholarships on the basis of need to Grange families with hearing-impaired children under the age of thirteen.

Gather-Round Pound Cake

1 cup butterscotch chips
2 tablespoons instant coffee granules
1/4 cup water
1 cup (2 sticks) butter, softened
1 1/2 cups sugar
3 cups flour
1/2 teaspoon baking soda
1/4 teaspoon salt
3/4 cup buttermilk or sour milk
4 eggs

Combine the butterscotch chips, coffee granules and water in a heavy 2-quart saucepan. Cook over low heat just until blended, stirring constantly; do not boil. Remove from heat. Cool to lukewarm. Beat the butter in a mixer bowl at high speed until creamy. Add the sugar gradually, beating constantly until light and fluffy. Add the butterscotch mixture. Beat at medium speed until blended. Add a mixture of the flour, baking soda and salt. Stir in the buttermilk. Beat at low speed until blended. Beat at medium speed for 2 minutes, scraping the bowl occasionally. Add the eggs 1 at a time, beating for 1 minute after each addition. Spoon the batter into a greased bundt or 10-inch tube pan. Bake at 350 degrees for 55 to 60 minutes or until the cake tests done. Cool in pan for 10 minutes. Remove to a wire rack to cool completely. **Yield:** 24 servings.

Virginia M. Smith, *Palmer Grange, Massachusetts*

Raisin Boil Cake

3 cups water
2 cups packed brown sugar
2 cups raisins
1 cup shortening
1 teaspoon cinnamon
1/2 teaspoon nutmeg
1/2 teaspoon allspice
4 cups flour
1 tablespoon baking powder
1 1/2 teaspoons salt
1 teaspoon baking soda
1 cup chopped nuts (optional)

Combine the water, brown sugar, raisins, shortening, cinnamon, nutmeg and allspice in a saucepan. Bring to a boil, stirring frequently. Boil for 3 minutes, stirring frequently. Let stand until cool. Sift the flour, baking powder, salt and baking soda together. Add to the raisin mixture and mix well. Stir in the nuts. Spoon into a 9x13-inch cake pan. Bake at 350 degrees for 1 hour or until the cake tests done. **Yield:** 15 servings.

Leon LaSalle, *Master, Alaska State Grange*

Red Velvet Frosting

3 tablespoons flour
1 cup milk
1 cup (2 sticks) butter, softened
1 cup sugar
1 teaspoon vanilla extract

Combine the flour with a small amount of the milk in a saucepan and stir until smooth. Add the remaining milk and mix well. Cook until thickened, stirring constantly. Chill in the refrigerator until very cold. Beat the butter and sugar in a mixer bowl for 15 to 20 minutes or until light and fluffy. Add the vanilla, beating until smooth. Add the chilled mixture and stir until blended. **Yield:** 12 servings.

Elizabeth Robinson, *First Lady, New Jersey State Grange*

Red Velvet Cake

2 ounces red food coloring
2 teaspoons baking cocoa
2 1/2 cups flour, sifted
3/4 teaspoon salt
1 tablespoon vanilla extract
1 cup buttermilk
1 1/2 cups sugar
1/2 cup shortening
2 eggs
1 tablespoon vinegar
1 teaspoon baking soda
Red Velvet Frosting (page 230)

Combine the food coloring and baking cocoa in a bowl, stirring until of a pasty consistency. Mix the flour and salt in a bowl. Stir the vanilla into the buttermilk in a bowl. Beat the sugar and shortening in a mixer bowl until creamy. Add the eggs and beat until blended. Beat in the baking cocoa mixture. Add the flour mixture alternately with the buttermilk mixture, mixing well after each addition. Fold in the vinegar and baking soda. Spoon the batter into three 8-inch cake pans. Bake at 350 degrees for 25 to 30 minutes or until the layers test done. Cool in pans for 10 minutes. Remove to wire racks to cool completely. Spread the Red Velvet Frosting between the layers and over the top and side of the cake. **Yield:** 12 servings.

Elizabeth Robinson, *First Lady, New Jersey State Grange*

Seven-Up Cake

1 (2-layer) package orange or pineapple
    cake mix
1 (4-ounce) package vanilla instant
    pudding mix
3/4 cup vegetable oil
4 eggs
10 ounces Seven-Up
1 large can juice-pack crushed pineapple
1 cup sugar
1/2 cup (1 stick) margarine
2 eggs, lightly beaten
2 tablespoons flour
1 (7-ounce) package shredded coconut

Combine the cake mix, pudding mix, oil and 4 eggs in a bowl and mix well. Add the Seven-Up, stirring until creamy. Spoon the batter into a greased 9x13-inch cake pan. Bake at 350 degrees for 25 to 35 minutes or until the cake tests done. Cool in pan on a wire rack. Combine the undrained pineapple, sugar, margarine, 2 eggs and flour in a saucepan. Cook over medium heat until thickened, stirring frequently. Stir in the coconut. Spread over the cake. Chill, covered, if desired. The cake will stay moist for several days. **Yield:** 15 servings.

Roger Halbert, *Director of Membership, National Grange*

Posters available for free distribution from the Deaf Activities Department include the Pledge of Allegiance in sign language, "Senior Americans' Guide to Better Hearing," and "Do You See the Signs?" describing speech development in children.

Sour Cream Fudge Torte

1 (2-layer) package devil's food cake mix
1 cup water
1/3 cup vegetable oil
3 eggs
2 cups sour cream
1 cup sugar
3 cups shredded coconut
3 cups whipped topping

Combine the cake mix, water, oil and eggs in a mixer bowl. Beat for 2 minutes. Spoon the batter into 2 round cake pans. Bake at 350 degrees for 30 to 40 minutes or until the layers test done. Cool in pans for 10 minutes. Invert onto wire racks to cool completely. Split each layer into halves. Combine the sour cream and sugar in a bowl and mix well. Stir in the coconut. Fold in the whipped topping. Spread between the layers and over the top of the torte. **Yield:** 12 to 15 servings.

Mildred Otte, *Nebraska Director of Women's Activities*

Sponge Cake

6 egg whites
1 teaspoon cream of tartar
1/2 cup sifted sugar
1 1/3 cups sifted cake flour
1 cup sifted sugar
1/2 teaspoon baking powder
1/2 teaspoon salt
6 egg yolks
1/4 cup water
1 teaspoon lemon extract

Combine the egg whites and cream of tartar in a mixer bowl. Beat at high speed until soft peaks begin to form. Add 1/2 cup sugar 2 tablespoons at a time, beating constantly until very stiff peaks form. Sift the cake flour, 1 cup sugar, baking powder and salt into a bowl and mix well. Add the egg yolks, water and flavoring. Beat with a spoon 75 strokes or just until blended. Fold into the egg whites. Spoon the batter into an ungreased 10-inch tube pan. Cut through the batter with a knife. Bake at 375 degrees for 30 minutes. Invert the pan on a sodapop bottle; do not remove pan. Cool for 1 to 2 hours. **Yield:** 12 to 15 servings.

Fannie B. Pease, *Ludlow Grange, Massachusetts*

Grand Champion Sponge Cake

1 1/4 cups sifted flour
1 cup sugar
1/2 teaspoon baking powder
1/2 teaspoon salt
6 egg whites
1 teaspoon cream of tartar
1/2 cup sugar
6 egg yolks
1/4 cup water
1 teaspoon vanilla extract
Creamy Pineapple Frosting (page 233)

Sift the flour, 1 cup sugar, baking powder and salt into a bowl and mix well. Beat the egg whites in a mixer bowl until frothy. Add the cream of tartar and mix well. Add 1/2 cup sugar gradually, beating constantly until stiff but not dry peaks form. Combine the egg yolks, water, vanilla and flour mixture in a mixer bowl. Beat at medium speed for 4 minutes or until light and fluffy. Fold into the egg whites. Spoon into an ungreased tube pan. Bake at 350 degrees for 45 minutes. Invert the pan on a soda pop bottle to cool. Remove the cake to a serving plate. Spread the side and top of the cake with the Creamy Pineapple Frosting. **Yield:** 16 servings.

Jean Ray, *Alfalfa Grange, Washington*

Creamy Pineapple Frosting

1/4 cup (1/2 stick) butter, softened
1/4 cup shortening
3 cups confectioners' sugar
1 (8-ounce) can crushed pineapple
1/2 teaspoon grated lemon zest
1/4 teaspoon vanilla extract
1/8 teaspoon salt

Beat the butter and shortening in a mixer bowl until creamy. Add the confectioners' sugar gradually, beating constantly until light and fluffy. Add the pineapple, zest, vanilla and salt and mix well. **Yield:** 16 servings.

Jean Ray, *Alfalfa Grange, Washington*

Hot Milk Sponge Cake

1 cup flour
1 teaspoon baking powder
2 eggs
1 cup sugar
1 teaspoon vanilla extract
1/4 teaspoon salt
1/2 cup milk
1 tablespoon butter

Sift the flour and baking powder together. Beat the eggs in a mixer bowl until pale yellow. Add the sugar, vanilla and salt and beat until foamy. Heat the milk and butter in a saucepan just to the boiling point. Add to the egg mixture. Beat until blended. Add the flour mixture and mix well. Spoon the batter into a greased glass 7x11-inch cake dish. Bake at 325 degrees for 45 minutes or until the cake tests done. Sprinkle with additional sugar, cinnamon and chopped walnuts before baking if desired or spread with your favorite frosting when cool. **Yield:** 8 servings.

Marian N. Plumb, *Litchfield Grange, Connecticut*

The Grange is the only agriculture family fraternity.

Ugly Duckling Cake

1 (2-layer) package yellow cake mix
1 (15-ounce) can fruit cocktail
1 cup flaked coconut
2 eggs
1/2 cup packed brown sugar
1/2 cup (1 stick) margarine
1/2 cup sugar
1/2 cup evaporated milk
1 1/3 cups flaked coconut

Combine the cake mix, undrained fruit cocktail, 1 cup coconut and eggs in a mixer bowl. Beat at low speed until mixed. Beat at medium speed for 2 minutes, scraping the bowl occasionally. Spoon the batter into a 9x13-inch cake pan. Sprinkle with the brown sugar. Bake at 325 degrees for 45 minutes or until the cake springs back when lightly touched. Bring the margarine, sugar and evaporated milk to a boil in a saucepan. Boil for 2 minutes, stirring occasionally. Remove from heat. Stir in 1 1/3 cups coconut. Spoon over the hot cake. Serve warm or at room temperature. **Yield:** 18 servings.

Donna Marous, *Jefferson Grange, Ohio*

Aunt Dee's Wacky Cake

3 cups flour
2 cups sugar
6 tablespoons baking cocoa
2 teaspoons baking soda
1 teaspoon salt
1/2 cup plus 2 tablespoons vegetable oil
2 teaspoons vinegar
2 teaspoons vanilla extract
2 cups water

Sift the flour, sugar, baking cocoa, baking soda and salt into a bowl and mix well. Make a well in the center of the flour mixture. Add the oil, vinegar and vanilla to the well. Add the water gradually, mixing constantly until smooth. Spoon the batter into a greased 9x12-inch cake pan. Bake at 350 degrees for 50 to 55 minutes or until the cake tests done. Cool in pan on a wire rack. May sprinkle with confectioners' sugar or spread with Chocolate Frosting (below). **Yield:** 12 servings.

Cynthia Finch, *Washington Grange, Connecticut*

Chocolate Frosting

1 cup sugar
1/4 cup baking cocoa
1/4 cup milk
1/4 cup (1/2 stick) butter or margarine

Bring the sugar, baking cocoa, milk and butter to a boil in a saucepan, stirring occasionally. Boil for 1 minute, stirring frequently. Remove from heat. Beat until of a spreading consistency. Spread over the cake immediately; this frosting hardens quickly. **Yield:** 12 servings.

Margaret Reed, *Ethel Grange, Washington*

Yum-Yum Cake

4 ounces chocolate
3 cups cold water
2 cups raisins
2 cups sugar
1¹/₃ cups butter
1 teaspoon cinnamon
1 teaspoon ground cloves
1 teaspoon salt
¹/₈ teaspoon allspice
2 teaspoons baking soda
¹/₂ cup cold water
4 cups flour

Combine the chocolate, 3 cups cold water, raisins, sugar, butter, cinnamon, cloves, salt and allspice in a saucepan. Bring to a boil, stirring frequently. Boil for 4 minutes, stirring frequently. Let stand until cool. Dissolve the baking soda in ¹/₂ cup cold water. Add to the chocolate mixture and mix well. Stir in the flour. Spoon the batter into a nonstick 9x13-inch cake pan. Bake at 350 degrees for 55 to 60 minutes or until the cake tests done. **Yield:** 15 servings.

Doris T. Shaw, *Tunxis Grange, Connecticut*

Butterfinger Candy

2 cups graham cracker crumbs
2 cups confectioners' sugar
¹/₄ cup (¹/₂ stick) butter, softened
2 cups peanut butter
1 pound milk chocolate
¹/₃ bar paraffin

Combine the graham cracker crumbs, confectioners' sugar and butter in a bowl and mix until of the consistency of pie dough. Add the peanut butter and mix well. Chill, covered, for 1 hour. Heat the chocolate and paraffin in a saucepan until blended, stirring frequently. Shape the peanut butter mixture into small balls. Dip each ball into the warm chocolate to coat. Arrange the balls on a sheet of waxed paper. Let stand until set. **Yield:** 50 servings.

Mildred Grim, *Walters Butte Grange, Idaho*

Grange halls throughout the country are community centers.

Grandpa Bert's Nut Caramels

1 (14-ounce) can sweetened
    condensed milk
1 cup corn syrup
1/2 cup sugar
1/2 cup (1 stick) butter or margarine
1/8 teaspoon maple flavoring
1 cup chopped walnuts

Combine the condensed milk, corn syrup, sugar, butter and flavoring in a saucepan. Bring to a boil. Boil for about 30 minutes over low heat, stirring constantly. Remove from heat. Stir in the walnuts. Spoon into a greased 7x11-inch dish. Let stand until cool. Cut into 1-inch squares. **Yield:** 60 servings.

Richard D. Stott, *Indian River Grange, Connecticut*

Divinity Fudge

2 cups sugar
1/2 cup light corn syrup
1/2 cup water
1/4 teaspoon salt
2 egg whites
1 teaspoon vanilla extract

Combine the sugar, corn syrup, water and salt in a 2-quart saucepan. Cook to 240 to 248 degrees on a candy thermometer, firm-ball stage; do not stir. Beat the egg whites in a mixer bowl until stiff peaks form. Add the hot syrup to the egg whites gradually, beating constantly. Add the vanilla. Beat until thick. Drop by teaspoonfuls onto waxed paper. Let stand until firm. **Yield:** 1 pound.

Randee Pound, *Edgemere Grange, Idaho*

Peanut Butter Fudge

1 (18-ounce) jar peanut butter
1 (7-ounce) jar marshmallow creme
2 cups sugar
2 cups packed brown sugar
3/4 cup milk

Combine the peanut butter and marshmallow creme in a bowl and mix well. Combine the sugar, brown sugar and milk in a saucepan. Bring to a boil, stirring occasionally. Boil for 2 minutes. Add to the peanut butter mixture and mix well. Spread in a buttered 9x13-inch dish. Let stand until firm. Cut into 1-inch squares. May add chopped nuts. **Yield:** 5 pounds.

Rosa Taylor, *Jaffrey Grange, New Hampshire*

Potato Fudge

1 medium potato, peeled
2 (1-pound) packages confectioners' sugar
2 (8-ounce) packages shredded coconut
1/2 teaspoon vanilla extract
4 ounces bittersweet chocolate, melted

Line a 9x9-inch dish with waxed paper, allowing an overhang. Combine the potato with enough water to cover in a saucepan. Cook until tender; drain. Mash the hot potato in a bowl. Stir in the confectioners' sugar, coconut and vanilla. Spread evenly in the prepared dish, pressing the fudge to the corners. Spread the melted chocolate over the fudge immediately. Let stand until firm. Lift the fudge out of the dish. Cut into 1-inch squares. **Yield:** 80 servings.

Ruth Tully, *Dunstable Grange, Massachusetts*

Microwave Peanut Brittle

1 cup sugar
1/2 cup light corn syrup
1 1/4 cups raw Spanish peanuts
1 teaspoon butter or margarine
1 teaspoon vanilla extract
1/4 teaspoon baking soda

Combine the sugar and corn syrup in a microwave-safe dish and mix well. Microwave on High for 4 minutes. Stir in the peanuts. Microwave on High for 2 1/2 minutes; stir. Microwave on High for 2 1/2 minutes. Stir in the butter and vanilla. Microwave on High for 2 minutes. Add the baking soda, stirring until light and foamy. Spread immediately on a buttered baking sheet. Let stand until cool. Break into pieces. Store in an airtight container. **Yield:** 1 pound.

Catherine Chase, *Oretown Grange, Oregon*

The National Grange stands for social and educational development of rural life.

Microwave Sunflower Seed Brittle

1 cup sugar
1/2 cup light corn syrup
1/8 teaspoon salt
1 1/2 cups raw sunflower seed kernels
1 tablespoon margarine
1 1/2 teaspoons baking soda
1 teaspoon vanilla extract

Grease a 12x18-inch sheet of foil. Combine the sugar, corn syrup and salt in a 3-quart microwave-safe bowl. Stir in the sunflower seed kernels. Microwave on High for 8 to 10 minutes or until light brown, stirring once or twice during the process. Add the margarine, baking soda and vanilla and stir until foamy. Spread as thin as possible on the prepared foil. Let stand until cool. Break into pieces. **Yield:** 1 pound.

Linda A. Wahl, *Edgemere Grange, Idaho*

White Chocolate Candy

8 ounces cream cheese, softened
4 cups confectioners' sugar
1 1/2 teaspoons vanilla extract
12 ounces white chocolate, melted
3/4 cup chopped pecans

Beat the cream cheese, confectioners' sugar and vanilla in a mixer bowl until smooth. Add the white chocolate and beat until blended. Stir in the pecans. Spread in a buttered 8x8-inch dish. Chill, covered, for 12 hours or until firm. Cut into squares. **Yield:** 24 servings.

Evelyn Davis, *Sheffield Star Grange, Ohio*

Texas Apple Pie

1 cup sour cream
1/2 cup sugar
2 eggs
2 tablespoons flour
1 teaspoon vanilla extract
4 medium apples, peeled, thinly sliced
1 unbaked (9-inch) pie shell
1/4 cup sugar
2 tablespoons butter or margarine, softened
1 tablespoon flour
1/2 teaspoon cinnamon

Combine the sour cream, 1/2 cup sugar, eggs, 2 tablespoons flour and vanilla in a bowl and mix until blended. Fold in the apples. Spoon the apple mixture into the pie shell. Combine 1/4 cup sugar, butter, 1 tablespoon flour and cinnamon in a bowl and mix with a fork until crumbly. Sprinkle or drop in clumps over the apple mixture. Bake at 300 degrees for 1 hour or until the crust is light brown. **Yield:** 6 servings.

Claire D. Gagnon, *Hudson Grange, New Hampshire*

Buttermilk Pie

1 cup buttermilk
1 cup packed brown sugar
1/2 cup (1 stick) butter, melted
2 eggs
2 tablespoons flour
1 teaspoon vanilla extract
1 unbaked (9-inch) pie shell

Combine the buttermilk, brown sugar, butter, eggs, flour and vanilla in a mixer bowl. Beat for 1 minute. Pour into the pie shell. Bake at 350 degrees for 45 minutes or until set.
Yield: 6 servings.

Ada M. Skiles, *Big Knob Grange, Pennsylvania*

Mom's Carrot Pie

3/4 cup sugar
1 egg, lightly beaten
1 tablespoon flour
1 teaspoon cinnamon
1/2 teaspoon nutmeg
1/4 teaspoon ground cloves
1/4 teaspoon salt
1 3/4 cups puréed cooked carrots
1 1/2 cups evaporated milk
1 unbaked (10-inch) deep-dish pie shell

Combine the sugar, egg, flour, cinnamon, nutmeg, cloves and salt in a bowl and mix well. Stir in the carrots. Add the evaporated milk and mix well. Pour into the pie shell. Bake at 350 degrees for 1 hour. Serve with whipped cream.
Yield: 6 servings.

Helen Stonebrink, *Hurricane Creek Grange, Oregon*

As of 1999, the states with the largest associate Grange membership are North Carolina and Washington.

Surprise Cherry Pie

1 (8-ounce) can juice-pack crushed
    pineapple
8 ounces cream cheese, softened
1/2 teaspoon vanilla extract
1 (21-ounce) can cherry pie filling
1/4 cup confectioners' sugar
1 cup whipping cream or whipped
    topping
1 (9-inch) graham cracker pie shell
1 pineapple ring

Drain the pineapple, reserving 2 tablespoons of the juice. Beat the reserved juice, cream cheese and vanilla in a mixer bowl until blended. Stir in 1/4 cup of the pineapple and 1/2 cup of the pie filling. Add the confectioners' sugar gradually to the whipping cream in a bowl and mix well. Fold into the cream cheese mixture. Spoon into the pie shell. Top with the remaining pie filling and remaining pineapple. Chill, covered, until firm. Arrange the pineapple ring in the center of the pie.
Yield: 8 servings.

Isabelle J. Lewis, *Pine Lake Grange, Indiana*

Chocolate Pie

1 2/3 cups milk
1 cup sugar
2 ounces unsweetened chocolate
1/3 cup milk
2 tablespoons (heaping) flour
2 eggs, lightly beaten
1 tablespoon butter
1 teaspoon vanilla extract
1 baked (9-inch) pie shell
Whipped topping
Chocolate sprinkles

Combine 1 2/3 cups milk, sugar and chocolate in a saucepan. Bring to a boil, stirring constantly. Remove from heat. Beat 1/3 cup milk, flour and eggs in a mixer bowl until blended. Stir the egg mixture into the chocolate mixture gradually. Bring to a boil, stirring constantly. Cook until thickened, stirring constantly. Remove from heat. Stir in the butter and vanilla. Beat with an electric mixture for several minutes or until smooth and creamy. Cool slightly. Spoon into the pie shell. Let stand until cool. Top with whipped topping and chocolate sprinkles. Chill until serving time. May substitute a mixture of 6 tablespoons baking cocoa and 2 tablespoons butter for the unsweetened chocolate.
Yield: 6 servings.

Mildred Ginger, *Hex Grange, Indiana*

Coconut Pies

2 cups shredded coconut
2 cups sugar
1 (12-ounce) can evaporated milk
6 tablespoons (3/4 stick) margarine,
    melted
3 eggs, lightly beaten
1 teaspoon vanilla extract
2 unbaked (9-inch) pie shells

Combine the coconut, sugar, evaporated milk, margarine, eggs and vanilla in a bowl and mix well. Pour into the pie shells. Bake at 350 degrees for 25 to 30 minutes or until a knife inserted in the centers comes out clean. May be frozen for future use.
Yield: 12 servings.

Thelma Hylton, *Prices Fork Grange, Virginia*

Custard Pie

1 recipe (1 crust) pie pastry
3 cups milk, scalded
¹/2 cup sugar
¹/4 teaspoon salt
4 eggs, lightly beaten
1 teaspoon vanilla extract
Nutmeg to taste

Line a 9-inch glass pie plate with the pastry, trimming and fluting the edge. Combine the scalded milk, sugar and salt in a bowl and stir until the sugar dissolves. Add the milk mixture gradually to the eggs in a bowl, stirring constantly until blended. Stir in the vanilla. Pour into the pie shell. Sprinkle with nutmeg. Place on the center oven rack. Bake at 475 degrees for 5 minutes. Reduce the oven temperature to 425 degrees. Bake for 25 to 30 minutes longer or until set. May sprinkle shredded coconut over the pie shell before adding the filling. **Yield:** 6 servings.

Pat Quick, *Colorado Director of Women's Activities*

Grape Pie

1 recipe (2-crust) pie pastry
4 cups Concord grapes
1 cup sugar
3 tablespoons flour
1 teaspoon lemon juice
¹/4 teaspoon salt

Line an 8-inch pie plate with half the pastry. Peel the grapes, reserving the peel and pulp. Place the pulp in a saucepan; do not add water. Bring to a boil, stirring frequently. Remove from heat. Press the hot grape pulp through a strainer to remove the seeds. Combine the strained pulp and reserved peel in a bowl and mix well. Stir in the sugar, flour, lemon juice and salt. Spoon into the prepared pie plate. Top with the remaining pastry, trimming and fluting the edge and cutting vents. Bake at 425 degrees for 35 to 45 minutes or until brown and bubbly. **Yield:** 6 servings.

Virginia L. Conner, *Five Corners Grange, New York*

The latest annual contest of the Women's Activities Department was started in 1997 and is called Harvest of Handicrafts. The categories, which are changed each year, offer everyone a chance to create an item made of wood, a quilted entry, and an entry in a sewing or craft media. The craft items are in keeping with the "fads" of the day.

Huckleberry Cream Cheese Pie

1 cup sugar
3 tablespoons cornstarch
1/4 teaspoon salt
4 cups fresh or frozen huckleberries
1 unbaked (9-inch) pie shell
8 ounces cream cheese, softened
1/2 cup sugar
2 eggs
1 cup sour cream

Combine 1 cup sugar, cornstarch and salt in a 2-quart saucepan and mix well. Stir in the huckleberries. Cook over medium heat until thickened, stirring frequently. Spoon into the pie shell. Bake at 425 degrees for 10 minutes. Remove from oven. Reduce the oven temperature to 350 degrees. Combine the cream cheese, 1/2 cup sugar and eggs in a mixer bowl. Beat at medium speed until smooth. Spoon over the huckleberry mixture. Bake at 350 degrees for 30 to 35 minutes or until set. Cool on a wire rack. Chill, covered, for 4 hours. Spread the sour cream over the filling and garnish with fresh huckleberries just before serving. **Yield:** 8 servings.

Margaret Bryant, *Priest Lake Grange, Idaho*

Italian Easter Pies

3 cups flour
2 1/2 teaspoons baking powder
1/4 teaspoon salt
3/4 cup sugar
1/2 cup vegetable oil
2 eggs
1 teaspoon vanilla extract
1/4 cup milk
3 pounds ricotta cheese
3/4 cup sugar
1/4 cup honey
6 eggs
Cinnamon to taste

Sift the flour, baking powder and salt together. Combine 3/4 cup sugar, oil, 2 eggs and vanilla in a bowl and mix well. Add the flour mixture and milk and mix well. Divide into 2 equal portions. Roll each portion into a circle on a lightly floured surface. Fit the pastry circles into two 9-inch pie plates; trim and flute the edges. Combine the ricotta cheese, 3/4 cup sugar, honey and 6 eggs in a bowl and mix well. Spoon into the prepared pie plates. Sprinkle with cinnamon. Bake at 350 degrees for 1 hour and 10 to 15 minutes or until a knife inserted in the centers comes out clean. **Yield:** 12 servings.

Marcella Vecchitto, *Westfield Grange, Connecticut*

Jelly Pie

4 eggs
1 cup sugar
3/4 cup any flavor jelly
1 1/2 to 2 tablespoons butter
1 teaspoon vanilla extract
1/8 teaspoon salt
1 cup chopped pecans
1 unbaked (9-inch) pie shell

Beat the eggs in a mixer bowl until pale yellow. Add the sugar, jelly, butter, vanilla and salt and mix well. Stir in the pecans. Spoon into the pie shell. Bake at 300 degrees until set. **Yield:** 8 servings.

Grace White, *David Crockett Grange, Texas*

Creamy Lemon Pie

1³/4 cups cold milk
2 (4-ounce) packages vanilla instant
    pudding mix
1 (6-ounce) can frozen lemonade
    concentrate, thawed
8 ounces whipped topping
1 (9-inch) graham cracker pie shell
Lemon slices (optional)

Pour the milk into a bowl. Add the pudding mixes. Whisk for 30 seconds. Add the lemonade concentrate. Whisk for 30 seconds. Fold in the whipped topping. Spoon into the pie shell. Chill, covered, for 4 hours or until set. Garnish with lemon slices. Store any leftovers in the refrigerator. **Yield:** 8 servings.

Ann J. Butterfield, *Dunstable Grange, Massachusetts*

Lemon Meringue Pie

1 cup water
³/4 cup sugar
¹/2 cup cold water
5 tablespoons cornstarch
2 egg yolks, beaten
6 tablespoons lemon juice
1 tablespoon butter
1 baked (8-inch) pie shell
2 egg whites
¹/4 cup sugar

Bring 1 cup water and ³/4 cup sugar to a boil in a saucepan, stirring occasionally. Add a mixture of ¹/2 cup cold water and cornstarch and mix well. Cook over low heat until thickened, stirring constantly. Remove from heat. Stir a small amount of the hot mixture into the egg yolks; stir the egg yolks into the hot mixture. Add the lemon juice and butter and mix well. Spoon into the pie shell. Beat the egg whites in a mixer bowl until foamy. Add ¹/4 cup sugar gradually, beating constantly until stiff peaks form. Spread over the filling, sealing to the edge. Bake at 325 degrees for 15 minutes or until light brown. May substitute a graham cracker pie shell for the pastry pie shell. **Yield:** 6 servings.

Louisa Hott, *Maryland Director of Women's Activities*

Conferences and training sessions for each department of Grange are held in Kansas City, Missouri, on a rotating basis. National Directors and leaders meet with their state counterparts to develop new programs, discuss problems, share ideas, and enjoy the friendships and fraternity which abound in the Grange.

Maple Chiffon Pie

1 tablespoon unflavored gelatin
1/4 cup cold water
1 cup pure maple syrup
3 egg yolks, lightly beaten
1/2 teaspoon salt
1/2 teaspoon vanilla extract
3 egg whites, stiffly beaten
1 cup whipping cream, whipped
1 baked (9-inch) pie shell

Soften the gelatin in the cold water. Combine the maple syrup, egg yolks and salt in a saucepan and mix well. Cook just until slightly thickened, stirring constantly. Remove from heat. Add the gelatin mixture, stirring until dissolved. Stir in the vanilla. Chill, covered, until partially set. Beat until light and fluffy and the color of caramel. Fold in the egg whites. Fold in the whipped cream. Chill, covered, until the mixture mounds when dropped from a spoon. Spoon into the pie shell. Chill, covered, until firm. **Yield:** 6 servings.

Margaret Richardson, *First Lady of the National Grange*

Oatmeal Pie

3/4 cup packed brown sugar
3/4 cup light corn syrup
3/4 cup quick-cooking oats
1/2 cup shredded coconut
1/2 cup (1 stick) margarine
2 eggs, beaten
1 teaspoon vanilla extract
1/2 teaspoon salt
1 unbaked (8-inch) pie shell

Combine the brown sugar, corn syrup, oats, coconut, margarine, eggs, vanilla and salt in a bowl and mix well. Spoon into the pie shell. Bake at 350 degrees for 45 to 50 minutes or until set. **Yield:** 6 servings.

Julia Elliott, *Bloomington Grange, Iowa*

Peanut Butter Pie

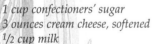

1 cup confectioners' sugar
3 ounces cream cheese, softened
1/2 cup milk
1/3 cup peanut butter
8 ounces whipped topping
1 (9-inch) graham cracker pie shell

Beat the confectioners' sugar, cream cheese, milk and peanut butter in a mixer bowl until blended. Fold in the whipped topping. Spoon into the pie shell. Freeze, covered, for 3 hours. **Yield:** 6 to 8 servings.

Lisa Malone Kirk, *Wesley's Chapel Grange, Tennessee*

Pecan Pie

1 cup corn syrup
1 cup sugar
3 eggs, lightly beaten
2 tablespoons margarine, melted
1 teaspoon vanilla extract
1/8 teaspoon salt
1 cup pecan halves
1 unbaked (9-inch) pie shell

Combine the corn syrup, sugar, eggs, margarine, vanilla and salt in a bowl and mix well. Stir in the pecans. Spoon into the pie shell. Bake at 400 degrees for 15 minutes. Reduce the oven temperature to 350 degrees. Bake for 30 to 35 minutes longer or until set. **Yield:** 6 servings.

Donna Keeton, *Flora, National Grange*

Impossible Pecan Pie

1 1/2 cups chopped pecans
3/4 cup packed brown sugar
3/4 cup milk
3/4 cup corn syrup
1/2 cup baking mix
1/4 cup (1/2 stick) butter or margarine,
    softened
4 eggs
1 1/2 teaspoons vanilla extract

Sprinkle the pecans in a greased 9-inch pie plate. Process the brown sugar, milk, corn syrup, baking mix, butter, eggs and vanilla in a blender until smooth. Pour into the prepared pie plate. Bake at 350 degrees for 50 to 55 minutes or until set. Let stand until cool. **Yield:** 6 servings.

Fannie Korol, *Ludlow Grange, Massachusetts*

The Lecturers Department of the Grange offers an opportunity called "With Pen In Hand," where essays are composed on assigned subjects. Prizes and awards are given in a number of categories.

Double-Layer Pumpkin Pie

4 ounces cream cheese
1 tablespoon milk
1 tablespoon sugar
1½ cups whipped topping
1 (9-inch) graham cracker pie shell
1 (16-ounce) can pumpkin
1 cup milk
2 (4-ounce) packages vanilla instant
    pudding mix
1 teaspoon cinnamon
½ teaspoon ginger
¼ teaspoon ground cloves

Place the cream cheese in a microwave-safe bowl. Microwave on High for 15 to 20 seconds. Add 1 tablespoon milk and sugar and stir until blended. Add the whipped topping and mix well. Spoon into the pie shell. Combine the pumpkin, 1 cup milk, pudding mixes, cinnamon, ginger and cloves in a bowl and mix well. Spread over the prepared layer. Chill, covered, for 4 hours or until set. Garnish with additional whipped topping.
Yield: 6 servings.

Maxine Kooch, *Hurricane Creek Grange, Oregon*

Shoofly Pie

¾ cup baking molasses
¾ cup boiling water
1 teaspoon baking soda
1½ cups flour
⅔ cup sugar
½ teaspoon cinnamon
¼ teaspoon ginger
¼ teaspoon salt
⅛ teaspoon ground cloves
⅓ cup butter
1 unbaked (10-inch) deep-dish pie shell

Combine the molasses, boiling water and baking soda in a bowl and mix well. Let stand until cool. Combine the flour, sugar, cinnamon, ginger, salt and cloves in a bowl and mix well. Cut in the butter with a pastry blender until crumbly. Spoon ¼ of the crumb mixture into the pie shell. Spread with the molasses mixture. Top with the remaining crumb mixture. Bake at 350 degrees for 40 minutes. Cool to room temperature.
Yield: 6 to 8 servings.

Florence E. Williamson, *Bottle Run Grange, Pennsylvania*

Raisin Crème Pie

2 cups milk
1 cup raisins
¾ cup packed brown sugar
2 tablespoons cornstarch
Milk
3 egg yolks, beaten
1 tablespoon butter
1 baked (8-inch) pie shell
3 egg whites
½ cup sugar

Combine 2 cups milk and raisins in a saucepan. Cook until heated through, stirring occasionally; do not boil. Remove from heat. Mix the brown sugar and cornstarch in a bowl. Add just enough milk to moisten and mix well. Stir in the egg yolks and butter. Add to the raisin mixture. Bring to a boil. Boil for 3 minutes or until of the desired consistency, stirring frequently. Spoon into the pie shell. Beat the egg whites in a mixer bowl until foamy. Add the sugar gradually, beating constantly until stiff peaks form. Spread over the filling, sealing to the edge. Bake at 350 degrees for 10 minutes or until light brown.
Yield: 6 servings.

Florence Hansel, *Woodland Grange, Iowa*

Sour Cream Raisin Pie

3/4 cup sugar
2 tablespoons cornstarch
1 teaspoon cinnamon
1/2 teaspoon nutmeg
1/4 teaspoon ground cloves
1/4 teaspoon salt
3 egg yolks, beaten
1 cup sour cream
1 cup raisins, ground
1 unbaked (9-inch) pie shell
3 egg whites
6 tablespoons sugar

Combine 3/4 cup sugar, cornstarch, cinnamon, nutmeg, cloves and salt in a bowl and mix well. Stir in the egg yolks. Add the sour cream and raisins and mix well. Spoon into the pie shell. Bake at 350 degrees for 40 to 45 minutes or until a knife inserted in the center comes out clean. Beat the egg whites in a mixer bowl until foamy. Add 6 tablespoons sugar gradually, beating constantly until stiff peaks form. Spread over the baked layer, sealing to the edge. Bake at 350 degrees for 12 to 15 minutes or until golden brown. **Yield:** 6 servings.

June Shambaugh, *Klondike-Piney Grange, Wyoming*

Best-Ever Rhubarb Pie

5 cups flour
1 teaspoon baking powder
1 teaspoon salt
1 teaspoon sugar
1 pound shortening or lard, chilled
3/4 cup cold water
1/4 cup vinegar
4 cups cubed rhubarb
2 cups sugar
2 eggs, beaten
1 tablespoon flour
1 tablespoon cornstarch
1 tablespoon butter, softened

Combine 5 cups flour, baking powder, salt and 1 teaspoon sugar in a bowl and mix well. Cut in the shortening until crumbly. Add a mixture of the cold water and vinegar and mix well. Shape the pastry into 6 balls each the size of a small softball and wrap each ball with waxed paper. Chill for 1 hour. Roll 1 of the pastry balls into a 12-inch circle on a lightly floured surface. Fit into the pie plate. Combine the rhubarb, 2 cups sugar, eggs, 1 tablespoon flour, cornstarch and butter in a bowl and mix well. Spoon into the pastry-lined pie plate. Roll another pastry ball into a 12-inch circle on a lightly floured surface. Place over the filling, trimming and fluting the edge and cutting vents. Bake at 425 degrees for 25 minutes. Reduce the oven temperature to 375 degrees. Bake for 20 minutes longer or until golden brown. The remaining pastry may be stored in the refrigerator for several days or frozen for future use. **Yield:** 8 servings.

Thelma Meyer, *Millville Grange, California*

Through the Lecturers Department a program is offered to each Grange where work done in the community by an individual citizen or by a group of people may be recognized and honored. Upon selection of a recipient, each Grange arranges a special evening and program when the guest is honored and presented with a plaque for outstanding public service.

Rhubarb Sour Cherry Pie

1 recipe (1-crust) pie pastry
1¹/2 to 2 cups sugar
2 tablespoons flour
2 tablespoons tapioca
2 cups chopped rhubarb
2 cups pitted sour cherries
1¹/2 teaspoons butter
¹/3 cup sugar
¹/3 cup flour
¹/2 teaspoon cinnamon
¹/4 cup (¹/2 stick) butter

Line a 9-inch pie plate with the pastry, trimming and fluting the edge. Combine 1¹/2 to 2 cups sugar, 2 tablespoons flour and tapioca in a bowl and mix well. Add the rhubarb and sour cherries and toss until coated. Spoon the rhubarb filling into the prepared pie plate. Dot with 1¹/2 teaspoons butter. Combine ¹/3 cup sugar, ¹/3 cup flour and cinnamon in a bowl and mix well. Cut in ¹/4 cup butter until crumbly. Sprinkle over the filling. Bake at 425 degrees for 40 to 50 minutes or until brown and bubbly. May substitute pastry for the crumb topping, sprinkling the pastry lightly with sugar and cutting vents.
Yield: 6 to 8 servings.

Rebecca Michalka, *Pennsylvania Director of Women's Activities*

Strawberry Pies

2 cups water
1¹/2 cups sugar
¹/4 cup cornstarch
1 (3-ounce) package strawberry gelatin
¹/4 cup water
2 baked (9-inch) pie shells
1 quart (about) strawberries, whole or
    sliced
Whipped topping

Combine 2 cups water, sugar and cornstarch in a saucepan and mix well. Cook until the mixture is clear and comes to a boil, stirring constantly. Remove from heat. Combine the gelatin and ¹/4 cup water in a bowl and mix well. Add to the hot mixture and stir until dissolved. Let stand at room temperature until partially set. Spoon just enough of the sauce into each pie shell to cover the bottom. Arrange the strawberries over the sauce. Spoon the remaining sauce over the strawberries. Let stand until cool. Spread with whipping topping. Chill until serving time. **Yield:** 12 servings.

Betty Bailey, *Mt. Nebo Grange, Ohio*

Sugar Pies

3 eggs
1¹/2 cups sugar
2 tablespoons margarine, melted
2 tablespoons milk
1 teaspoon lemon extract
2 unbaked (9-inch) pie shells

Whisk the eggs in a bowl until pale yellow; do not use an electric mixer. Add the sugar gradually, beating constantly. Stir in the margarine, milk and flavoring. Spoon into the pie shells. Bake at 250 degrees for 1 hour. **Yield:** 12 servings.

Elizabeth G. Myers, *Colonial Grange, South Carolina*

Index

What's Cookin' IN THE Grange

**Family Recipes From Grange
Homes Over The Years**

The National Grange
1616 H Street, NW
Washington, D.C. 20006-4999
Attention: Georgia M. Taylor

Please send me _____ copies of **What's Cookin' IN THE Grange** at $15.00 per book (includes postage and handling). Enclosed is a check payable to The National Grange for $ _____.

_____
Name

_____
Address

_____
City   State   Zip

What's Cookin' IN THE Grange

**Family Recipes From Grange
Homes Over The Years**

The National Grange
1616 H Street, NW
Washington, D.C. 20006-4999
Attention: Georgia M. Taylor

Please send me _____ copies of **What's Cookin' IN THE Grange** at $15.00 per book (includes postage and handling). Enclosed is a check payable to The National Grange for $ _____.

_____
Name

_____
Address

_____
City   State   Zip

Photocopies will be accepted.

A New Century
A New Grange